Natural Healing for
DEPRESSION

Solutions from the
World's Great Health Traditions
and Practitioners

Edited by

JAMES STROHECKER &

NANCY SHAW STROHECKER

CONTRIBUTORS

David E. Bresler, Ph.D., L.Ac.; Hyla Cass, M.D.;
Roger C. Hirsh, O.M.D., L.Ac., B.Ac. (UK), Dipl. Ac. (NCCA); Shri Kant
Mishra, M.D., M.S., Doctor of Ayurveda;
Joseph Pizzorno, N.D.; Carlos Warter, M.D., Ph.D.;
Melvyn R. Werbach, M.D.; Jacquelyn J. Wilson, M.D.; Janet Zand, O.M.D., L.Ac.

A PERIGEE

Most Perigee Books are available at special quantity discounts for bulk
purchases for sales promotions, premiums, fund-raising or educational use.
Special books, or book excerpts, can also be created to fit specific needs.

For details, write: Special Markets, The Berkley Publishing Group, 375
Hudson Street, New York, New York 10014.

A Perigee Book
Published by The Berkley Publishing Group
A division of Penguin Putnam Inc.
375 Hudson Street
New York, New York 10014

Copyright © 1999 by James Stuart Strohecker and Nancy Shaw Strohecker
Introduction copyright © 1998 by Leo Galland, M.D.
Interior illustrations by Jeff Wells
Book design by Tiffany Kukec
Cover design by Jill Boltin
Cover photo copyright © by H. Okamoto/Photonica

First edition: October 1999

Published simultaneously in Canada.

The Penguin Putnam Inc. World Wide Web site address is
http://www.penguinputnam.com

Library of Congress Cataloging-in-Publication Data

Natural healing for depression: solutions from the world's great
health traditions and practitioners / edited by James Strohecker &
Nancy Shaw Strohecker; contributors, David E. Bresler . . . [et
al.].—1st ed.
    p.   cm.
Includes bibliographical references and index.
ISBN 0-399-52537-8
    1. Depression, Mental Popular works. 2. Depression,
Mental—Alternative treatment. I. Strohecker, James. II.
Strohecker, Nancy Shaw. III. Bresler, David E.
    RC537 .N38 1999
    616.85'2706—dc21   99-34778
                                                        CIP

Printed in the United States of America

10 9 8 7 6 5 4 3 2 1

We dedicate this book with love and gratitude to the memory of Nancy's mother, Patricia Ann Shaw, who left this world during the final stages of writing this book.

To all of those who have suffered from depression—sometimes making the ultimate sacrifice with their lives. This book has been created to raise awareness of the abundance of natural healing solutions from around the world in the effort to help eliminate unnecessary suffering.

I am convinced that my life belongs to the whole community; and as long as I live it is my privilege to do for it whatever I can, for the harder I work the more I live. I rejoice in life for its own sake. Life is no brief candle for me. It is a sort of splendid torch which I got hold of for a moment, and I want to make it burn as brightly as possible before turning it over to future generations.

—George Bernard Shaw

Contents

Foreword

If you are reading this book because you or someone you care about suffers from depression, please understand that you are not alone. The symptoms of depression trouble more than 25 percent of Americans. The frequency of depression is increasing and its debilitating symptoms are striking people at younger and younger ages. If you were born after World War II, you are four times more likely to experience severe depression than your grandparents were. The increase in depression parallels an increase in other epidemic diseases of modern society, all of which have become frighteningly prominent during the twentieth century: cancer, heart disease, asthma and allergic disorders, arthritis, inflammatory bowel disease, attention deficit disorder, and childhood autism. The response of conventional medical care to all these problems has been to define new diagnostic standards, develop new drugs for treatment, and search for the genes that "cause" the disease. Yet all our modern diseases result from complex, interacting factors that include stress, social and cultural changes, the effects of environmental toxicity and nutritional imbalances.

Depression, because of its impact on all aspects of one's life, demands a holistic approach to its understanding and its treatment. Depression always involves both mind and body, the individual person, and the environment in which the person lives. Depression disrupts social relationships. It may destroy friendships and marriages or result from the destruction of friendships and marriages. Depression alters the chemistry of the brain and may also result from abnormalities in the chemistry of the brain. By affecting appetite it may alter nutrition. Nutritional deficiency and excess on the other hand may cause depression. Depression may be the result of physical illness and may cause physical illness. It is just as significant in causing death from heart disease as are smoking or high blood pressure; lifelong depression increases the risk of cancer.

Because depression rarely has a single cause, complete recovery from depression usually requires that many paths be taken. It's important to know what factors in a person's life trigger symptoms and how the various components of life modulate moods and thoughts. Diet and nutrition, the daily pattern of sleep and exercise, memories and expectations, social interactions, the time of year, the weather, stage of the menstrual cycle, the use of drugs and medication, exposure to toxins—chemical, psychological and spiritual—must all be considered.

Although depression has increased dramatically in today's world, the problem of depression is ancient. We can therefore draw on the wisdom of many different healing traditions, modern and ancient, in our quest to overcome the burden of depression and discover the vibrant energy that each of us possesses.

This unique book brings together the expertise of doctors skilled in different healing traditions. They all share a common understanding: that good health and vitality result from harmony and balance and that illness or disease is the result of disharmony and imbalance. This understanding separates all systems of natural healing from conventional medicine, which is built around the theory of diseases. The key question for the conventional physician is, What *disease* does this person have? The treatment then is the treatment of the disease, in this case depression, not an attempt to help the individual restore health by creating harmony and balance. The distinction between the two approaches—natural healing and conventional—can be profound. The conventional approach to depression has been increasingly based upon the use of drugs that alter the chemistry of the brain. Alternative therapies focus on the person with the goal to empower the individual to regain health, emotional and physical, by restoring balance and harmony of function. These methods may complement or substitute for conventional psychiatric care and are often useful in helping people who resist or oppose the concepts that underlie conventional psychiatric methods. They represent a wonderful resource for people in the stressed/depressed modern world.

Not only is each of the contributors to *Natural Healing for Depression* an expert in the particular field he or she discusses; each writer brings a holistic perspective to his or her work that recognizes the importance of integrating therapies. The awareness that guides this book is the same awareness that underlies Integrated Medicine. Specific therapeutic techniques are helpful, but what is most important for restoring and maintaining health is the holistic perspective. Each of us is a unique individual living in an environment we share with others. Each of us has special needs for achieving and maintaining a state of inner balance and harmony with the environment in which we live. Depression is one outcome of the breakdown of balance and harmony. Restoration of health begins with empowerment, the decision each person makes to take an active role in health restoration. To realize personal empowerment, we need tools. *Natural Healing for Depression* gives its readers those tools and the resources with which to seek additional help.

For many people, diet and nutrition are a good place to start because food can have profound physiological effects—alcohol, sugar, and caffeine affect the body like drugs. People who are depressed frequently medicate themselves with these foods, producing an unstable internal state that aggravates depression. Four chapters in this book use nutrition as the point of departure for the journey of self-healing. Their perspectives are different but complementary, allowing readers to choose tactics with the greatest personal appeal.

Patterns of thought have a profound influence on the symptoms of depression. It's common to believe that sad feelings are the cause of negative thoughts. Extensive research and abundant experience show us that the converse is true. Our thoughts and activities determine our feelings. Seven chapters of this book present strategies for promoting thoughts, beliefs, and habits of physical activity that enhance emotional well-being. Although their techniques differ, they share the belief that personal activation can help people overcome depression. Control of your thoughts, actions, eating, and drinking is the beginning of empowerment.

Several chapters proceed from the recognition that natural substances, including nutritional supplements, full strength herbs, and homeopathic remedies, can help enhance energy and vitality. It is important to understand the difference between this nutriceutical/ homeopathic approach and the pharmaceutical approach of conventional medicine. Like drugs, nutriceuticals influence the physiology of the body. Unlike drugs, however, nutriceuticals are not used to suppress symptoms or to treat diseases. They are used as part of a system that has as its primary focus the restoration of harmony of function for the whole person.

James and Nancy Strohecker have brought together some of the best healers practicing today. Search through their insights and their wisdom. Embrace those concepts and techniques which make the most sense to you. Use this book to empower yourself and those you love.

Leo Galland, M.D.
Director, Foundation for Integrated Medicine
Author, *Power Healing* (Random House, 1998)

Acknowledgments

We would like to acknowledge the following people for helping to make this book a reality.

Terry and Phyllis Jacobs, friends and partners in producing the original "Healing Depression" seminar in Santa Monica, California. Halim Provo-Thompson, for being a spiritual brother who opened doors. Joe Bruggeman, for his generous spirit, friendship, and encouragement. Ling Lucas, our spirited agent, for her humor, professionalism, and insight.

To all of the contributors for their vision and courage as leaders in their respective fields and for helping to further the revolution in natural medicine and integrative health care. For their patience and commitment in the endless rounds of brainstorming, edits, and updates that were essential to bringing out the most valuable ideas, current information, and resources for preventing and treating depression, as well as maintaining health in body/mind/spirit.

Special thanks to all the people who have honored us with their personal stories, solutions, and courage in the face of suffering.

We would like to offer our heartfelt thanks and appreciation to the countless generations of healers and health professionals who have kept the ancient traditions of herbal medicine, Ayurveda, and Chinese Medicine alive, and to the contemporary practitioners who have battled to make these forms of health care available to all of us here in the United States.

To Samuel Hahnemann, the fearless visionary and pioneer of homeopathy who endured sixty years of persecution for his enlightened views on medicine, and those resolute healers who have kept homeopathy alive in the United States for the past 150 years despite overwhelming resistance from mainstream medicine.

To the pioneers of naturopathic medicine in America and those who have followed who carried the torch of natural medicine burning for the past one hundred years.

To the pioneers of nutritional medicine who remained steadfast in their knowledge and beliefs while modern medicine took a detour down the path of chemical drugs for the better part of this century.

To the pioneers of mind/body medicine who followed their hunches on what the physiology and neurophysiology of yoga and meditation could teach us about the mind/body relationship.

To those healers who could never understand why modern medicine chose to divorce the spirit from the equation of good health and continued to teach and practice the art of dealing with the whole picture of health: body, mind, and spirit.

To all of our dear friends for their encouragement and support.

To our parents, John William Strohecker and Elizabeth Bond Strohecker, and Joseph Armitage Shaw and Patricia Ann Shaw, for their enduring love, wisdom, and common sense.

To Swami Muktananda Paramahansa, for reminding us that our state of mind is the ultimate source of our happiness or unhappiness. His love of natural therapies—diet, yoga, meditation, herbal medicine, and Ayurveda—created a living workshop for studying and practicing holistic lifestyles.

Many Paths to Healing Depression

James Strohecker & Nancy Shaw Strohecker

It's supposed to be a professional secret, but I'll tell you anyway. We doctors do nothing. We only help and encourage the doctor within.
—*Albert Schweitzer*

There is no shortage today of media stories on depression. Newspaper headlines from this year cover a wide range of issues surrounding depression: "Herb Is Found to Aid Mild Depression," "Researchers Probe Heart Disease–Depression Link," "Millions of American Teenagers Suffer from Depression," "A Hidden Epidemic of Male Depression," "Feeling Blue? Check Your Thyroid," "Medicating Kids: A Pacifier for Depression," and "Prozac Keeps Drugmaker Feeling Good After 10 Years." Why this sudden fascination with depression? Is it because depression is rapidly becoming recognized as one of the biggest health problems facing our society, affecting not only adults, but teens and children?

This current climate is a far cry from the amount of public interest and media coverage of depression just a few years ago in 1994, when we produced a conference called Healing Depression in Santa Monica, California, which inspired this book. At that time, depression was still a taboo subject socially, a frightening and mysterious condition that was treated medically with powerful psychotropic antidepressants such as Paxil and Zoloft which had disturbing side effects. The controversial antidepressant drug Prozac had been on the market for several years and was just penetrating the public consciousness and beginning to make headlines. There seemed to be little or no interest in, nor knowledge of, natural alternatives to treating depression.

Today, thanks to the barrage of media stories and a number of well-known public figures who have disclosed their battles with depression, including television journalist Mike Wallace, actor Rod Steiger, novelist William Styron, and Tipper Gore, wife of Vice President Al Gore, much of the social stigma surrounding depression has been removed. Discussion of depression in our culture has become more commonplace, and it can now be mentioned in the same breath as being "anxious" or "stressed out." Concurrently, there is an increasing public interest in natural approaches to dealing with this health condition. Even conventional medical doctors who have historically been known to only prescribe antidepressants, are now responding to the public demand and are beginning to recommend natural remedies like St. John's wort for mild to moderate depression.

A NATIONAL HEALTH PROBLEM

One in four Americans will experience some degree of clinical depression or mood disorder during their lifetime, and each year over 25 million people will be diagnosed with a depressive illness. Two-thirds of those suffering from depression are women. However, the recent focus upon a "silent epidemic" of depression among men indicates that these figures are in need of adjustment.[1]

All told, it is estimated that depression will cost our economy more than $44 billion and an annual loss of 200 million work hours. These numbers may be deceiving, however, given people's reticence in the past to talk to their physician about depression. Today over 17 million people, including teens and children, are currently on Prozac, the second most commonly prescribed drug in America. Pharmaceutical giant Eli Lilly, the maker of Prozac, engages in major media campaigns to raise public awareness about depression and Prozac. With the rising tide of awareness of depression, many who would have never considered themselves depressed will be taking Prozac, or some other antidote, pushing the statistics even higher.

It appears we are bringing our children along for the ride. It is estimated that close to 13 percent of teenagers and approximately 3 percent of children under thirteen suffer from depression.

According to the Center for Mental Health Services, until recently no one has wanted to recognize that teens and children suffer from depression. To make matters more difficult, childhood depression is hard to identify and diagnose because it is so easily confused with other health conditions, and because children lack the verbal skills to explain what they are experiencing. As a result they act out their depression in the only way they know how—what we commonly describe as moodiness, irritability, anger, and even rage and violence.

Are we becoming a "Prozac nation"? Prozac, despite its ability to transform personality, appears to be a short-term solution to a long-term problem. Food and Drug Administration (FDA) statistics reveal unsettling reports of adverse side effects ranging from loss of sexual appetite to suicide and death. These serious shortcomings, the rising incidence of depression, and the growing popularity of natural health care clearly demonstrate the need for safe and reliable drug-free treatments. It is no surprise then that the antidepressant herb St. John's wort, despite having been successfully used for centuries, was barely on the radar screen in the United States four years ago, but is now the number four–selling herb in the United States and is outselling Prozac in Germany.

WHERE DOES THE ANSWER LIE?

We have spoken with an endless number of people whose psychiatrist or psychologist reflexively prescribed antidepressant medication for their depression as the only available option. Modern medicine, with its focus on treating disease with a single "standard of practice," has created a serious situation for those being treated for depression with the class of psychotropic antidepressant drugs. Many suffering from depression complain they have been on a treatment merry-go-round for years, going from one antidepressant to another, and are still seeking help. They report that they have had some relief but at the cost of unpleasant and grave side effects. Others, however, have received little or virtually no relief or have gotten worse and are becoming increasingly desperate.

Two things are clear. The human suffering resulting from depression is real and impacts every aspect of one's life—family, work, and relationships. Secondly, depression is not an illness that can be explained by a single cause or reversed by a single cure, as demonstrated by the problems associated with the succession of antidepressant drugs produced over the years. There are no magic bullets for depression.

Where then does the answer lie to relieving the toll of human suffering brought on by depression? We have discovered that there are many answers to solving this complex malady. The key is in understanding the many underlying causes of depression and becoming aware of the variety of natural approaches to its treatment.

Many of the solutions come from the world's great systems of traditional health care. Some have ancient roots such as herbal medicine, the oldest form of health care on the planet, and the Greek medicine of Hippocrates. Chinese Medicine and Ayurveda from India, both of which have been practiced continuously for 5,000 years, can rightly be called the original systems of holistic medicine.

Other systems of traditional health care have more modern origins, such as homeopathy and naturopathic medicine, each of which originated in early- to mid-nineteenth century Germany before taking root in the United States. After having fallen into obscurity for most of the twentieth century because of the advent of miracle drugs, both are now enjoying a major renaissance.

What all of these systems of traditional health care have in common is a focus on health maintenance, prevention, treating the whole person, reliance on natural therapies, and taking a more integrative, multidisciplinary approach to treatment in order to restore health and internal balance. These systems also share another commonality—for most of this century, each has remained outside the accepted standards of conventional Western medicine but is now becoming increasingly in demand by people like yourself who are in search of solutions to their health problems.

In order to prevent illness and achieve an optimum level of personal health, it is important to be familiar with the tools that can help build a wellness-based lifestyle, and become aware of all your treatment options. The approaches in this book represent the collective wisdom of thousands of years of the great healing traditions as well as the best of the emerging field of integrative medicine—nutrition, healthy lifestyles, mind/body therapies, and spiritual practices.

We have brought together a team of nine leading experts from each of these fields to present, for the first time, a comprehensive and integrated picture of depression, including an understanding of its many causes, prevention, and time-tested natural approaches to its treatment.

This team of health professionals will provide an understanding of the following primary systems of natural medicine:

- **Ayurveda:** The traditional system of medicine in India, the practice of Ayurveda extends to 3500 B.C. The term *ayurveda* means "science of life," and it has a long history working with rejuvenation, longevity, and mental health through diet, lifestyle, herbs, massage, yoga, and meditation.

- **Chinese Medicine:** Practiced for over 5,000 years, Chinese Medicine includes the use of herbs, acupuncture, dietary therapy, massage, and lifestyle changes as well as Qigong, a system that uses movement, energy, and breath. This medicine is based on balancing the flow of *Qi*, or life force, through the body's meridian system or energy pathways.

- **Herbal Medicine:** The therapeutic use of herbs to alter physiology and mental/emotional states. Both Western and Chinese herbs are explored here in the treatment of depression, with an emphasis on St. John's wort as the most highly researched and publicized herb for treating depression today.

- **Homeopathy:** Homeopathic remedies are designed to stimulate the body's own natural powers of recovery to aid in overcoming the disease rather than simply suppressing symptoms. Homeopathy aims to treat the patient rather than the disease and has effective treatments for mental/emotional disorders.

- **Mind/Body Medicine:** The use of stress-reduction techniques, guided imagery, biofeedback, meditation, and other modalities to achieve higher levels of mind/body integration, greater capacities for self-regulation, and inner peace in order to better control anxiety and mood swings.

- **Naturopathic Medicine:** A comprehensive and natural approach to medicine which looks at all of the factors needed to help move a person toward health. This form of medicine looks to understand the underlying causes of illness, and then addresses these causes with natural therapies such as diet, lifestyle, herbs, homeopathy, nutritional supplements, hydrotherapy, and acupuncture.

- **Nutritional Medicine:** This approach involves the use of diet and nutritional supplements to correct nutritional deficiencies that may contribute to biochemical imbalances in the brain, resulting in depression. Nutritional medicine also utilizes nutrients in higher, pharmacological doses in order to push biochemical reactions in the desired direction to bring about a return to balance and health.

- **Qigong:** The Chinese art and science of gathering, circulating, and storing body/mind energy (*Qi*) through breath and energy work. These techniques involve movements and visualizations while standing, sitting, and moving.

- **Spiritual Medicine:** An emerging field that explores the spiritual dimension of health and psychology, utilizing psychospiritual disciplines such as meditation, yoga, breathwork, self-inquiry, and other spiritual disciplines. In the more ancient systems of traditional health care, the spiritual dimension of health was an integral part of a comprehensive, holistic approach to health and well-being.

- **Yoga:** A spiritual discipline practiced in India for many thousands of years, employing diet, lifestyle, relaxation, physical postures, breathing practices, meditation, and awareness to promote physical, mental, and spiritual health.

(For a complete list of therapies covered in this book see "Appendix A: Quick Reference to Therapies in *Natural Healing for Depression*.)

MANY PERSPECTIVES ON THE CAUSES OF DEPRESSION

There are many underlying causes of depression beyond the conventional biomedical perspective that focuses solely on imbalances in brain chemistry. We now know that numerous biochemical and physiological factors can induce depression. Many physical illnesses can be the cause and, conversely, depression can lead to physical illnesses. Depression may be caused by emotional, psychological factors or life circumstances. On an energetic level depression can be viewed as an imbalance of vital energy, and on a spiritual level it can be seen as stemming from spiritual disconnection or lack of soul awareness.

From an overall systems perspective, depression can be viewed as a "warning sign" that the body/mind is off course in some manner—biochemical, physiological, psychological, energetic, or spiritual—and is signaling that there is a need to make some change in your life.

Psychological/Emotional Causes of Depression

Depression often has emotional or psychological roots in the experience of loss, which may involve the death of a loved one, a job, a change of circumstances, or divorce. Depression that accompanies the grieving process following a significant loss is a natural phenomenon that we all experience at one time or another in our lives. In many cases, this type of depression can run its course without professional intervention, and in these cases it is not appropriate to "medicalize" the experience and classify it as "mental illness." On the other hand, more severe and enduring forms of emotional and psychological depression due to preoccupation with a loss, long-term disappointments in life, or chronic pain and physical trauma may require psychological intervention or counseling to help guide one through the often dark and difficult process of emotional healing.

Biochemical/Physiological Causes of Depression

Contrary to conventional wisdom, numerous biochemical and physiological factors can induce depression. These elements include diet, stress, sleep, exercise, environmental toxins, nutritional deficiencies, or hormonal imbalances. Similarly, depression may be a symptom of other underlying health conditions such as candidiasis, hypothyroidism, hypoglycemia, or hormonal imbalance. Cases of chronic, psychologically based depression may eventually result in altered biochemistry, which in turn may reinforce depression as a psychological state, making it even more difficult to alleviate. In these cases, it may be beneficial to deal with the biochemical factors while simultaneously addressing the psychological level. The contributing health professionals in this book will cover the following underlying factors that can cause or contribute to depression:

- Alcoholism: Depletes levels of many essential nutrients and amino acids that are necessary for proper brain physiology

- Candidiasis: Chronic overgrowth of yeast in the gut

- Chronic pain: The experience of ongoing physical or emotional pain

- Dietary imbalances: Excess sugar and caffeine consumption

- Environmental factors: Toxic reactions to neurotoxins such as solvents and heavy metals—aluminum, cadmium, and lead

- Food and chemical sensitivities: Allergies to foods such as dairy and wheat as well as to chemicals such as aspartame

- Hormonal imbalance: When the endocrine glands (thyroid, ovaries, testes, pituitary, and adrenal) are under stress or not functioning properly, hormone levels may fluctuate and profoundly effect mood

- Hypoglycemia: This condition of low blood sugar can lead to chronic mood swings and depression

- Hypothyroidism: Low levels of thyroid hormone can lead to exhaustion and depression

- Infectious diseases: Such diseases as strep throat, especially in children, affect the autoimmune system

- Intestinal parasites: Symptoms of parasitic infection include brain fog, depression, and feelings of doom

- Lack of exercise: Nonexercisers are three times more likely to have depression as exercisers

- Leaky gut syndrome: Caused by candidiasis and intestinal parasites, this can lead to allergic reactions, poor absorption of food, and malnourishment

- Lifestyle: High stress levels, smoking, and lack of exercise can lead to depression

- Low levels of neurotransmitters: Low levels of serotonin and norepinephrine

- Malabsorption: Inability to properly absorb nutrients due to deficiency in stomach hydrochloric acid (HCL), pancreatic enzymes, or bile acids

- Nutritional deficiencies: Deficiencies in vitamin B complex, vitamin C, iron, calcium, magnesium, potassium

- Pharmaceutical drugs: Antipsychotics, barbiturates, benzodiazepines, beta-blockers, cholinergics, corticosteroids, estrogens (including contraceptives), levodopa, reserpine

- PMS/menopause: Often accompanied by mood swings, anxiety, and depression

- Seasonal affective disorder (SAD): Caused by lack of exposure to sunlight

Energetic Basis of Depression

According to Traditional Chinese Medicine (TCM) illness results from an energetic imbalance of *Qi*, or life force, in the body's meridians and internal organs. TCM views depression as resulting from a blockage or stagnation of emotional *Qi*. Similarly, the Chinese system of energy training known as Qigong and the Indian system of yoga recognize the link between the mind and the life force (*Qi* or *prana*), while utilizing breathing and awareness practices to help regulate the flow of life energy in the body/mind.

Spiritual Basis of Depression

According to the "perennial philosophy" found in the world's great spiritual traditions, we have essentially forgotten who we are—our true nature and divine heritage—and feel disconnected from our spiritual source. This disconnectedness or separation is viewed as the primary source of unhappiness. Many sacred traditions view mental illness and conditions such as depression not as a disease of the mind, but as a lack of connection to and awareness of soul. When we lose touch with our essential spiritual nature and forget our true purpose in life, we become subject to depression and other illnesses.

IS DEPRESSION PREVENTABLE?

> *The doctor of the future will give no medicine, but will inter-est his patients in the care of the human frame, in diet, and in the cause and prevention of disease.*
>
> —*Thomas Edison*

When looking at the many faces of depression, a logical question arises: is depression preventable? In many cases the answer is yes if we can learn to minimize or avoid the previously mentioned causes by living a balanced, wellness-based lifestyle and maintaining a healthy psychological and spiritual perspective. Until recently, however, prevention has been a hard sell in America, as our system of health care has actually been a "sick-care" system focused on treating disease, not in preventing illness and maintaining health. In this book, each of the health traditions discussed by our team of health experts offers solutions to not just treating, but preventing depression through a healthy lifestyle and having tools and resources at hand to help deal with depression at its onset.

WHAT DO THE WORLD'S SYSTEMS OF TRADITIONAL HEALTH CARE OFFER?

Throughout history, the world's great systems of traditional medicine have provided a more balanced approach to health care, echoed in the World Health Organization's (WHO) classic definition of health:

> *Health is a state of complete physical, mental, and social well-being, and not merely the absence of disease or infirmity.*

The World Health Organization uses the term "traditional medicine" to describe established systems of health care worldwide considered "unconventional" by modern, standardized Western medicine. Most people are surprised to learn that according to the WHO, 80 percent of the world's population receives its health care from the various forms of traditional medicine considered to be "alternative" or "unconventional" in the United States. These systems include Ayurveda, Chinese Medicine, herbal medicine, unani (Graeco-Arab medicine), Native American medicine, traditional African medicine, naturopathic medicine, homeopathy, chiropractic, and osteopathy, among others.

Maintaining health and preventing disease form the basis of Ayurveda, Chinese Medicine, naturopathic medicine, and other forms of traditional health care. The therapeutic protocols in these systems are intended to restore balance to the body systems in order to reestablish health. Samuel Hahnemann, the late eighteenth- to early nineteenth-century founder of homeopathy, wrote volumes on hygiene, health maintenance, and mental health, as well as the prevention of disease. These systems all understood the connection between diet and mental health, the influence of lifestyle factors, the strong connection of mind and body, and finally the importance of the spiritual dimension in physical and mental health.

Yoga and Qigong are psychospiritual practices aimed at integrating body, mind, and spirit. Meditation, now regularly prescribed by many physicians, is one of the eight limbs of classical yoga. In fact, the basis of much of today's mind/body medicine, including guided imagery, biofeedback, and other relaxation techniques, have strong ties to the practices of yoga and meditation.

The following poetic passage written thousands of years ago in the *Yoga Vasistha,* a Sanskrit text of yoga and spiritual philosophy, demonstrates a profound and timeless understanding of how illness can originate in the mind—an understanding that is now weaving itself into the fabric of today's medicine:

> *When the mind is agitated, then the body also follows in its wake. And when the body is agitated, then there is no proper perception of the things that are in one's way and prana (vital force) flies from its even path onto the bad road, staggering like an animal wounded by an arrow. Through such agitations, prana, instead of pervading the whole body steadily and equally, vibrates everywhere at an unequal rate. Therefore, the nadis (subtle channels for circulation of prana) do not maintain a steady position, but quiver. Then to the body, which is the receptacle of partially or completely digested food, the nadis are simply death, because of the fluctuations of the pranas. The food which settles down in this body amidst such commotion is transformed into incurable diseases. Thus through the primary cause (of the mind) the disease of the body is generated. If this*

primary cause be annihilated at its root, then all diseases will be destroyed.[2]

The formation of a truly global medicine in the spirit of the World Health Organization's vision of integrating modern Western medicine with the world's traditional medicines is more and more becoming a reality. This process involves a revitalization of medicine, inspiring the evolution of even greater numbers of safe and effective forms of naturally based approaches to health care, side by side with the cutting-edge developments in the field of mind/body medicine and energy medicine.

HOW TO GET THE MOST OUT OF THIS BOOK

The information and resources in this book will empower you to be more proactive and self-reliant in dealing with cases of mild or transient depression, showing you how it can be managed through the appropriate self-care and wellness-based lifestyle practices. It will also show you how to work in partnership with a health professional in more moderate or serious cases of depression to create an effective treatment program that incorporates the leading-edge natural approaches.

Choosing a specific program or approach for any health condition can be a very personal process. For healing depression, some of you may choose to work primarily with an acupuncturist or Doctor of Oriental Medicine, while others may prefer to work with a homeopathic or naturopathic physician. Still others will choose a psychiatrist or a physician who is knowledgeable of both alternative and conventional therapies. Some of you may find that taking a more multidimensional approach in designing a program that utilizes several different health practitioners and forms of therapy including exercise, massage, meditation, a healthy diet, nutritional supplements, and herbs, is the right solution for your condition.

Look over each chapter and see if the approach is relevant to your situation and whether or not its basic principles resonate with your own philosophy and belief system. Each of these approaches has been effectively used for treating depression, and can work if it is the appropriate approach for you. With the broader acceptance of alternative/complementary therapies we are no longer restricted to standardized, conventional medicine that looks for one solution to each health problem as if

Alternative, Complementary, or Integrative Medicine? What's in a Name?

"Alternative medicine" is a relative term that refers in large part to the systems of traditional medicine that until recently were considered to be outside of the mainstream of Western medicine. Today, courses on many of these systems, including Chinese Medicine, acupuncture and Qigong, Ayurveda, herbal medicine, mind/body medicine, nutritional medicine, homeopathy, naturopathy, and chiropractic, are now being taught in over fifty U.S. medical schools. There is a growing number of traditional patient-care organizations that now offer alternative medicine services in their clinics as well as insurance reimbursements.

Many in conventional medical circles, however, still refer to "alternative" as unproven therapies that purport to replace or act as alternatives to conventional medical treatment. The issue as to what constitutes proof—conventional double-blind studies as opposed to hundreds or even thousands of years of favorable or successful outcomes—remains a contentious issue in conventional medicine. We often see conventional medical experts erroneously stating that there is no research on herbal or nutritional medicine. The *German Commission E Reports,* probably the single most important collection of botanical research in the world, have been publicly available in Germany for over ten years. Few in this country were aware of its existence, and of those who were, many discounted its significance as it was not "American" research. However, the *German Commission E Reports*[3] have now been translated into English (1998) in a project spearheaded by the American Botanical Council, and is beginning to gain its due respect. Similarly, Dr. Melvyn Werbach's classic book, *Nutritional Influences on Illness*[4], now a CD-ROM containing over 4,000 pages of nutritional research on over one hundred health conditions, was until recently little known outside alternative medicine circles.

Two other terms coming into greater use are "complementary" medicine and "integrative" medicine. Complementary medicine complements, but does not replace, conventional health care—for example, the use of acupuncture for pain control in the treatment of diabetic neuropathy. The Office of Alternative Medicine (OAM) at the National Institutes of Health now promotes the use of the term Complementary and Alternative Medicine (CAM). Integrative medicine refers to a form of health care that integrates both alternative/traditional and conventional medicine.

Whatever name you choose, the strengths of this approach to health care are in maintaining a high level of health and well-being, treating the whole person, preventing illness, and offering safe and nontoxic natural therapies for treating illness, particularly chronic illness.

The public demand for alternative medicine is very strong. A national survey conducted in 1998 by the Stanford Center for Research in Disease Prevention showed that the public does not differentiate between alternative and conventional medicines. Those polled wanted the options of going to both conventional and alternative health practitioners and using those medicines and services that proved most effective without being restricted by arbitrary definitions. Over 69 percent of the respondents had used some form of complementary and alternative medicine in the past year. Clearly, consumers want choice in the forms of treatments they pursue—they want the best of both worlds.

physicians were treating "disease units" rather than a whole person with both biochemical and psychological individuality.

Because the various systems of traditional medicine and the more modern systems of alternative medicine share a common perspective— a holistic focus on prevention, health maintenance, the use of natural therapies, and a comprehensive treatment plan—you will find throughout the various chapters some of the same therapies as part of an overall treatment plan. For example, St. John's wort is included in the chapters on herbal medicine and naturopathic medicine, as well as in an integrated approach to women's depression. This overlapping is not only because of this herb's high success rate with depression, but because the description of each approach would be incomplete without a discussion of this herb.

Finally, you can use this book to help increase your general level of health and well-being by incorporating the dietary, lifestyle, and stress management guidelines presented here. Every chapter provides tools to help you develop a wellness-based lifestyle and to address imbalances that may occur in your physical and mental health.

We have provided additional resources in the appendices for each specific therapy included in the book: recommended reading, national organizations and educational institutes, professional referral sources, as well as Internet resources. The Internet has played a strong role in disseminating information and resources about alternative medicine to consumers, health professionals, and health care organizations. More importantly, as a global delivery system it supports the formation of an integrated global system of health care that can utilize the best of traditional and modern medicine.

The Need for Self-Managed Care

The next major advance in the health of the American people will be determined by what the individual is willing to do for himself.

—*John Knowles, former president of the Rockefeller Foundation*

With the current direction of managed care, it is vital for the individual to take more control over his or her own health care. The abundance of information about medical options and alternatives necessitates that we become educated brokers of our own health care. Consumers are doing much of their own medical research today and assessing alternative treatments before conferring with their health professional. The accessibility and wealth of information on the Internet has only accelerated this process.

The philosophy of Self-Managed Care emphasizes maintaining health and well-being, consumer empowerment, partnership with one's health care provider, and increased utilization of natural remedies and alternative medicine services. The baby-boomers, many of whom are now managing their own health as well as that of their children and aging parents, are opting for less-invasive and more cost-effective natural approaches as their primary strategy, tending to avoid the medical system when possible in nonemergent cases. Savvy health consumers today want a full range of treatment options from both conventional and alternative medicine. More than ever the key word is *choice*.

MANY PATHS TO HEALING DEPRESSION

This book offers contributions from nine nationally recognized experts in the major fields of alternative/complementary (traditional) medicine, which as a whole presents a comprehensive and holistic vision of depression. Five of the contributors are experts in the major systems of traditional medicine: Ayurveda, Chinese Medicine and Qigong, herbal medicine, homeopathy, and naturopathic medicine. Three contributors are experts in mind/body medicine, nutritional medicine, and spiritual medicine. The final contributor, a psychiatrist and expert in women's mood disorders, represents the true integrative approach by blending Western medicine with nutritional medicine, herbs, and leading-edge psychotherapy.

In reading this book you will witness the true art of medicine as you are intelligently and compassionately guided by dedicated health professionals who look beyond the apparent symptoms to address the deeper, underlying causes of depression through natural and humane approaches. Reading each chapter will take you on a journey of hope and discovery. You will be exposed to healing solutions, both ancient and modern, that will expand your view of the nature of depression and illness as well as educate you in the many paths to healing this condition.

The following summaries of the nine chapters of this book will give you a sense of each healing system or approach and help you or your loved one begin developing the components of an effective treatment plan.

Depression As Emotional Pain: A Mind/Body Approach—
David E. Bresler, Ph.D., L.Ac.

Depression is a part of the natural healing process and does not always require therapeutic intervention, says clinical psychologist and mind/body pioneer Dr. David Bresler, who is an associate clinical professor at the UCLA School of Medicine and cofounder of the Academy for Guided Imagery. In this compelling and human picture of the psychological dimension of depression, he explains how our real concern should be not with people who experience depression, but with those who have become stuck in the healing process. From this perspective, we can view depression as a form of chronic emotional pain or an emotional habit that results in one becoming "stuck" in a depressed state of consciousness. In order to break the habit of depressed thinking, we can employ mind/body approaches such as interactive guided imagery that can have powerful physiological and psychological effects and put us in touch with our own inner resources.

Guided imagery can help us learn to "focus attention on the part of the nervous system that may have answers to our questions and solutions to our problems," according to Dr. Bresler. Most of us are unaware of the powerful inner resources we have at our disposal, and guided imagery techniques can help us to discover these resources and use them to provide new insights and creative solutions to our problems. The reader is guided through an evocative imagery experience designed to identify the particular qualities that are needed to help get one through a current challenge or difficulty. Additional imagery tools are given for dealing with depression: exploring the origin and meaning of symptoms, encountering the Inner Critic, and accessing your Inner Intelligence or Inner Advisor. According to Bresler, of vital importance in healing depression is keeping the human spirit alive through hope and faith: "When we lose hope, we lose the very thing that offers the greatest help in healing our problem."

Natural Medicine and Depression: A Naturopathic Approach— Joseph Pizzorno, N.D.

The true role of a naturopathic physician is not in treating disease but in helping people to reestablish health, says Dr. Pizzorno, president and cofounder of Bastyr University and an internationally recognized expert in natural medicine and author of the acclaimed book *Total Wellness: Improve Your Health by Understanding the Body's Healing Systems*. Identifying a disease can provide a useful label to help people understand their health problems; however, the naturopathic approach looks beyond the label of "depression." It looks at the whole person and identifies the underlying causative factors to determine what steps are needed to eliminate those causes and help a person move toward a balanced state of health.

This approach has many advantages. Stressing prevention and honoring the healing power of nature, naturopathic medicine relies upon natural therapies including diet, nutritional medicine, herbs, homeopathy, acupuncture, massage, and bodywork as well as psychological and lifestyle counseling. The patient is able to utilize a combination of therapies determined by the naturopath at very safe dosages, rather than using a single therapy at a higher, toxic dosage. Naturopathy also views the role of the physician to be an educator, teaching and motivating people to take more personal responsibility in maintaining good health and a state of wellness. All of these factors allow the patient to be highly involved in the treatment process.

Dr. Pizzorno's naturopathic approach to treating depression identifies five primary determinants of mood: physical factors; social factors (family and social patterns); mental factors (a person's thinking patterns); emotional factors; and spiritual factors. For example, on the physical level we may need to eliminate toxins, normalize endocrine function and neurotransmitter metabolism, increase exercise and light exposure, and utilize natural mood elevators. On the mental and emotional levels we may need to deal with family of origin issues, employ psychodynamic approaches when necessary, or even follow a prescription for having fun if we need to lighten up our lives.

Dr. Pizzorno offers a fascinating case study to illustrate naturopathic medicine's comprehensive and effective approach to dealing with depression, an approach that provides the necessary and immediate symptomatic relief while also treating the primary causes.

Women's Depression: An Integrated Approach— Hyla Cass, M.D.

Psychiatrist and author Hyla Cass, an expert in integrating leading-edge natural medicine with innovative psychotherapy and assistant clinical professor at the UCLA School of Medicine, encounters many women in her private practice with typical psychiatric complaints: depression, addiction, impaired concentration, eating disorders, weight gain, insomnia, anxiety, fatigue, and sexual dysfunction. Rather than approaching her patients from a standard psychiatric, drug-prescribing perspective, Dr. Cass examines other possible underlying causes for their depression and related symptoms: genetic predisposition, hormonal imbalances, food and chemical sensitivities, chronic fatigue syndrome, candidiasis, toxic reactions, and nutritional deficiencies.

Her integrative approach to treating depression and mood disorders in women utilizes a wide range of therapies depending upon the specific history and biochemistry of the patient as determined by laboratory tests. These therapies include dietary therapy and nutritional medicine, amino acid therapy, herbal medicine, and natural hormone therapy, as well as mind/body therapies, leading-edge forms of psychotherapy including Voice Dialogue, and when necessary, conventional antidepressant medications. Dr. Cass's integrative approach to treating depression and its underlying metabolic causes is also relevant to men, with the exception of the specific hormonal imbalances.

A Comprehensive Approach to Depression: Nutritional Medicine and Biofeedback—Melvyn R. Werbach, M.D.

Psychiatrist Melvyn Werbach presents a "new" model for looking at depression based on the natural and holistic principles of Hippocrates, the ancient Greek physician/healer recognized as the father of Western medicine. Depression can be viewed in three different ways according to Dr. Werbach: as a failure of a body system, a psychological defense, and a physical or psychological warning of the imbalance between mind and body. Optimal treatment involves a holistic approach that integrates the best of psychiatry, nutritional medicine, and mind/body therapies.

Dr. Werbach, an internationally recognized authority in nutritional medicine, an early pioneer in biofeedback research at UCLA, and assistant clinical professor at the UCLA School of Medicine, provides a clear and in-depth explanation of the nutritional treatment of depression through diet and nutritional supplementation, based on solid scientific research. Dietary factors and common foods associated with depression are examined; these include caffeine, sugar, and alcohol as well as specific nutrient deficiencies including vitamin B complex, folic acid, vitamin B_6, vitamin B_{12}, and vitamin C. Neurotransmitter precursor therapy may be used to raise serotonin levels. A case study emphasizes the importance of integrating therapies such as biofeedback and relaxation response training into a more comprehensive model of treating depression.

The Natural Pharmacy: Herbal Medicine and Depression— Janet Zand, O.M.D., L.Ac.

Depression is an enigmatic and complex phenomenon according to Dr. Janet Zand, a Doctor of Oriental Medicine, author, and a nationally known expert in herbal medicine. In fact, many of the numerous symptoms of depression—chronic fatigue, insomnia, loss of appetite, headaches, backaches, bowel disorders, and feelings of worthlessness and inadequacy—can, in other circumstances, be the cause of depression. Herbal medicine has a long and respected history and holds a valuable place in the treatment of mental/emotional disorders such as anxiety and depression as well as the vast majority of health problems. The proper use of herbs not only helps to alleviate symptoms but also helps to treat the underlying problem and strengthen the overall functioning of a particular organ or body system.

Dr. Zand profiles the Western and Chinese herbs that have proven effective in treating depression, anxiety, and mood disorders, including St. John's wort, kava, Siberian ginseng, *Ginkgo biloba,* astragalus, *Dong quai*, bupleurum, milk thistle, ginger root, and valerian. She also provides a list of essential oils that are helpful in alleviating depression as well as a useful herbal chart for quick reference. This chart lists the herbs and the corresponding symptoms of depression that it addresses, along with how the herb is taken, plus any possible side effects.

Homeopathy and Depression—Jacquelyn J. Wilson, M.D.

Homeopathic remedies use minute doses of a medicinal agent that stimulate the body's own natural powers of recovery to restore balance and health rather than to simply suppress symptoms. Dr. Wilson, a nationally recognized authority in homeopathy and past president of the American Institute of Homeopathy, has found this system of natural medicine to be consistently effective in treating mental and emotional problems as a method of individual self-care and, in more serious cases, when administered under the care of a health professional. In classical homeopathy, however, there are numerous forms of depression, as depression is not considered to be a single disease but a specific symptom-picture. Classical homeopathic prescribing matches a single remedy with a patient's detailed symptom profile. The key to the homeopathic approach to treating depression, therefore, is to find the medicine that corresponds or is similar to the depressed person's mind and body traits and complaints.

The most important homeopathic remedies for depression are described in this chapter, along with the appropriate Bach Flower remedies and cell salts, including each remedy's matching symptom profile. Dr. Wilson also distinguishes between the advantages and disadvantages of the two primary forms of homeopathy—classical single remedy prescribing and complex homeopathy, which uses combination remedies. She provides a fascinating account of a seriously depressed woman who did not respond to antidepressants and conventional medicine but significantly benefited from a specific homeopathic remedy.

Ayurveda and Yoga for Depression and Promoting Mental Health—Shri Kant Mishra, M.D., M.S., Doctor of Ayurveda

Ayurveda, the traditional system of medicine in India, has been practiced continuously for over 5,000 years. The principal goal of Ayurveda is the preservation and promotion of health with special emphasis on preventing illness. The secondary goal of this form of medicine is the treatment of physical, mental, and spiritual illness, according to Dr. Shri Kant Mishra, an internationally renowned neurologist, and the only Western-trained M.D. working in the United States with a formal degree in Ayurveda from Benares University in India. In addressing one's overall health, Ayurveda embraces a holistic perspective, integrating all aspects of life—nutrition, hygiene, sleep, seasonal changes, lifestyle, and physical, mental, and sexual activities. Diagnosis and treatment in Ayurvedic medicine revolves around determining the individual's constitutional profile, which is based upon the unique combination of the three *doshas*, or humors (*vata, pitta*, and *kapha*). Illness and depression result when there is a *dosha* imbalance.

This ancient system of natural medicine has a long history in the areas of mental health, rejuvenation, and longevity through the use of diet and lifestyle practices, herbs, massage, yoga, and meditation. Dr. Mishra explores the Ayurvedic approach to attaining a balanced state of mental health and focuses on specific approaches to treating *vata, pitta*, and *kapha* forms of depression. He also provides yogic practices such as *pranayama* (breathing practices) and meditation to help promote optimal health, mental clarity, and balance.

Qigong, Chinese Medicine, and Depression— Roger C. Hirsh, O.M.D., L.Ac., B.Ac. (UK), Dipl. Ac. (NCCA)

Chinese Medicine, as well as the many Chinese healing arts and martial arts, is based on the concept of *Qi*, or vital force. Chinese philosophy believes that the free and unobstructed flow of *Qi* throughout the organ meridian system of the body brings radiant health, whereas its blockage or stagnation results in reduced energy that can lead to health problems. There is a strong recognition in Chinese Medicine of the role of the emotions in health and illness. When the body and mind move in harmony, positive emotions prevail. Depression, however, is due to a stagnation of emotional *Qi* within an individual's internal organs, especially the liver, kidneys, and lungs. If the *Qi* is deeply stagnated for a period of time, it can affect every organ meridian system and cause severe depression.

Dr. Hirsh, a respected doctor of Chinese herbal medicine, acupuncture, and a longtime teacher of Qigong and *Taiji* (Tai Chi), leads the reader in a journey into the secrets of Qigong, an ancient Chinese art of energy training and rejuvenation. Qigong is increasingly utilized in health care settings worldwide for both the prevention and the treatment of depression. For those experiencing either acute or deep-seated depression, Hirsh provides some simple Qigong exercises that involve breathing, visualization, and movement to stimulate and energize. The first set of Qigong exercises are warm-ups that can be performed either individually or in a group to help deal with mild to moderate depression. The second group, "The Eight Silken Brocades," is a set of ancient exercises that help to stimulate and tonify the whole biomechanical system of the body in order to relieve stress, maintain youthfulness, and promote general well-being.

The Spiritual Dimension of Depression— Carlos Warter, M.D., Ph.D.

The great spiritual traditions of the world tell us that pain and suffering are rooted in the forgetfulness of our true divine nature—our separation from the universal source. Psychiatrist Carlos Warter, M.D., Ph.D., a pioneer in spiritual psychology and psychospiritual integration, shows us how depression can manifest through ignoring or forgetting our true identity as spiritual beings. In treating hundreds of individuals with symptoms of depression, Dr. Warter recognizes the validity of each treatment modality, and the importance of looking at the physical, biochemical, mental, and emotional causes of depression. To be really effective, however, he has discovered that one must cross into the realm of the spiritual to create a truly comprehensive treatment approach. "In the majority of depression cases that I have treated," says Warter, "the essential problem is that the individual's identity is firmly established in the smaller story of the personality and their larger, divine identity has been 'forgotten.' "

The solution, according to Warter, is to help the individual to move from the small, contracted story where depression is able to develop, to the awareness of a larger dimension of one's being, the big story of human life. This elevation in awareness entails a fundamental shift in the very notion of who we are, thereby undercutting the very basis of the existing depression. In this chapter, Dr. Warter charts out the spiritual terrain of healing, by combining both Eastern and Western spiritual traditions and providing many practical tools and exercises to help us reclaim our wholeness and spiritual birthright.

Where Do I Go from Here?

The final chapter gives you important tips to further educate yourself about the therapies in this book and the criteria for selecting the most appropriate approach for a specific condition. This includes referrals to the various appendices of the book, which provide resources on alternative and complementary health care, recommended reading, and Internet resources. The chapter also provides guidelines for finding the most suitable professional services, including health professionals, diagnostic laboratories, and compounding pharmacies.

Treat this book like a treasure chest of healing approaches to depression and mood disorders. By opening and examining its unique and valuable contents, you can discover and take with you the map to healthier living.

two

Depression As Emotional Pain: A Mind/Body Approach

David E. Bresler, Ph.D., L.Ac.

Happiness is finding without looking; unhappiness is looking without finding; depression is looking without finding and then feeling guilty about being presumptuous enough to even look.

—Anonymous

Statistics concerning depression in America today are truly staggering. Over 25 million Americans are being treated for depression, two-thirds of whom are women, and these figures do not take into account all the people who are depressed but are not being treated.

The statistics concerning suicide are equally alarming. It's been reported that over 1 million people attempt suicide each year and over 50,000, or approximately 5 percent, are successful. Women have a much greater incidence of attempting suicide, while men have a much greater incidence of success in committing suicide.

Patients who actually attempt suicide typically go through four recognizable stages. The first stage is "passive suicidal ideation," in which they ruminate or think about the possibility of suicide and what it would be like not to be alive. This is a philosophical, "What if?" scenario.

The second stage is "active suicidal ideation," in which they examine the implications of the act and how it will affect their family and friends. They are contemplating the practical reality of committing suicide that includes how, when, and where they will do it.

The third stage is the "preparation to act" stage, in which they might write a will and personal letters and get their affairs in order. The fourth stage is the actual suicide attempt.

I make it a practice to ask every client or patient about suicidal ideation, and I am shocked how common it is in people with pain. Even more shocking is patients who tell me that I am the first health professional who's really questioned them on this issue!

To me, depression is a form of emotional pain, and for many desperate people in pain, suicide is seen as the ultimate pain reliever. Patients will often say, "You know I'm not crazy. These suicidal thoughts don't mean that I'm out of my mind. I'm in pain all the time, not able to do anything useful, relate to my family or friends, have restful sleep, or enjoy life. This is no way to live. It's just torture."

I tell clients who are contemplating suicide two things: "Suicide is a permanent solution to what might very well be a temporary problem," and "If you act on these thoughts, you won't be around later on to change your mind." As simplistic and obvious as these statements sound, it is often profound food for thought for those considering suicide and its consequences.

Many clients who seek help for depression have two parts of themselves (or "subpersonalities"), one of which has very strong suicidal ideation or intent, while the other resists the thought and wants to move through the problem and get on with life.

How do I know there's a part that wants to survive? I know it because they came to see me for help. Something inside made them call for an appointment and made them walk through my door. That's the part of the person I want to talk to about the changes needed to move through depression.

STAGES OF LOSS

Psychological depression is, by and large, a very natural occurrence. While some people feel stigmatized by depression, we all experience depression at one time or another, especially following a loss. I genuinely believe that depression is an essential part of the healing process and the transformational experience that follows loss.

There are several characteristic stages that individuals go through following loss. The first stage will usually be one of shock, which often provides a degree of anesthesia for the pain. The loss may seem like an unreal experience, and during this stage, you may dissociate and even "leave your body" for a day or two. Usually this is a short-lived stage and is followed by the second stage, which is characterized by protest, denial, or anger. People often feel "This is not fair. Why is this happening to me?"

As the initial protest subsides, the experience of loss then moves to the third stage, which is characterized by grief, mourning, and depression. This depressed, grieving stage is a very natural part of healing and usually does not require any therapeutic intervention except perhaps some additional support.

If we stay with our feelings and work through them, we next move into a stage of detachment where we remember the loss, but no longer feel pain about it. Finally, after a period of time, we are ready to reattach. I think of this entire process as a kind of "emotional healing," for it is how we normally heal ourselves and recover following a loss.

THE SYMPTOMS OF DEPRESSION

It is interesting to see how most psychiatrists and psychologists view depression. According to the American Psychiatric Association's DSM-IV,[1] for example, in order to diagnose a patient with a major depressive episode, the patient must have "a depressed mood" and "a loss of interest in usual activities" for a period of at least two weeks, and at least four out of the following seven symptoms:

1. Loss of appetite accompanied by weight loss or overeating

2. Insomnia or hypersomnia

3. Fatigue or loss of energy

4. Feelings of worthlessness or excessive or inappropriate guilt

5. Poor concentration or difficulty in making appropriate decisions

6. Suicidal thoughts or actions

7. Psychomotor agitation or retardation

According to this DSM-IV characterization, nearly everyone who is going through a period of loss can be categorized as having a "major depressive episode." In fact, you can look at other emotional states, such as being in love, as a "pathologic condition" in which you have loss of interest in your usual activities, loss of appetite, weight loss, insomnia or sleep dysfunctions, psychomotor retardation, and decreased ability to concentrate.

Isn't it amazing that despite all the research that's being done on clinical depression and all the attention that is being focused on this condition, we still do not really have a solid way to identify, define, categorize, or classify it?

In simple terms, depression is a natural phenomenon that occurs frequently in most of us. Think about a disappointment related to a time when you experienced some loss in elementary school. You can probably remember that this was a significant loss or disappointment, but it is very unlikely that you are still depressed about it today. In most cases, we move through depression, heal ourselves emotionally, and go on with our lives. While people dealing with loss may need support and probably some direction, depression is usually part of the normal healing experience, and thus, it generally does not need to be fixed.

Sometimes, I find myself concerned about people who do not get depressed following a loss, because it may mean they are emotionally shut down, in denial, or stuck in shock. Possibly they may have skipped the grieving process and moved on to detachment. However, when you do not adequately grieve a significant loss, you are likely to grieve it even more deeply the next time you have loss.

PSYCHOLOGICAL VIEWS OF DEPRESSION

According to Freud, and the analytic school that followed him, depression was "anger turned inward" or anger directed against the self. If the diagnosis was depression, the treatment was to let all those feelings out. The difficulty with this approach is that when they "let all the feelings out," people can do strange and destructive things, such as jump out of windows or shoot someone. While there is abundant literature discussing this analytic perspective, there is little evidence to support the notion that psychological depression is primarily anger against the self.

In current times, there is great interest in the biochemical notions that consider depression to be a disease of the brain and spinal cord. As with many other diseased organs, the most common medical approach today is to treat it with medications, and we certainly do. (I sometimes wonder how many people are not taking antidepressants, rather than how many people are.)

On the other end of the spectrum are the disciples of cognitive therapy who consider depression to be a "tyranny of shoulds." Depression is a disordered, inappropriate way of thinking, causing stupid behavior by nonstupid people. Cognitive theorists see the symptoms as the disease and believe that to treat depression, you need to treat the symptoms of disordered thinking.

The analysts counter by saying that if you simply treat the symptoms, they will emerge in other ways through cathexis or sublimation. Treating only the symptoms of depression may also deprive people of the emotional and spiritual growth that occurs as you explore the root causes and meaning of the depression, and ultimately, heal it.

THE MEANING OF PAIN AND DEPRESSION

A confusion surrounding the definition and diagnosis of pathologic depression is very reminiscent of the situation we see in trying to define an experience such as pain. In our language and culture, we often talk about pain as if it is a "thing" like a splinter. If I bang my hand on a table, I might say, "I have pain in my hand." If you experience low back pain radiating down your leg, you may describe it as if it is a tangible, physical entity that exists somewhere in the back and lower leg.

Upon some reflection, however, it is obvious that pain is not a "thing." Let's look at the other side of the coin: pleasure. For example, if you had breakfast this morning and were eating a delicious Danish pastry, I doubt very much that you said, "Ummm . . . That tastes so good, my mouth is full of pleasure. Not only do I have a lot of pleasure in my tongue and mouth right now, but that pleasure is radiating all the way down the back of my throat to my stomach, and now my stomach is filling with pleasure." Although it sounds ridiculous in this context, this is actually how we talk about pain.

It is important to understand that there is no such "thing" or object as pain. When I bang my hand on a table, that injury triggers a barrage of electrochemical messages that ascend the neuraxis into the central nervous system. Depending upon how that information is interpreted by the brain and spinal cord, it may or may not be considered painful. For example, have you ever scratched an itch really hard? Does it hurt? Does it feel good? It's really hard to say, isn't it?

There are many important implications to realizing that pain is not a "thing" or a sensation. This is not to say that metabolic disturbances, physical injuries, nutritional deficiencies, environmental toxins, or other factors can't trigger the experience of pain or depression, but it is far too simplistic to say that pain is simply a sensation or that depression is simply an emotion.

PAIN AND DEPRESSION AS PERCEPTIONS

To some extent, one could consider pain or depression to be a "perception" because, like other perceptions, they are very much influenced by early learned experiences. For example, it was reported that dogs raised in a pain-free environment were relatively insensitive to pain later on in life. This insensitivity caused many problems in dealing with changing environments, for pleasure and pain are important feedback experiences that help us navigate successfully through life. Pleasure tends to facilitate behavior, and pain tends to inhibit it. Without both an accelerator and brakes, navigation can be perilous.

When you look at pain as a learned perceptual experience, it is easy to see why two patients with the same degree of physical pathology can have very different experiences of pain. The same applies to the realm of depression, when two people who suffer the same type of loss experience their resulting depression in very different ways.

To illustrate, I like to compare the X-rays of two patients with knee injuries. One patient was a professional football player who had undergone eight or nine surgical procedures to his knee. When looking at his X-ray, it's hard to imagine that he could stand or walk, much less continue to play professional football. However, he was not complaining of pain, and refused to take any pain medications because they made him less "ferocious" when he played football. He didn't care about the pain but wanted greater stability and strength in his knee.

The second knee X-ray belongs to a patient injured in a workers' compensation case. There was absolutely nothing in the X-ray to indicate any physical abnormality whatsoever, yet this patient was in agonizing pain, completely disabled, and unable to stand, bend, lift, carry, or walk.

Likewise, whether or not we become depressed depends less upon the nature of the loss, and more upon how we tolerate or deal with it.

DEPRESSION AS A LEARNED BEHAVIOR

Another perspective for understanding depression comes from the work of Martin Seligman, a psychologist who conducted several fascinating studies on what he called "learned helplessness." In a typical experiment, a dog is placed into a shuttle box that has a grid floor and a little hurdle in the middle. When shock is turned on, the dog will bark, howl, and seem very distressed. After a time, the dog will eventually jump over the hurdle to the other side, at which point the experimenter immediately turns off the shock. After very few trials, dogs rapidly learn that as soon as the shock comes on, they can avoid pain by jumping over the hurdle to the other side and the shock will be turned off. This is called "escape learning," and it is well known that dogs can learn this very quickly.

Dr. Seligman, however, pretrained a group of dogs by first putting them into hammocks and giving them unavoidable, inescapable, random shocks. There was nothing the dogs could do about the shocks except sit there and take it. At first, the dogs would howl, bark, and carry on, but after a period of time, the dogs would give up hope and just sit there victimized. When he put these animals into the shuttle box and turned on the shock, all they had to do was jump over the hurdle to avoid the shock, but they just sat there.

Seligman called this phenomenon "learned helplessness" and suggested that it represents an animal model of depression. First, all the same types of biochemical abnormalities seen in human depression also showed up in these "learned-helpless" dogs. Second, the therapeutic interventions used to treat human depressives (e.g., electroconvulsive shock, tricyclic antidepressants, monoamine oxidase (MAO) inhibitors, etc.) facilitated the return of jumping behavior in these dogs.

What was particularly intriguing to me were the behavioral interventions that Seligman tested to see if they were effective in returning jumping behavior (i.e., treating depression). For example, he would turn off the shock and put food on the other side of the shuttle box. The dogs were not interested—they had depressed appetite. He put female dogs in heat on the other side of the shuttle box, and again, the dogs were not interested—they had depressed libido. However, when he turned on the shock, grabbed them by the collar, and dragged them over to the other side, then turned off the shock and repeated this a few times, the dogs started jumping again on their own. Once they started jumping again, all the biochemical abnormalities also disappeared.

In a sense, Seligman "empowered" the dogs and showed them that there was something they could do to get relief. This experiment clearly demonstrates the importance of self-management and further that hope, learning, memory, and prior experiences are vitally important in how we experience depression.

DEPRESSION AS A HABIT

Depression can also be thought of as an "emotional habit" in which we get stuck in an obsessive-compulsive rut consisting exclusively of negative thoughts and feelings that are like a bad habit or impulse we can't control. How do we break such a habit? We seemingly cannot, because even if we withdraw all reward or reinforcement from the habit, it will often continue to persist. For example, if a rat is trained to run down a maze and turn left to get a piece of food, he will continue to do so long after the food has been removed. This is called "resistance to extinction" of a habit. If we want to teach the rat to turn right, the fastest way to do so is to put the food on the right.

In other words, the most effective way to break an old habit is to learn a new habit that is incompatible with the old one (the rat cannot turn left and right at the same time). It is also important that we systematically reward and reinforce the new habit in order to allow it to gain strength. When people are stuck in the habit of depressed thinking and feeling, it is often helpful to embrace a new belief system, point of view, or personal reality that contains more positive thoughts and feelings. This new reality must then be consistently reinforced until it gains sufficient strength to maintain itself.

For example, it is common to find that when one experiences depression following the death of a loved one after a prolonged illness, it is often a shock to discover that part of the person feels relieved by the death; commonly this can cause additional feelings of guilt. It is important to see that feeling relief is healthy and demonstrates a hopefulness that the pain is coming to an end and that a new beginning is around the corner. One must not overlook the importance of reinforcing this new belief system.

TRAUMATIC LEARNING

I have long believed in the concept of "traumatic learning" and the vital role it can play in perpetuating pain and depression. If trauma is significant enough, permanent learning can occur in one session. For example, a cat that steps on a hot stove once will never step on a stove again, hot or cold.

How do we learn through trauma? When we are traumatized, we often go into a trancelike state similar to hypnosis. In a sense, hypnosis can be defined as "a state of focus, concentrated attention in which there is increased openness to suggestion." Suggestions that are made around a traumatic experience produce images that can be very enduring, and the feelings that are associated with these images can quite literally last a lifetime. These internal images formed around trauma contain sensitive and vital information about what happened, how we reacted, how we think and feel about it now, and how concerned we are about it happening again. As a result, these images can create negative views of ourselves and our ability to handle trauma, leading to long-term depression and low self-esteem. These images can also drive (unconsciously) our behavior in ways that are counterintentional and even bewildering.

Interactive Guided Imagery is one of the most effective ways to take people back in time to explore the origins of their problem or situation. For example, I might invite a patient with low self-esteem to "go back in your mind to the very first time you felt that you were not as good as other people. Allow an image to spontaneously form, and describe it when it appears." One of my patients responded, "I'm about seven years old, and it's recess time at school. I'm out on the playground and two other kids are choosing teams. Everybody else has been chosen, and I'm sitting there all alone watching the two kids argue with each other about which one has to take me on their team."

Was this person in "a state of focused, concentrated attention" in which there was "increased openness to suggestion" when teams were being chosen on the playground? This is pure hypnosis, for in this case, a traumatic "self-image" formed that this person was not as good as other people. Long after this episode has been denied or repressed, or some other psychological defense against pain has come into play, that self-image can remain and produce psychological, emotional, or even physical damage until the roots of the problem are uncovered and finally resolved.

When you think about all the different ways that we learn to deal with loss and trauma throughout our early years, it's easy to see why there's great individual variation on how people handle or experience depression.

DEPRESSION AS A SYMPTOM

We can also look at depression as a symptom, depending upon how we define the term. To me, a symptom is the way the body tries to heal itself or prevent further injury. For example, consider a low-grade fever. In Chinese Medicine, a low-grade fever is a healthy thing, for the body is raising its core temperature to burn out some invading microorganism. It is not seen as a "disease" or "illness," but as a way in which the body works to maintain homeostasis and heal itself.

Symptoms are also the way an organism tries to call attention to a need for change. To me, real healing is almost always about change, not about adjusting or covering up symptoms as is emphasized in our contemporary health care delivery system.

A typical physician might say, "Your blood pressure is too high, so we will give you some medication to lower it," or "Not getting enough sleep? We will give you some medicine to reduce your insomnia," or "Feeling depressed? Here's some medicine to raise your mood." To me, the real issue is: Why is that person's blood pressure too high? Why is she not able to sleep? Why is he depressed? Symptoms have meaning, and that's what we should be exploring.

For example, sometimes people with headaches ask, "Why do I have these headaches?" I often respond, "Well, there are at least two possibilities we can consider. The first possibility is that the Martians are doing it. You were walking down the street and stepped into some kind of Martian headache ray and got zapped. Unfortunately, we don't have any antidotes to the Martian ray, and we haven't yet established communication with the Martians, so we can't negotiate, but maybe sometime in the future, there may be hope.

"There is another hypothesis, however, that we can also consider," I continue. "That is that your nervous system is giving the experience of headaches for a reason. It may involve an endocrine imbalance, nutritional deficiency, metabolic disorder, environmental toxins, stress, your relationships, or other factors occurring in your life, but it is attempting to get your attention regarding an issue that needs change.

Once we understand the reason why your nervous system is giving you headaches, we might be able to make some changes in your life so that headaches will no longer be needed."

THE EXPERIENCE OF DEPRESSION

Although it may be helpful to "adjust" symptoms by giving medications so that patients are more comfortable as they explore the meaning of their symptoms, the critical step in the healing process is to understand what needs to change.

Because we can experience depression and pain physically, emotionally, cognitively, motivationally, perceptually, and spiritually, it is easy to get lost in it. By stepping back and getting "the big picture," we can more easily see that depression is a life experience that we all go through. Sometimes, it is a natural way to be detached, feel the pain, and grow following a loss. Sometimes, it is also a way to stop forward movement, change direction, and regroup forces before moving on. I smile when I remember the pioneering Humanistic psychologist Abraham Maslow saying, "If there's no pain, there's no growth."

DEPRESSION AND STATE DEPENDENCY

The most common things that need to change following a loss are our beliefs and attitudes. In order to do this, we need to understand the concept of "state dependency." This notion maintains that a specific emotion is attached to a specific state of consciousness that holds a set of beliefs, attitudes, values, and drives that are different from those we experience in other states of consciousness.

For example, think back to a time when you were in an argument with your spouse or close friend, and he or she brought up an incident that occurred five or ten years earlier. You may be incredulous and say, "That was over five years ago!" To that person, however, it felt like it happened yesterday.

This illustrates state dependency. When you get into an angry state of consciousness, you have access to all the information, memories, beliefs, values, and drives that were available the last time you were angry. Conversely, when you are in a loving state of consciousness, you have access to all the things you thought about the last time you were in that loving state of consciousness.

Of course, it follows that when you are in a depressed state of consciousness, you have access to all the things you thought about the last
time you were depressed. If you are not awake and aware of this phenomenon, you can easily get stuck in this self-perpetuating nature of
depression.

As a quick illustration of how to change your state of consciousness
when you are wrestling with depression, try smiling at yourself in a mirror. You'll find that at first, it's difficult to do, but as you continue to smile
and leer at yourself, you'll find that after a few moments, it's almost
impossible not to break into laughter and to realize how ridiculous everything is. As you laugh, you may also notice that your depression has been
relieved and that the things you were worried and concerned about don't
seem to be quite as worrisome.

EVOCATIVE IMAGERY

When depression is viewed as a "stuck" state of consciousness, many
nondrug interventions can be helpful, including a guided imagery technique called Evocative Imagery. With this technique, you first identify the
particular quality that you need right now to help you get through a current challenge or difficulty. Perhaps hope, courage, patience, or strength is
needed, but identify the exact quality you would like to have more of in
your life. Then, allow your mind to go back to a time when you actually
experienced having that quality, and through guided imagery, you can
bring that quality forward in time as you now look at your situation from
a different point of view or state of consciousness.

Here is an example of Evocative Imagery that can be taped and
played back, or read aloud by someone else.

> *Close your eyes and take a few moments to allow yourself to
> become more comfortable and at ease. You might find it help-
> ful to take a few breaths: inhale deeply, and as you exhale let it
> be a real letting go.*
>
> *You might also find it helpful to imagine a ball of pure energy
> or white light that starts at your lower abdomen, and as you
> inhale, it rises up the front of your body to your forehead, and as
> you exhale, it goes down your spine, down your legs, and into
> the ground. Again, just imagine a ball of pure energy or white
> light that starts at your lower abdomen, and as you inhale, it goes*

up the front of your body to your forehead, and as you exhale, it goes down your spine, down your legs, and into the ground. . . .

Take a few moments to circulate that ball of energy around, allowing it to move you into an even deeper state of relaxation and comfort.

As you allow yourself to feel even more relaxed and at ease, bring to mind some issue or challenge that's going on in your life right now. It may be a symptom, an emotion such as depression, a problem, or a goal or aspiration. As you think about it, consider what quality would be most helpful to you in working through this situation, this challenge, or this problem or what quality would be most helpful in reaching your goals or aspirations. What quality would you like to have a lot more of to be successful in working through this experience?

Once you clearly identify this quality, let your mind wander back to a time when you actually experienced this quality, and manifested it very strongly in your life. Imagine that you are there now, and notice where you are, who you are with, and your posture as you're in touch with this quality.

Notice your tone of voice as you're in touch with this quality. Imagine that you can experience this quality in every cell of your body to the deepest core of your being.

If you like, imagine that you have a volume control knob that you can use to turn up how much you experience this quality, so that it fills every cell of your being as it begins to radiate not only to every part of your body, but outside your body as well. Feel it as an aura an inch away from you, two, three, or four inches away from you, filling up all the space around you as well.

Use the volume control knob to turn it up as much as you like, and then to turn it down a little. See how that feels, and if you like, you can now turn it up even more to find the level that feels most comfortable for you. As you feel the fullness of this quality so strongly in yourself, bring it back with you to the present time, as we take another look at the issue that is going on in your life right now.

Is it the same, or does it look or feel a little different to you in some way? In what way does it look or feel different? Let yourself know that you can turn up this quality in yourself any time you wish by simply going through the same steps that we just took. When you are ready, allow yourself to return to this time and this place, to this outside world as you open your eyes feeling refreshed, comfortable, at ease, and ready to meet any demands that arise. You might want to take a little stretch at this time.

Evocative Imagery offers a fast and simple way to get out of an "emotional rut" like depression and move into a more positive state of consciousness.

DEPRESSION AND STRESS

The relationship between depression and stress is an important one. I once had the good fortune to teach a workshop with several of the world's experts on stress, including Hans Selye, Ken Pelletier, and Mayer Friedman, the researcher who conducted the pioneering studies on the relationship between Type A behavior and heart disease. On one occasion, Dr. Friedman told us formally about an unpublished study he had conducted at Mt. Sinai Hospital in San Francisco. He was interested in comparing stress levels and their biochemical correlates in a population of depressed patients with those of a control group known to be under intense stress.

For this control group, he chose the parents of children with leukemia who had been admitted to the hospital for one last attempt at aggressive chemotherapy. While few things are more stressful than having a dying child, the results of the study indicated that the depressed patients had been under even more stress than the parents of these children.

Living with depression is extraordinarily stressful, and even though depressed patients usually do not look as though they are "stressed out," it is always helpful for them to learn some type of stress management technique to cope more effectively with their emotional pain.

Stress vs. Stress Tolerance

The concept of stress was first advanced by Hans Selye, who defined it as "a demand on the organism." Dr. Selye distinguished two types of stress: distress, which is negative stress, and eustress, which is positive stress.

I once asked Dr. Selye, "What do think is the single most stressful human experience?" He replied with a twinkle in his eye, "Probably a

passionate kiss," and went on to describe changes in adrenal corticos-
teroid levels, blood pressure, and heart rate that correlated with high
stress levels during lovemaking.

Positive things can certainly be stressful, which is why I always
remind my patients about the difference between a vacation and a rest.
Vacations are typically very stressful (although fun), and often we need
to have a period of rest following a vacation in order to recover and
protect our health.

While there is a huge amount of scientific literature that suggests
strong relationships between high stress levels and illness, I believe that
the relationship is a more complex one and that high stress levels do not
necessarily lead to illness.

For example, two researchers named Thomas H. Holmes, M.D.,
and Richard H. Rahe, M.D., developed a well-known test called the
"Schedule of Recent Life Experience," which assigns a point value to
the various demands that we encounter in modern-day living. For
instance, the death of a spouse is valued at 100 points, divorce is 90
points, a change of job is 85 points, and so forth. By adding up the
point values associated with the demands we experience, this scale is
said to have high validity in determining the likelihood that stress-
related illness will develop.

Although these data may have validity over a large population of
people, I often question their accuracy when dealing with an individual
patient, for many people experience a decrease in stress following a
divorce, the death of a loved one after a prolonged illness, or leaving a
job that was unsatisfying.

The key factor determining how we will be affected by stress is not
the external situation or demands that are placed upon us, but rather
how we deal with or tolerate those demands through the coping strategies we use to deal with change.

Dealing with Stress: Two Migraine Patients

The variability in how people handle stress was brought home to
me dramatically by two patients with migraine headaches whom I was
treating at the same time. The first patient was a narcotics officer for
the LAPD. While taking his history during our first session, I asked him
what a typical day was like.

He responded, "Well, I get up in the morning, do my stretching, then go downstairs to work out and do my exercises. Then I come back up, shower, shave, do all my toiletries, get dressed, put on my bullet-proof vest, remind myself I'm going to get shot, and go down for breakfast. Usually I have a bowl of cereal and some fruit . . ." I broke in and said to him, "Wait, back up a minute. What did you say about getting shot?"

He replied, "Yeah, I make it a practice to remind myself in the morning that it is likely that I'll get shot. In this business, we all get shot at, and some of us get hit. We're mostly concerned about how badly we may get hit and how well our partner is able to back us up." In a sense, this police officer considered himself to be an urban garbageman, raiding crack houses and cleaning the junk off Los Angeles streets. His job was like a game to him ("catching the bad guys"), and he did not seem to be very stressed by the dangers that were involved.

As I continued to take his history, however, he revealed that shortly before his headaches began, his eighteen-year-old daughter had started dating a "very questionable character" in his opinion, and his daughter's response to his concern was, "Tough. I'm going to do what I want."

At about that time, he had also discovered that his sixteen-year-old son was beginning to experiment with drugs. Imagine what a narcotics officer for the Los Angeles Police Department sees in a typical week! While he could tolerate the stress of being in very dangerous situations and possibly even getting shot, he could not handle what was going on with his children.

The second patient with headaches was a Beverly Hills matron whom I rated high on the obsessive-compulsive scale. For example, she would have the windows in her mansion cleaned inside and out seven days a week and showed up at my office with a blistering migraine because a bird had "dumped" on one of her windows just before an important cocktail party.

When you see these two patients on the same day, it becomes very clear that it's not what's "out there" or the demands that life places upon us that make us sick, but rather, how we tolerate or handle those demands.

The same is true for depression. I always find it interesting to observe how differently people respond to loss, particularly very profound and significant loss. Why do some of us completely fall apart and find ourselves unable to deal with loss, while others seem to have tremendous resilience? Resilient types of people are not necessarily unfeeling or uncaring, but they certainly seem to handle the stress caused by life's changes. In my opinion, the reason that resilient people do so well following loss is directly related to their belief systems and the way that they perceive reality.

PERSONAL REALITY SYSTEMS

Have you ever been in a situation where two of your friends were in a terrible argument? After you talk to the first one and hear his point of view, you might think to yourself, "I can't believe that other person would do that! It's outrageous, but I've got to talk to him right away." You then talk to the other person and get his point of view which is, of course, completely different.

What really happened? They both occupied the same space at the same time, yet their personal realities as to what occurred are completely different. This is called the Uncertainty Principle in quantum physics, a statement that reality is based on a personal "frame of reference," "point of view," or "personal belief system."

People who tolerate high levels of stress well tend to have more positive beliefs about the reality of what's happening. For example, the Chinese *gua*, the character for "crisis," has two components to it: the upper portion represents "danger," and the lower portion represents "opportunity." When most people go through crisis, they are usually well aware of the dangers involved. Resilient people are aware of the opportunities.

THE CRITICAL IMPORTANCE OF ATTENTION

How do we as health care professionals help our patients reframe a crisis or a loss so that they can see it from a more positive point of view? For me, it's by teaching them how and where to place their attention. I like the old saying that states, "Whatever you give attention to grows," whether it's your garden, your children, or your worries, anxieties, and depressed thinking. In a sense, the more you pay attention to the reasons why you feel depressed, the more depressed you become.

As a psychologist, I am expected to know what "consciousness" is. That's part of the job description, but I've never found a satisfactory definition that fits all we know about it. Although I can't define consciousness, I am certain it has to do intimately with this process of attention.

In our particular culture, we are usually rewarded for paying attention to our "conscious mind," the little voice inside our head that talks to us all the time. This voice originates from the part of our nervous system that is rational, logical, analytic, and articulate. It's the part of our mind that we try to quiet when we meditate or do biofeedback.

I used to believe that the voice inside of my head was who I was, and that I was my mind. Upon further reflection, however, it is clear to me that saying "I am my mind" is like saying "I am my kidneys," or "I am my liver." My mind is certainly an important part of who I am, but it is not all that I am. I am much more than my mind, for who I am includes my emotions, fantasies, memories, drives and desires, my physical body, my memories and beliefs, and my spiritual nature.

In addition to that voice inside our head that talks to us all the time, there are other languages that the nervous system utilizes to communicate with itself. One of these is the language of imagery and symbolism, which is more highly valued and utilized in other cultures. While the language of imagery is more subtle, it is extremely informative and powerful, and it communicates critical information about our life through our insights, intuitions, fantasies, and dreams.

Have you ever been in a situation where you've said to yourself, "I knew that was going to happen." Who told you? The Martians? Where did that information come from? It probably came in the form of an "insight" or "intuition" that utilized the language of imagery to grab your attention.

Our nervous systems are constantly broadcasting information through the language of imagery, but in our culture, most of us have not learned to pay attention to this type of communication, and thus we often miss a great deal of important messages from our inner world.

GUIDED IMAGERY

Guided imagery is an extremely powerful technique that can be used to focus attention on the part of the nervous system that may have answers to our questions and solutions to our problems. An ancient concept central to alchemy states that "The answer is in the question and the solution is in the problem."

When patients come to see me, I try to remember that they bring in not only their problems, but also their solutions. While patients are typically not aware of how many powerful inner resources they already have, guided imagery and related techniques can help them discover these resources and guide them through their inner world to find new insights and creative solutions to their current life challenges.

My partner, Dr. Marty Rossman, a gifted teacher and clinician, has a wonderful way of describing this inner wisdom that I often share with my clients:

When you are first conceived, your mother's egg and your father's sperm cells come together so that each can contribute a set of chromosomes. A little flash of light goes off somewhere and that single-celled ovum begins to divide. From one cell, it becomes two, then four, then eight, then sixteen, and so forth. If you could dissect those cells and carefully analyze them, you would find that each one is an exact replica of the other, just a floating ball of absolutely identical cells somewhere in your mother's uterus.

However, before too long, something quite extraordinary begins to happen. Some sort of intelligent process takes over cell duplication, and by reading information contained in the DNA/RNA, it causes some of the dividing cells to form into a tiny tube, which ultimately becomes your central nervous system. This intelligent process causes other cells to form into another tube, which becomes your gastrointestinal tract.

This intelligent process, whatever it is, continues to read the unique blueprint stored on your DNA/RNA, and it proceeds to construct one of the most complex organisms on the face of the planet—you. This intelligent process doesn't stop at birth. For example, think about puberty. It's a complete remodeling job, isn't it? The whole body undergoes radical change during puberty, and it's clear that this intelligent process continues to control cell division for our entire lifetime.

Therefore, the analogy continues, if there is an intelligence inside each of you that is smart enough to start with one microscopic cell and proceed to design, create, and produce one of the most complex organisms on earth, namely you, maybe it would be a good idea to get a second opinion from it about your depression. Maybe it has some thoughts or opinions about it, and maybe it also has some wisdom to share about what to do in order to resolve it.

Physiologic Effects of Imagery

Imagery is not only the language of the unconscious mind, but it is also the language of the autonomic nervous system, the "housekeeping" part of our nervous system that controls various physiological functions within the body.

Images have important physiologic consequences. For example, if you wanted to increase salivation, you can read all that is known about salivary glands and the nerves that innervate them, but it wouldn't necessarily help you to create more saliva.

On the other hand, if you imagine sucking on a slice of a fresh, plump, juicy lemon, feeling the sour, tart lemon juice swirl all around your mouth, and your taste buds curdling in response to it, within a few moments you will begin to salivate automatically. You don't need to suck on an actual lemon to do this, only to experience it in your imagination.

If thinking about a lemon causes salivation, what happens when you think of yourself as a helpless, hopeless victim of some insoluble problem? What kind of message does that give the immune system, the endocrine system, or the nervous system? Doesn't it tell them, "Why bother?" Conversely, giving our attention to more positive images can have a powerfully enhancing effect on the body's ability to heal itself.

Our thoughts give physiologic instructions to the body, both positive and negative. In the case of long-term depressive thinking, the body can receive a range of negative physiologic instructions that can produce significant consequences. Observe in Figure 1 the picture drawn by a depressed patient with postlaminectomy syndrome and chronic pain following three back surgeries.

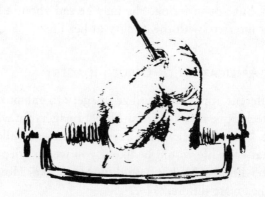

Figure 1

At first glance, it is obvious that this image is created by someone who is experiencing agonizing back pain. If you step back and embrace a broader perspective of this picture, we see that the patient is also suffering from "victim consciousness," in which he has completely surrendered to his pain. It controls him and everything he can or cannot do in his life.

They say a picture is worth a thousand words, and the picture in Figure 2 was drawn by a second patient with postlaminectomy syndrome who embraced quite a different worldview.

Figure 2

Strong images of hope and healing can have profoundly beneficial effects upon the immune system, nervous system, and other regulatory systems within the body. Stepping back, this picture shows a person who is in pain, but not suffering. She may be sad about a loss, but she is not letting it interfere with the quality of her life.

Therapeutic Application of Guided Imagery

Several different approaches utilize imagery to enhance the healing process. One technique is called Ideal Model Imagery, in which we suggest to a client, "Close your eyes for a few moments and allow an image to form of what your life would be like if you weren't depressed. How would things be different? What would they look like? How would you know that things were different?"

I find it interesting that some people are absolutely unable to imagine this. This often occurs when some resistant part of them is vested in maintaining the depression and does not want to let it go, even if only in their imagination.

Focusing on "what it might be like if you weren't depressed" is also a way of doing state-dependent work to help a client move into a more positive state of consciousness, just like the Evocative Imagery technique described earlier.

In another imagery technique, called Space Control, I invite people to close their eyes and imagine a beautiful, safe, serene place in which there is no depression and no pain. This helps them to create "an inner sanctuary" that they can visit in their imagination for a "time out" from their depression. I sometimes give them a "ride ticket," or a piece of paper that gives them written permission to take a trip inside to a place where there is no depression, pain, or sadness—a wonderful, positive, enlightening place.

Another imagery technique is Time Control, which is similar to Evocative Imagery, but in this case, people are invited to go back to a time when they did not feel depressed, to fully reexperience that time, how they felt, and how others reacted to them, and then to bring it forward to the present. Space Control techniques can also be used to invite people to imagine a future time when they have overcome their depression, much like Ideal Model Imagery.

Many people do not realize that we spend most of our time in the imaginal world. One of the most typical ways that we image is to worry! People often say, "Oh, I can't do imagery," and I respond, "Do you worry?" because what we worry about is happening only in our imagination. Another time that we commonly use imagery is whenever we are planning something like a trip or remodeling a part of our house.

Frequently we "time warp" into the past and ruminate like a cow chewing its cud over and over—constantly bringing the past into the present moment, reliving it in our imagination and contaminating our present with negative memories from the past. We also frequently "time warp" forward in our imagination to fear what has not yet even happened—the future.

These types of negative imagery can have serious physiologic consequences. It is well known that people can worry themselves into hypertension and other health problems, and I suspect that the experience of helplessness, hopelessness, and depression can also have serious

consequences for the body's regulatory systems, especially our autonomic nervous system and immune system. As Dr. Marty Rossman frequently asks, "If our thoughts can make us sick, can they also make us
well?" A vast body of information concerning hypnosis, suggestion,
and guided imagery suggest that they can.

THE MEANING OF DEPRESSION

By far, the most powerful way to utilize imagery applications in
treating depression is to explore the meaning and ideology of the
depression through imagery dialogue. While some think that depression
"just happens," or is caused by something alien to our being, depression, like other symptoms, occurs for a reason.

Causes may be biochemical imbalances, environmental toxins,
nutritional deficiencies, traumatic losses, and hormonal imbalances, to
name but a few. In my opinion, it is vitally important to explore the
meaning of the symptom before administering treatments or therapy.
Imagery dialogue, like the following, is one of the most powerful ways
to do this:

> *Close your eyes for a moment and allow yourself to get in
> touch with any feelings of helplessness, hopelessness, worthless-
> ness, or depression, however you may experience it. . . . As you
> get in touch with these feelings, allow an image to form that sym-
> bolizes or represents your experience of depression and when an
> image comes to mind, take a few moments to observe it.*
>
> *What do you notice about this image? What sort of qualities
> does it have? How do you feel as you experience this image?*
>
> *Tell the image how you feel, and let it respond to you in a
> way you can understand.*

As the dialogue with the image of depression unfolds, opportunities arise to ask, "Why are you here? What do you want? What do
you need? What do you have to offer? What part of my nervous system do you represent? What do I need to change in my life?"

The answers to these kinds of questions shed a great deal of light concerning the dynamics of the depression and often include physiological,
environmental, metabolic, or psychological situations from the past that
contribute significantly to the current problem. This information may not

present itself in contemporary medical terminology, but when one understands the language of imagery, the message it reveals from the inner wisdom of the organism often opens new opportunities for treatment interventions that can alleviate the problem.

One of the most common imagery techniques utilized for inner resources and support systems is to invite an image to form of an Inner Advisor. By definition, this image has the qualities of compassion, support, and wisdom needed to effectively explore one's inner world. People experiencing depression tend to have minimal support systems in the outside world, and no support whatsoever in the inside world, where they tend to focus attention on nonsupportive and self-destructive inner images. One of these figures is called the Inner Critic, the superego-like part of ourselves that judges, criticizes, and puts us down. A well-trained practitioner of this technique, called an imagery guide, can help sort out the variety of inner figures who may appear and help select a true Inner Advisor who is supportive, loving, and caring.

Imagery techniques can also be used to help patients go back to earlier experiences that may have etiologic influences on their current experience of depression. These are usually related to significant loss experiences that were not completely resolved.

Imagery can also be used for Parts Work that enables a person to get in touch with the part of oneself who wants to move through the depression and feel better, as well as with the coexisting part that is invested in maintaining the depression in order to get more attention, to avoid responsibilities, or for other reasons. A well-trained imagery guide can help mediate the conflict between the parts, much like conducting marriage and family counseling sessions inside the skin.

As is the case with most psychotherapeutic interventions, it is critically important to seek care from a well-trained, experienced, and ethical practitioner. For recommended practitioners of Guided Imagery see "Appendix B: Resources for Alternative and Complementary Health Care."

THE IMPORTANCE OF HOPE AND FAITH

Depression, on a spiritual and emotional level, can be extremely dangerous. Like the AIDS virus, which attacks the very system that defends us against disease, depression is insidious because it attacks what most keeps us alive—our will to live.

When we lose hope, we lose the very thing that offers the greatest help in healing the problem. Nothing keeps the human spirit alive more than hope and faith. Unfortunately, our contemporary health care delivery system has caused a tremendous erosion in our faith in the effectiveness of our doctors and the medications and procedures they prescribe.

Positive expectant faith is one of the most important ingredients in healing, and in scientific circles, the most common term used to describe faith healing is called the "placebo effect." Few things are more effective than placebos ("sugar pills"). In most typical experiments, one in three people given a placebo obtain a positive response, even though the pill contains no active therapeutic ingredients.

The placebo effect is so powerful that it works even when people know they are receiving a placebo. For example, in one study, researchers told a group of postoperative pain patients, "There are no active ingredients in these pills, but one in three people who take them get pain relief. Would you like to try?" Even though they revealed this information, they still found that one in three people who took the placebos reported significant pain relief.

I believe that many of the alternative or complementary therapies that are becoming popular today receive their power to some extent from our expectations and beliefs that they are going to be effective. Marty Rossman and I often joke that there should be a new specialty in medicine called Placebology that teaches doctors and other health professionals how to optimize the power of the placebo effect in their patients. Few things are more powerful than positive expectations, and when we can enhance the will to live and the belief that healing is possible, we are facilitating some of the most powerful healing systems in the human body.

three

Natural Medicine and Depression: A Naturopathic Approach

Joseph Pizzorno, N.D.

The natural force within each one of us is the greatest healer of disease.

—Hippocrates (460–377 B.C.),
father of Western medicine

As a naturopathic physician, I have come to recognize that my true role is not in treating disease but in helping people reestablish health. When we view depression from the naturopathic perspective, we understand that this condition is often the result of an accumulation of many interrelated factors. In a more general sense, depression can be viewed as a loss of energy for life. Depression therefore requires a more comprehensive perspective and solution—there is no single magic bullet.

One advantage to the naturopathic approach is that a combination of natural therapies can be utilized at very safe dosages rather than relying upon one pharmaceutical drug at a high or toxic dosage. Most important, this approach allows the patient to be highly involved in the healing process.

In order to illustrate the naturopathic approach to treating a patient with depression, I will present a simulated patient profile much as I would in my classrooms at Bastyr University. First, I will examine the principles of naturopathic medicine. Then I will explore the determinants of mood, or factors that cause depression, and examine how the various personal and lifestyle elements in the patient's life may relate to depression. Finally, I will demonstrate the various ways in which depression can be treated and develop a customized therapeutic plan for our hypothetical patient.

PRINCIPLES OF NATUROPATHIC MEDICINE

Naturopathic medicine is based on six principles: do no harm; a belief in the healing power of nature; treating the whole person; treating the cause; physician as teacher; and prevention is the best cure.

Do No Harm

The first principle, "Do no harm," is based on a very powerful belief in the ability of the body to heal itself and clarifies the real role of the physician as a person who provides the patient with tools with which to heal himself and to stimulate within the patient the belief in his ability to get healthy.

The Healing Power of Nature

Naturopathic medicine places great emphasis on the healing power of nature and the power of each individual to heal oneself. We work well with the conventional medical community, but one of the greatest frustrations we have with the medical profession is that practitioners often will tell patients that they have an *incurable* disease. In naturopathic medicine there is no such thing as an incurable disease; there are only diseases for which we may not know a cure. Equally important is the fact that a person's sense of hope and beliefs have a significant impact on their health. In other words, patients have a tremendous amount of control over their health, and the practitioner's role is to help reestablish that control.

Treating the Whole Person

Naturopathic medicine looks at the individual as a whole system composed of physical, mental, emotional, and spiritual components.

Treating the Cause

Practitioners of natural medicine have to be very cautious about addressing the underlying cause of a condition, because we have excellent natural therapies at our disposal that are just as good as allopathic medicines at suppressing symptoms and making people feel better without treating the causes. We do have to relieve symptoms to help the patient feel better, but if we do not deal with the cause, the person will keep getting sick. Dealing with symptoms is a very effective way to build a medical practice to keep patients for a long time, but it is not a very good role for a physician.

Physician As Teacher

Naturopathic physicians go beyond treating disease to educating and motivating people to take more personal responsibility in maintaining good health and a state of wellness through proper diet, lifestyle, and attitude.

Prevention Is the Best Cure

Naturopathic physicians are specialists in preventive medicine. Prevention is best accomplished through education, empowerment of the patient and the promotion of wellness and a health-enhancing lifestyle.

DEPRESSION: A SAMPLE CASE HISTORY

Our typical patient is one that any mental health practitioner or physician has seen. She is a forty-five-year-old woman who comes in complaining of depression and wants an alternative to the antidepressants she has been taking for two years. She wants to take a different pill that is safer and more natural. On examination we see a single woman who is sedentary and works as a secretary in a highly stressful office environment at an aluminum plant in southern Washington. She lives near where she works. She is thirty pounds overweight and eats a standard American diet high in fat, cholesterol, meat, dairy, and refined sugar and flour, with plenty of processed and fast foods. She eats chocolate to boost her spirits, takes oral contraceptives because her periods are irregular, and her depression is much worse in the winter than the rest of the year.

How do we approach this patient? First, we do not look specifically at depression, but at the overall mood of the patient. When we examine mood, we recognize that it is a continuum and people are at various points on that continuum. Our role is not necessarily to push them up the continuum, but to help them find their own level of balance on this continuum.

The standard medical approach focuses on killing disease. People who have depression are given drugs to deal with the depression. If they have mania, they are given drugs to deal with the mania. If they are manic-depressive and bounce back and forth between the two poles of depression and mania, they are given drugs to try to stop them from bouncing between the two extremes. On the other hand, the approach of natural medicine, or the wellness approach, is to reestablish balance, equanimity, and emotional poise for the patient. This approach is intended to help individuals to become strong emotionally, physically, and socially so that regardless of the stressor to which they are exposed, they are able to respond to it while maintaining health and well-being.

WHAT ARE THE DETERMINANTS OF MOOD?

There are five primary determinants of mood: physical; social (the family and social patterns); mental (thinking patterns); emotional; and spiritual. A person's moods and emotions have equally strong impact upon the other aspects of his or her life. We know, for example, that people with depression have a greater incidence of cancer. We do not know whether cancer makes people more depressed or depression makes people more susceptible to cancer. We do know, however, that mood and beliefs have a tremendous impact on health.

THE PHYSICAL DIMENSION OF DEPRESSION

The physical dimension of depression has been vastly underestimated by conventional medical thought. Naturopathic medicine places a strong emphasis on the physical dimension of depression, which can be divided into six key areas:

- Eliminate toxins

- Normalize neurotransmitter metabolism

- Increase physical exercise
- Increase light exposure
- Normalize endocrine function
- Use mood elevators when necessary

Eliminate Toxins

There are many toxins that have an impact on a person's physical and emotional well-being. Mood can be seriously influenced by both endogenous and exogenous toxins (endogenous refers to toxins produced internally, such as from the bowel, and exogenous refers to toxins produced from the outer environment, such as chemicals). If the brain is being poisoned, counseling the patient will be fruitless and will not positively affect the underlying physiological cause of the imbalance and depression.

Smoking.

Smoking is a serious health problem, and we know that approximately 30 percent of the adult population smokes. On the one hand, the smoker gets a boost from the nicotine in a cigarette. On the other hand, however, the smoker is simultaneously getting carbon monoxide poisoning of the brain. Cigarette smoking also increases the secretion of the stress hormone cortisol, which in turn decreases the production of serotonin, and it is documented that people who are depressed have lower serotonin levels. Smoking decreases vitamin C levels in the bloodstream, and this deficiency also causes a loss of serotonin production. It is crucial that anyone who is a smoker and is depressed needs to stop smoking if he or she is serious about getting well.

Solvents.

Solvents are another common toxin that can affect mood. Every time a person opens a can of paint (particularly oil-based paint) or is exposed to chemicals in a chemical factory, he is being exposed to solvents. It is well documented that solvents are neurotoxins to the brain.[1]

I remember a particular patient, from Port Townsend, Washington, one of the boat-building centers of the Pacific Northwest. He was a fiberglass boat builder who was very good at his craft and loved his work. Over the years, however, he had become progressively more and more depressed. We ended up having to take him out of his work environment because as long as he continued to be exposed to the neurotoxins there, he remained depressed. Finally, he decided that he did not have to build boats anymore and discovered that he wanted more sunshine. So he moved to the Virgin Islands and is doing very well.

Lead.

Lead is another well-documented brain toxin related to depression and mood disorders and is especially dangerous to children.

Aluminum.

One very interesting statistic is that 89 percent of workers in aluminum smelting plants suffer from clinical depression, while 84 percent of them lack coordination and 85 percent have memory impairment.[2] In the case of workers at hazardous waste incinerators, 94 percent suffer from depression.[3] Where do the toxins from the hazardous waste incinerator go? They go into the air. You can imagine what happens to the homes nearby that receive direct, continuous exposure to these toxins. If you are living near an aluminum smelter or a hazardous waste incinerator and suffering from depression, you can undergo extensive psychological counseling, but you will have little long-term benefit until you eliminate the source of the toxins you are carrying in the body.

Aspartame.

Another key toxin in mood disorders and depression is aspartame, which is found in Nutrasweet, diet colas, and other artificially sweetened and processed foods. Aspartame decreases serotonin levels in the brain, and low serotonin levels cause depression.[4]

Let's return to our hypothetical patient. What do we know about her? She both works at and lives near the aluminum plant. She is also thirty pounds overweight and is probably drinking diet sodas. Now are we getting a picture of the various factors that may be contributing to her depression?

Drugs.

Two major side effects of prescription drugs are significant memory impairment and depression. This is a particularly troublesome problem for the elderly, as they often do not remember which drugs they are on or why they are taking them. In fact, forty-three classes of drugs have been implicated in depression, especially in the elderly.[5] Some of the well-documented drugs that cause depression include[6]:

- ACTH
- alpha-methyldopa
- antipsychotics
- barbiturates
- benzodiazepines
- beta-blockers (propranolol)
- cholinergics

- cimetidine
- corticosteroids
- estrogens (including contraceptives)
- levodopa
- ranitidine
- reserpine

For those who want to decrease their usage of prescription drugs and whose doctor is open to natural medicine, there may be a corresponding natural alternative to treating the illness without the troubling side effects.

Normalize Neurotransmitter Metabolism

Normalizing neurotransmitter metabolism involves correcting nutritional deficiencies and, when necessary, stimulating the availability of neurotransmitters.

Correcting Nutritional Deficiencies.

Correcting nutritional deficiencies is an important part of helping to normalize neurotransmitter metabolism. Vitamin B_{12} is very commonly deficient in depressed patients, and as their depression improves, their B_{12} levels return to normal. In addition, antacids and a common class of drugs typically given to men with ulcers, specifically blocks the absorption of B_{12}. If you are on ulcer medications and are having problems with depression, you might check with your doctor to see if you are having problems with B_{12} deficiency. Of course, aluminum-based antacids should be avoided at all cost as exposure to aluminum has been linked to depression.

Research has shown that 30 percent to 40 percent of depressed patients are deficient in folic acid, and another 20 percent are deficient in magnesium.[7] In fact, virtually any nutritional deficiency can result in depression, so it is important to look at all possible nutritional problems a depressed patient may have. This is one reason why I automatically put a patient who comes to see me on a multivitamin and multimineral plan. Supplements are also a good form of health insurance, in case a particular nutritional deficiency is overlooked.

Stimulating the Availability of Neurotransmitters.

The Biogenic Amine Hypothesis is based on the concept that depression is due to inaccurate neurotransmission of monoamines, especially norepinephrine and serotonin.[8] Most clinically effective antidepressants affect neurotransmitter levels, especially serotonin. When direct measurements are taken of these chemicals in the brain, however, you do not consistently find differences between people who are depressed and those who are not depressed. You will often see that serotonin levels are low, but not in all cases. This may indicate that depression is related not only to the level of the neurotransmitters, but also to the receptivity of the nerves to the neurotransmitters. This demonstrates again that depression is not caused by any one factor and that it is important to take a comprehensive approach to the problem.

Tryptophan—Precursor to the Mood-elevating Neurotransmitter Serotonin.

The amino acid tryptophan is converted in the body to serotonin through several steps. If agents are used to either increase tryptophan levels or increase rates at which tryptophan is converted to serotonin, mood elevation results. If agents are used that block the rate at which serotonin is converted to melatonin, mood elevation results. If agents are used that block the rate at which serotonin is broken down, i.e., monoamine oxidase inhibitors such as Prozac, the result again is mood elevation.

Tryptophan levels in depressed women have been shown to be decreased.[9] This was demonstrated when researchers took a group of women with a history of depression but who were currently normal and put them on a tryptophan-deficient diet. Within ten days, 60 percent of them were back into clinical depression.[10]

There are several known factors that affect the levels of tryptophan that get into the brain. Three factors decrease the levels of tryptophan in the brain, including cortisol. What causes an increase in cortisol levels in the body? What is cortisol a measure of? Stress. Stress decreases the brain levels of tryptophan. Aspartame also decreases the levels of tryptophan,[11] and a high-protein meal decreases the levels of tryptophan.

Niacin and niacinamide are two factors that increase brain tryptophan. One of the things the body does is to convert tryptophan into niacin, or niacin analogues. If there is a great deal of niacin or niacinamide in the bloodstream, however, it decreases the rate at which tryptophan is converted into niacin. SAMe (S-adenosylmethionine) also increases the amount of tryptophan in the brain.[12] Sugar on a short-term basis increases the amount of tryptophan in the brain, although it decreases it on a long-term basis.

It is very unfortunate that tryptophan was taken off the market in 1989 and thus is no longer available as a clinical agent. Many foods contain tryptophan, but because the amino acids in food compete with the tryptophan for absorption, it is important to find foods that have a good tryptophan-to-amino-acid ratio. Among them are almonds, cashews, pumpkin seeds, raisins, and avocados.

Avocados are one of the very best foods containing tryptophan, with a 14:1 ratio of tryptophan to other amino acids. You would, however, have to eat about thirty avocados a day to get therapeutic levels of tryptophan. If you take foods that have a relatively high proportion of tryptophan compared to other amino acids, like raisins, and combine them with a high carbohydrate meal, with both simple and complex carbohydrates, this will decrease the other amino acids while not affecting the tryptophan levels.

Serotonin and Epinephrine Pathways.

There are two basic neurotransmitter pathways: serotonin and epinephrine. If a patient receives a high dose of tryptophan, it will stimulate the serotonin pathway, and if she receives a high dose of the amino acid tyrosine, it will stimulate the epinephrine pathway. Tyrosine can help a depressed patient who feels better when on stimulants, and tryptophan is effective with patients who are suffering from depression and a sleeping disorder. My clinical experience has been that far more patients tend to respond to tryptophan than tyrosine.

The recommended supplemental dosage of the amino acids tryptophan and tyrosine is 3 grams. The B vitamins can be helpful when added to either of these amino acids, and niacinamide can be combined with tryptophan to get a better effect without having to use a high dosage. As tryptophan is no longer available, I now use a more activated form of this amino acid, called 5-hydroxytryptophan, which is now sold in health food stores although it was only available by prescription in the past. A low dosage of 5-hydroxytryptophan—100 milligrams—is needed for clinical efficacy.

Increase Physical Exercise

The data on the significance of exercise in depression are very clear; nonexercisers are three times as likely to be depressed as exercisers.[13] This is probably as important as anything we can do nutritionally with the patients. Exercise increases energy production and monoamine synthesis in the brain. Whether you need more serotonin or more epinephrine, exercise increases both. To achieve the maximum benefit, however, it is important to exercise at least thirty minutes, three times a week at 70 to 85 percent of the maximum heart rate.

I am very careful about using the word "exercise" with my patients, because when most people hear that they need more exercise, they say, "I hate to exercise" and will not listen to anything else I have to say. For this reason it is important to understand the wide range of activities people enjoy, encourage them to add a physical component to these activities, and then slowly increase these physical components until they have the appropriate amount of exercise in their lives.

Increase Light Exposure

Light increases serotonin levels and light exposure is a very simple and effective therapy for elevating mood. If you expose a person to full-spectrum or special bright light for two hours a day, the average depressed person experiences a 50 percent decrease in symptoms. This therapy is even more effective in people who suffer from seasonal affective disorder (SAD).

Research has shown that morning light is better than evening light because it helps to reestablish the appropriate circadian rhythms (the natural twenty-four-hour rhythms of the body).[14] If you have to use artificial light to treat depression, white and green light are the best forms, while blue and red light are the least desirable.[15] One of the problems with our Western lifestyle is that we tend to get up late in the morning and go to sleep late at night, spending our days in artificial light, which throws off our circadian rhythms. My preference, then, is to encourage depressed patients to take a walk in the morning, one of the most beautiful times of the day, in which they get exposure to the light and physical exercise as well as reestablish their connection with nature.

Seasonal affective disorder can be a big problem in areas such as Seattle in the Pacific Northwest, where there is a high level of rainfall and the weather is overcast and cloudy much of the time. This area has one of the highest suicide rates in the country, occurring primarily in the wintertime, and this high incidence is believed to be primarily due to seasonal affective disorder. SAD officially affects about 5 percent of the population, but somewhere between 16 percent and 38 percent of clinically depressed people also have SAD. This condition worsens between the months of October and April, and the typical patient is a woman between thirty and fifty years old suffering from PMS.

Looking back at our patient, what more do we now know about why she is depressed? She lives in southern Washington, where it is really gray and overcast. She is sedentary and does not get much exercise. These are both good indicators of the possible source of her depression. Does this woman need Prozac or other antidepressants? An antidepressant may work temporarily, but it will neither address her underlying problem nor improve her general level of health.

Normalize Endocrine Function

The next step in treating depression on the physical level is to normalize endocrine function. About 20 percent of patients with clinical depression suffer from hypothyroidism, or low thyroid hormone levels. The thyroid gland controls your metabolic rate, and if you have low thyroid function and a low metabolic rate control, it can lower your energy level and cause depression.

Many doctors believe that an iodine deficiency is the cause of hypothyroidism; however, at Bastyr University we uncovered another possible cause that is also related to the age-old naturopathic concept that disease begins in the bowels and a first line of treatment is to detoxify the bowels. I thought that this concept was outdated until one of my students wrote a chapter for *A Textbook of Natural Medicine* on bowel toxemia.[16] One of the things he discovered was that there is a form of bacterium in some people's bowels called *Yersinia enterocolitica*. It is interesting to note that the body produces antibodies to fight this bacterium, and these antibodies cross-react with thyroid tissue. In other words, when the body starts fighting this bacterium and encounters thyroid tissues, it forms antibodies to the thyroid. People with hypothyroidism have an elevated level of anti–*Yersinia enterocolitica* antibodies. Therefore, when a patient has hypothyroidism, I check for yersinia infection.

How do you get *Yersinia enterocolitica*? And how many people have this bacterium? The answer is not clear at this time; however, we had an interesting experience in Seattle about fifteen years ago, when there were reports of increasing incidence of people with yersinia. To help the public health officials out with this problem, we did a survey at Bastyr University and discovered that approximately 20 percent of the students at the school were eating tofu, and 20 percent of the students had yersinia infection in their intestines. The problem was ultimately traced to a contaminated production facility at a tofu company.

Another cause of hypothyroidism is a deficiency of the trace mineral selenium. While the thyroid gland produces thyroid hormones, these hormones do not have much effect until converted into a more active form in the cells. The enzymes that make this conversion require selenium, zinc, and/or copper.

Use Mood Elevators When Necessary

After exhausting all options in dealing with the underlying causes of depression, we will then consider the mood elevators. They include St. John's wort (*Hypericum perforatum*), Siberian ginseng (*Eleutherococcus senticosus*), *Ginkgo biloba,* hawthorne berry (*Crataegus oxyacantha*), as well as chocolate and sugar.

St. John's wort (Hypericum perforatum).

This is an herb that has a long folk history of use as a nervine, a substance that is beneficial to nerve function and helps people feel better. Hypericum is clinically documented as a mood elevator and may be a monoamine oxidase inhibitor. The standard dose of the standardized extract (an extract with 0.3 percent hypericin) is 300 milligrams, three times a day. Caution must be taken in using Hypericum, however, because if taken in medium to large doses over a long period of time, it may cause photosensitivity (sensitivity to sunlight) reactions. I consider Hypericum a temporary aid to get a person off Prozac or other antidepressants and do not depend upon it for a long-term solution.

A few years ago many AIDS patients using Hypericum were feeling a lot better, and there was a belief that Hypericum might be a cure for AIDS. The laboratory research indicated that hypericin, one of the components of Hypericum, was a reverse oxidase inhibitor that inhibited the HIV virus replication. The downside, however, is that you cannot orally consume or inject sufficient levels of Hypericum to actually get an anti-HIV effect. Apparently, the patients were feeling better because Hypericum is a great mood elevator, but it was unable to do anything for the underlying disease in this case. This is one reason why research is so important in natural medicine. Although the very best measure of a therapy's effectiveness is how a patient feels, this may not always present an accurate picture of the patient's condition.

Siberian ginseng (Eleutherococcus senticosus).

This herb is a classic adaptogen, an agent that helps normalize body function and makes it work more efficiently. If a person is low in a particular physiological function, it helps it go up; if a person is high in a physiological function, it helps it go down. Not only does Siberian ginseng increase the sense of well-being, it also increases brain neurotransmitter levels. The recommended dose of Siberian ginseng is 2 to 4 milliliters, three times a day, in the form of a fluid extract (in a 1:1 concentration). Traditionally herbs are used in the form of tinctures and extracts because these forms tend to be more stable.

Ginkgo Biloba.

This herb is excellent for improving the blood supply to the brain. Because inadequate blood supply to the brain causes memory loss and depression, particularly in the elderly, *Ginkgo biloba* has been used with remarkable results. I normally recommend supplementing with 80 milligrams, three times a day, in a standardized extract usually available in health food stores.

Hawthorn berry (Crataegus oxyacantha).

Hawthorn berry improves the contractivity of the heart by dilating the blood vessels that go to the heart, allowing the heart to beat stronger. It also helps dilate the blood vessels going to the brain.

A seventy-seven-year-old friend visited me about four years ago, and I did not think she was going to live for another two years. She was not mentally depressed because she did not have that type of personality, but she was so physically lethargic that all she could do was crawl out to the lawn chair and sit there all day and gaze out at the water. Concerned, we took her to Bastyr's Natural Health Clinic, but they could not find anything wrong with her. We decided to have her start taking hawthorn berry. In two weeks, she felt and acted twenty years younger and maintains that level of behavior and activity today. Her active lifestyle now includes swimming and weight training.

She, however, had a temporary relapse while visiting us once. One night she became very lethargic and passed out on the way to the bathroom. We discovered that she had left her hawthorn berry at home because she thought that as a liquid it would not travel well on the airplane, we put her back on it and she returned to normal within twenty-four hours.

Although my friend did not have a diagnosable disease or heart failure, the blood supply to her brain had been getting weaker. Hawthorn berry helped reestablish her blood supply and had a remarkable and positive impact on her mood and behavior. Dramatic cases like this reinforce your belief in a therapeutic agent, particularly when you see the effects of both taking and not taking it.

Chocolate.

As we all know, chocolate is an incredibly addictive substance, and it is not surprising that our sample patient was eating chocolate whenever she was feeling blue. Many people crave a candy bar when they are feeling down, because it is a mood elevator high in sugar and caffeine analogues.

Most importantly, however, chocolate is high in phenylethylamine (PEA), an amphetamine-type stimulant that is a highly addictive mood elevator. The PEA levels in depressed patients are always low. It is typical of chocolate and similar substances to give the individual a short-term boost, but the long-term impact ends up lowering your mood and resulting in more depression.

Let's return to our patient again. She is overweight and has low energy, is probably suffering from hypothyroid, and is addicted to chocolate because it makes her feel good, temporarily. Because it is hard to tell people to stop eating something that makes them feel good, I instead supplement them with the appropriate nutrients in order to change what is going on in their body, so they can feel well enough to taper off chocolate or a similarly addictive substance.

Sugar.

Sugar, as simple carbohydrate, increases serotonin production. This is probably due to an increase in insulin levels that, in turn, facilitates absorption of tryptophan into the brain and decreases the levels of other amino acids in the brain competing for absorption. Long-term sugar consumption, however, can lead to depression. There is good research, including the Framingham studies, showing that consumption of a healthy low-fat, high–complex carbohydrate diet will help reduce depression.

Social and Family Aspects of Mood: Treating the Family System

Dr. Don Williamson, one of the country's leading family therapists and part of the family counseling program at the Leadership Institute of Seattle, an affiliate of Bastyr University, has demonstrated the importance of treating not just the individual but the family system in cases of depression or mood disorders.

When there is pain or sadness in the family, one member tends to absorb the family's pattern through his or her own emotional or physical symptoms, feeling "recruited" to do the duty of maintaining the cohesiveness of the family or social system. This person may be playing the role of scapegoat or even overachiever. Some children, in absorbing the dysfunctional parental system, exhibit their symptoms through social delinquency or physical illness.

As a part of the dysfunctional family dynamic, the family will often be very concerned about the individual who has taken on the family's pain and as a result will take that person to a number of doctors and therapists. The family will, however, slowly sabotage the effort by not allowing the core family issues to be directly addressed. Even if the individual refuses to continue carrying the responsibility for the family's emotional well-being, another family member will be forced to take that responsibility in order to keep the status quo and hold the family unit together. This pattern will continue until the family is guided to recognize and break the pattern.

According to Dr. Williamson, the member of the family who has taken on the role of absorbing the family's pain is the person who is depressed. As long as there is a family system that reinforces that individual's depression and taking on the family's pain, it will be very hard to break him or her free of that particular dynamic and heal the depression without treating the family.

Faced with the choice of going into family therapy, many times the family members will resist this opportunity. The skill of the counselor comes into play in negotiations with the family to encourage them to become engaged in the process. A skilled therapist is often the one who is able to get the whole family to recognize their patterns and motivate them to engage in the healing process. It is therefore crucial for the health professional in dealing with depressed patients to develop the skills in this area of communication and family dynamics and be able to refer the patient to the appropriate therapist. It is equally important for the depressed patient to bring up this subject with the health professional.

MENTAL AND EMOTIONAL ASPECTS OF MOOD

When we view depression as a loss of energy for life, the significance of the mental and emotional aspects of mood become more clear. Often people experience "situational depression," in which their emotional state of depression is due to an immediate loss of a loved one or an external situation such as losing a job. On a longer-term basis, people can develop negative, limiting belief systems that substantially impact their mental and emotional health. And one element that seems to be missing from life when one is suffering from a depressed mood is fun—when we lack energy for life, it is unlikely that we will truly enjoy ourselves and have fun.

Situational Depression

When looking at depression of a situational nature, or an event outside oneself, we take a direct approach that is immediately supportive of the patient. In other words, if they have just had a death in the family or something equally tragic, we are supportive of who they are as a human being and their experience, ensuring that they have a solid structure within to work. We first make sure that they know where their next meal is coming from and that their particular human needs are being met. We then work, when possible, at healing the precipitating event with counseling. The final and most important thing is to stimulate the life force through building healthful, creative activities in order to bring about the restoration of normal living.

Prescribing Fun

When the basic needs of a depressed patient are met, we then like to address the need for positive life-giving experiences by prescribing fun. I use the word "prescribe" because many patients will not go out and have fun unless you make the prescription part of their therapy. These fun activities can be very diverse and designed to fit the patient's life and emotional needs. It may involve going to the movies at least twice a week and seeing the latest exciting film, going to visit the park at least twice a week in the morning, or a weekly visit to a museum or art gallery. It may involve spending more time with one's children and playing some computer games with them. We also try to make the patient's actual experience in the clinic an enjoyable one. What we are doing for the patient is modeling fun behavior and bringing the concept of fun and enjoyment back into his or her life.

Psychodynamic Approaches

Sometimes we need to take a much deeper psychodynamic approach with patients, which requires more advanced skills. In this approach we try to identify a person's chronic negative beliefs and replace them with more positive metaphors. For example, a depressed woman came in to see me who had three stories to tell. One was that her son had just gotten a ticket for driving under the influence of alcohol. The next story was that she used to have good sex with her husband but now it had developed into S&M. Finally, she said that when she was a child, she moved into her grandmother's house and a week later, the house burned to the ground. What is the internal message this woman has received? What is her internal belief? Anything she comes into contact with turns bad.

In her case we needed to help her change her belief system from negative, life-taking metaphors to positive, life-affirming metaphors. Many times for people whose belief systems are filled with life-taking metaphors their life becomes a self-fulfilling prophecy. They are unable to be successful because their underlying negative behavior patterns arise to sabotage any success that begins to happen. These negative beliefs can even follow one into dreams. Research performed with depressed patients concluded that their nighttime dreams have depressing endings. When the therapist asked them to rewrite their dreams to have happy or resolved endings, the patients experienced an improvement in their psychological well-being.

For this and other reasons, I look at healing depression as an ongoing process, and do not try to accomplish everything with one approach in one session. Instead I gradually move forward, improving one thing at a time in a step-by-step fashion, until greater health and well-being are achieved.

TREATING OUR HYPOTHETICAL PATIENT

Now we have a fairly complete picture of our patient and are ready to develop a treatment program. She is a forty-five-year-old woman who complains of depression; wants a natural alternative to her antidepressant drugs; is sedentary and overweight; lives alone near her work in a highly stressful office environment at an aluminum plant; is thirty pounds overweight; eats a standard American diet high in fat, cholesterol, meat, dairy, and refined sugar and flour, with plenty of processed and fast foods; eats chocolate whenever she needs a boost; takes oral contraceptives for irregular periods; and has symptoms that worsen in winter. How will we treat this woman?

Social Life

We know that she is lonely, has no physical contact, and lives under high stress. What are we going to recommend to her? Research shows that people with inadequate or unsatisfactory love relations and physical contact are more depressed than people who have satisfactory love relations and physical contact. Research has also shown that simple physical contact will have a mood-elevating effect on people.

We may recommend that she become involved in a dating service. Although this does not appeal to everyone, we have used this approach with very good success. We will also recommend that she join a gym. This may be a touchy issue because she may not feel very comfortable with her body and physical appearance in a gym environment. Therefore, we try to work this issue out so we can set up this program, because the advantage of a gym is not only the physical environment but the social environment. We will also help her explore other fun activities.

Massage

Because our patient has little or no physical contact, I would recommend massage, which is very nurturing and helps one to feel better. In an article in the January 1993 *New England Journal of Medicine*, Dr. David Eisenberg reported that one-third of Americans use alternative medicine; he also states that a large percentage of those people receive massage or chiropractic therapy because the touch made them feel so much better.

Thyroid Function

In attempting to balance the endocrine system, we will try to determine how well the thyroid is functioning because it is likely that our patient is hypothyroid. We will not just run a thyroid test to check out her thyroid levels, however, because these tests will usually show thyroid hormone levels to be normal, although the functioning of the person's thyroid can be quite low. We like using the test methodology of Dr. Broda Barnes which involves measuring a person's basal body temperature. This is done by putting a basal thermometer under the arm for ten minutes upon waking in the morning and before getting out of bed. A normal reading should be over 98 degrees. Some people, however, have a basal temperature as low as 96 degrees.

We will then try to determine what she needs to normalize thyroid function. This may involve supplementing nutrients that are necessary for optimal thyroid function, or it may be necessary to give her small amounts of thyroid hormone. One way to supply the necessary nutrients is by supplementing with desiccated thyroid, which is derived from the whole thyroid gland, but with the thyroid hormones removed. All of the nutrients necessary for proper thyroid function are present in the gland.

Another method is to provide the nutrients necessary for the thyroid gland to produce hormones, as well as the nutrients necessary for the thyroid hormones to be utilized by the cells and converted into their most active forms. Copper is necessary for the production of the thyroid hormone T_4, and selenium and zinc are necessary for the conversion to T_3. Depressed people tend to be deficient in these trace nutrients.

Detoxification

Our patient is also taking oral contraceptives and has been exposed to aluminum waste products. I address this by asking her to stop taking the oral contraceptives because irregular periods can be the result of low thyroid function and, having normalized her thyroid, she will not need the estrogens contained in the oral contraceptives any longer because her periods are now regular. I would also encourage her to change her job and move to another location away from the toxic dangers of the aluminum plant before putting her on a detoxification program that will rid her body of these toxins. Although moving and changing her job is a harsh requirement, I have become quite firm with patients in recognizing that unless they are willing to change unhealthy situations in their lives, they cannot truly be helped to reestablish health.

Exercise, Diet and Nutrition, Light Exposure

Our patient is getting little or no exercise, so I will recommend thirty minutes of exercise a day, three times a week, and a type that is appropriate and matched to her interests. On a nutritional level, she probably has subclinical deficiencies, so I will recommend that she eat a healthy, whole foods diet, take a multiple vitamin and mineral supplement, and stop drinking diet cola. Because she lives in southern Washington, I would also suggest that she add two hours of light exposure in the morning. I would also recommend an artificial light source to supplement what she is doing. This can be accomplished with full-spectrum lights, which are now available in both fluorescent and incandescent forms.

PROMOTION OF WELLNESS

The final element of our treatment for our hypothetical patient is the promotion of wellness, a key principle of naturopathic medicine. Wellness is defined as "a state of being healthy" and is characterized by positive emotion, thought, and action as well as the belief that it is inherent in everyone, regardless of the discomfort or disease they are experiencing. When a patient seeks help, a doctor's normal inclination is to figure out what disease he or she has. What we are trying to do in naturopathic medicine is rethink this way of approaching patients and instead ask, "What is their state of health or wellness and how do we stimulate them to a higher level of health and wellness?" To look at the patient in this way—to see the person's state and to help health and wellness emerge—is a constant challenge. Clearly it is a choice, and sometimes you have to treat the disease first, but every time you must also treat the level of wellness.

An important part of the promotion of wellness is creating a health alliance with one's physician. A health alliance can be defined as a partnership between physician and patient that focuses on the health and well-being of the patient, despite the patient's physical and/or psychological concerns. In the alliance, the patient demonstrates wellness along with positive emotion, thought, and action. Each time I interact with a patient, I help him to express some aspect of his health. For example, if the patient comes in saying, "Here are all my symptoms, here's why I'm not feeling well," I respond with, "Will you also tell me when you are feeling well?"

If our hypothetical patient comes in feeling depressed and says, "Well, I'm feeling a little better, but I'm still feeling depressed," I will ask her to look back over the week and tell me how she felt when she woke up each morning. She may respond, "You know, Tuesday I woke up and felt pretty good. Of course, by the time the day progressed, I wasn't feeling very good." At that point what I do is help her to remember and reinforce the positive moods and times. If our patient's experiences of wellness are recognized and really emphasized, then her depression may heal more quickly than through direct treatment alone, allowing her "energy for life" to return.

Women's Depression: An Integrated Approach

Hyla Cass, M.D.

First, do no harm.
—Hippocrates

Anxiety and depression seem to be the price we pay for our complex lifestyles. We feel the pressure to keep up with jobs, family, and the myriad responsibilities of everyday life. Women in particular are performing a constant juggling act between their roles as supermom, wife, and usually, member of the workforce, all thrown into the mix. Any extra stressors can become just too much to handle, and symptoms such as anxiety and depression drive us to seek psychotherapy or counseling.

Compounding these psychological symptoms, there are often underlying physical or metabolic problems, usually undetected and underdiagnosed by physicians, that can actually be the root cause of emotional problems. Once properly diagnosed, these disorders can be effectively treated by alternative medical means. Treatment can be at the hands of an enlightened health practitioner or even self-care by an educated patient.

While psychotherapy has an important role in treating depression, we certainly cannot expect the brain to work without the body's metabolism being in proper balance. Every disorder or deficiency in the body affects the brain. This organ is extremely sensitive to imbalances caused, for example, by low blood sugar, water retention, or oxygen deprivation. Some depressed patients do not respond well to psychotherapy, but when their conditions are properly—metabolically—diagnosed and treated, their response accelerates. When in balance the individual is able to be more present and to retain and integrate the material learned in therapy.

UNDERLYING CAUSES OF WOMEN'S DEPRESSION

In my private practice I see many women with typical psychiatric complaints: depression, addiction, impaired concentration, eating disorders, weight gain, insomnia, anxiety, fatigue, PMS, sexual dysfunction, and loss of interest in sex. I prefer, however, to begin psychotherapy only after excluding any underlying physical cause. This can run the gamut of any of the following:

- genetic predisposition

- hypoglycemia

- viral and fungal infections

- hormonal imbalances

- allergies, including food and chemical sensitivities

- toxic chemical or metal overload

- deficiencies of vitamins, minerals, or amino acids

Women are particularly prone to hormone-based depression. The combination of stress, toxic chemicals, and inadequate diet all contribute to upsetting the delicate balance of female hormones, which affect mood. While men's moods are also responsive to hormone levels, they do not have the complex cycles that women do, and they are less sensitive to hormonal shifts on a daily or monthly basis. Their hormonal changes are more apparent through the observation of testosterone levels, which dwindle with age and affect the level of aggression and sexual desire.

DIAGNOSING DEPRESSION

How do we diagnose depression and these conditions? Understanding the mind/body connection is extremely important in diagnosis.

All of these physical, physiological, and metabolic disturbances reside in a whole human being. Before the patient even comes in to see me, I send out a questionnaire that introduces him to my "mind/body" way of thinking. This prepares both of us, saving time during the visit for a better quality of interaction.

As a psychiatrist, even when it appears that I am taking a regular medical history, I am listening with what is known as "the third ear" in psychiatry. Who is this person? How is she interacting with me? What is her anxiety level? Is she more depressed than she thinks she is? Is she less depressed? Does she make eye contact with me? How does she feel about herself? How does she see herself? All of these observations play a valuable role in diagnosis.

Often, it can be therapeutic for patients simply to know that they are being taken seriously and are understood. Someone is finally paying attention to the symptoms they have presented to doctor after doctor. Often, during an initial evaluation, I do not have to do much psychotherapeutic work because the patient already feels better. People are incredibly relieved to hear that they are not "crazy," that their symptoms have a real metabolic basis and are treatable.

Based on my findings in the initial visit, I will order laboratory tests, the simplest (and least expensive) being a complete blood count and a chemistry panel. However, I will often add other tests as needed, such as antibody tests for candida or thyroid, and different viruses such as the Epstein-Barr virus, cytomegalovirus, and the herpes group. These last three are retroviruses that lie dormant, becoming active under stress. The antibodies are markers, evidence of the body's immune response to the virus. The tests can determine if someone has had an infection in the past (IGG antibodies) and/or a current infection (IGM antibodies). The antibody levels can then be monitored to measure response to treatment.

TREATING THE UNDERLYING CAUSES OF WOMEN'S DEPRESSION

Although many conditions can cause depression, there is a common treatment pattern to them all. Because many of these conditions overlap, treating one will often handle others, as you will see in the following case examples. Underlying causes run the gamut from viral and fungal infections to hypoglycemia, anemia, hormonal imbalance, and deficiencies in nutrients such as vitamins, minerals, and amino acids.

Chronic Fatigue Syndrome

Catherine, a successful thirty-two-year-old professional woman, described herself in desperate terms: "I feel like I'm losing my mind. I'm absentminded, simple tasks overwhelm me, and I'm in tears at the drop of a hat. I'm exhausted most of the time. I can barely get up in the morning. All day there's a constant struggle to stay awake. I feel my life is over at thirty-two!" Although she did have an obvious problem with workaholic habits, a high stress level, and a driving need to be a successful professional like her father, Catherine's medical history revealed other, unaddressed explanations for her desperation.

In her history, I discovered that she had the flu eight months prior to her appointment with me. Despite her apparent recovery after about a month, she never fully regained her former strength and energy. For example, she could no longer exercise as before and found that it depleted rather than energized her. In addition, she drank coffee to boost her energy, but after a while even that did not work. She suffered from intermittent swollen glands, sore throat, high fever, and a run-down, exhausted feeling. She also had numerous thought-processing symptoms: She said she could not "think straight," was absentminded, and sometimes could not think of the right word to say. She was depressed, anxious, tired, and had a sleep disturbance, waking up several times during the night.

Diagnosing Chronic Fatigue Syndrome

Based on her history, I ordered several blood tests. These revealed a number of problems, any one of which could cause fatigue, anxiety, and depression: iron-deficiency anemia, elevated viral antibodies, and hypoglycemia. Except for the anemia, for which I prescribed an iron supplement, orthodox physicians do not typically diagnose or treat these conditions. Alternative practitioners, however, are able to treat them with diet and a variety of nutritional supplements.

Catherine's flu turned out to be Epstein-Barr virus, a chronic, relapsing form of infectious mononucleosis, and part of a syndrome called chronic fatigue syndrome (CFS).[1] It appears to be caused by a member of a group of viruses that can lie dormant for months or years at a time, then be reactivated by physical or emotional stress. Symptoms include depression, extreme fatigue, nonrestorative sleep, impaired memory and concentration, anxiety attacks, intermittent low-grade fevers, sore throat, swollen lymph glands, muscle aches and pain (fibromyalgia), and allergies.

One feature that distinguishes CFS from depression or other causes of fatigue is a negative response to exercise. While most individuals feel energized after exercise, chronic fatigue patients feel worse. A special brain scan called a SPECT scan demonstrates a clear difference in the cerebral blood patterns before and after exercise, clarifying the two diagnoses.[2]

Treating Chronic Fatigue Syndrome

Despite orthodox physicians' propensity to ignore CFS or advise their patients that "You just have to get a lot of rest and learn to live with it," there are specific remedies for this syndrome. I put my patient on an immune-stimulating program: megavitamins, megaminerals, a therapeutic diet (the same as a hypoglycemic diet), high doses of vitamin C, magnesium, zinc, the amino acids lysine and cysteine, aloe vera, and the herbs echinacea, goldenseal, licorice, and astragalus. Herbs such as astragalus, echinacea, and goldenseal boost the immune system, helping it to fight viral invaders.

Within a week or two, Catherine started to get her energy back and began once again to think clearly. It took a few months for her condition to stabilize. As she continued the immune-building supplement program and maintained a good diet, she felt better than ever. This case shows us how crucial it is to get the right diagnosis when an individual is suffering from depression.

Candidiasis (Candida albicans)

Alexandra, an overweight, depressed, thirty-six-year-old secretary, was in tears. "Everything I eat makes my stomach bloat like I'm six months pregnant, I keep dieting, and I can't lose weight. My brain is like mush: I'm absentminded and afraid I'm going to lose my job. Yesterday, I went to get coffee for my boss, went to the file drawer instead, and couldn't remember what I was doing!" She craved sugar and bread, and had repeated vaginal yeast infections and severe PMS, with water retention, irritability, and depression. She was sensitive to perfumes and chemicals, such as printer's ink. She scored high on the candida questionnaire, and a candida antibody blood test confirmed the diagnosis.

Presenting a picture in some ways similar to both CFS and hypoglycemia is a systemic yeast infection called chronic candida albicans, systemic candidiasis, or candida hypersensitivity syndrome. There are a number of books on the subject, including Dr. William Crook's *Yeast Connection* and Dr. John Parks Trowbridge's *Yeast Syndrome.*[3] *Candida albicans* is a yeast that normally inhabits the gastrointestinal tract, mostly in the esophagus and colon, and is kept in balance by the friendly bacteria that aid in digestion, such as acidophilus, bifidus, and bulgaricum. It is only when candida overgrowth occurs that it begins to release poisons, called endotoxins, which can leak through the gut wall, which has become damaged from the yeast, and lead to an antibody response[4] (see "Leaky Gut Syndrome," page 87). These antibodies to the candida can be measured both qualitatively and quantitatively by specific blood tests.

The result of this invasion can be a multitude of diverse symptoms which, though often labeled psychosomatic, are due to the immune-suppressive effect of the yeast. The leaky gut syndrome may also lead to food allergies, because the digestion is incomplete and causes the immune system to see food as alien molecules, rather than as a source of nutrition. Food allergies are discussed in greater detail beginning on page 83.

Some factors predisposing to candidiasis include long-term use of antibiotics and/or steroids. The former kills the competing friendly bacteria. In addition, along with the steroids, they suppress the immune system. Repeated pregnancies and prolonged use of either birth control pills or progesterone can change the hormonal balance, thereby precipitating candidiasis. A diet high in sugar will promote it both because the yeast grow on sugar and because sugar has an immune-suppressant effect. Mercury fillings have also been implicated in its etiology, and their removal has led to relief from candidiasis.[5]

Symptoms of Candidiasis

Symptoms may include depression, mood swings, fatigue, PMS, impaired memory and concentration, food cravings, nasal congestion, vaginal yeast infections, abdominal bloating and gas, constipation or diarrhea, recurrent fungal infections, and urinary tract infections. Candida is a controversial diagnosis in orthodox medical circles, usually acknowledged only in severely debilitated patients. Nonetheless, its constellation can be diagnosed by a specific lab test for anti-candida antibodies and/or a stool test and treated with dietary changes, antifungal herbs and/or drugs, and an immune support program.

Treating Candidiasis

Diet.

The typical anti-candida diet consists of a good basic diet of fresh foods (not canned or processed), lots of vegetables, whole grains, and low fat, and eliminating sugar and other refined carbohydrates.

Natural Antifungals.

It is essential to repopulate the gut with a friendly bacterium, *Lactobacillus acidophilus*, which is supplied in liquid or powder that requires refrigeration or freeze-dried in capsules, not requiring refrigeration; pau d'arco, brewed as a tea or taken as a tincture, grapefruit seed extract (Citricidin), tannic acid, and caprylic acid.

Prescription Medications.

Nystatin powder—in gradually increasing doses as recommended by a physician or health practitioner; Nizoral—has potentially toxic effects on the liver, so must be carefully monitored; Diflucan—most effective, but very expensive at fifteen dollars per 200-milligram capsule, the average daily dose, for two months or so.

Supplements.

Basic immune system–building program as discussed in Catherine's case (see pages 73–74).

Candida treatments, especially the stronger ones, can cause a die-off reaction, a flulike syndrome for a day or more caused by the candida, in their death throes, giving off toxins. As these are eliminated by the body, the symptoms will clear.

Alexandra had taken antibiotics as a teenager to combat acne, and this predisposed her to an overgrowth of yeast in the digestive tract. She began taking birth control pills at the age of twenty-four, continuing to the present, leading to a hormonal state that also encouraged candida growth. The yeast in her intestinal tract kept multiplying, causing consistent self-reinfection, leading to vaginitis. The candida hypersensitivity syndrome affected her mental and emotional processes. Fortunately, she responded well to treatment: she adopted the therapeutic diet; eliminated sugar and bread, made easier by allergy desensitization (see pages 84–85); and took acidophilus, two capsules one-half hour before each meal, and two tannic acid capsules, three times daily. Her abdominal bloating cleared, as did her PMS, mood swings, and her brain fog. Chemicals and perfume were far less bothersome, and she was able to lose weight as well.

Although candida is not commonly diagnosed in traditional medicine, as we see here, it can be diagnosed by a specific lab test for anti-candida antibodies, then treated with dietary changes, antifungal herbs and/or drugs, and an immunity-enhancing support program.

HORMONAL IMBALANCES

There are many hormones that run our bodily processes that are secreted by the endocrine glands or the ductless glands. The endocrine glands include the thyroid, ovaries, testes, pituitary (the master gland), and the adrenals. They manufacture and release minute amounts of these chemical messengers to target areas of the body, having profound effects on many functions, as we will see.

Sex Hormones (Estrogen, Progesterone, Testosterone, and DHEA)

Laura, a forty-year-old secretary, was referred to me by her psychotherapist to explore the possibility of an underlying physical imbalance. Despite a year of weekly therapy sessions, some with her husband in a couples' group, Laura was still depressed, anxious, irritable, and tired. She was dissatisfied with her job, her family, and life in general. She argued daily with her husband and teenage daughter. She had severe premenstrual syndrome (PMS). Although she had been told by her gynecologist that she was nowhere near menopause, and that her problems were all psychological in origin, her psychological state resembled that induced by shifting female hormones. While still having periods, she was experiencing perimenopause, the time preceding full menopause.

First, we addressed her PMS. This syndrome has a wide range of symptoms: bloating, water retention, fatigue, cravings for sweets or caffeine, weight gain, irritability, insomnia, depression, and weepiness. I find, however, that most women need the same solution—to eliminate caffeine, dairy, and salt and add essential fatty acids in the form of flaxseed oil, evening primrose oil, or borage oil. I also suggest tyrosine, good for PMS as well as depression, and high doses of magnesium and vitamin B$_6$. The herb St. John's wort is also excellent for treating PMS, at 100–300 mg per day, of 0.3 percent standardized extract. I recommend taking all of these throughout the month, increasing as necessary during the premenstrual period.

When we looked at Laura's blood levels of the sex hormones estrogen, progesterone, and DHEA (dehydroepiandrosterone), we found low levels of progesterone and DHEA. Progesterone deficiency can lead to depression, PMS, water retention, and weight gain. To smooth out these imbalances, I prescribed natural progesterone, a derivative of the Mexican wild yam. This is not the commonly sold, over-the-counter "wild yam cream," which the body does not metabolize into progesterone on its own, but rather a laboratory extract supplied, by prescription, from a compounding pharmacy. There are special compounding pharmacies that cater to alternative/complementary physicians (see list in Appendix F).

The progesterone derived from this process is not to be confused with the synthetic hormone Provera, used in conventional hormone therapy with many negative side effects. The compounded natural product is similar to the body's own hormone and acts in the same way. It relieves water retention; depression; irritability; swollen, sore breasts; and over the long term, prevents osteoporosis, a form of bone loss associated with menopause. Natural progesterone is supplied either in capsule form or as a skin cream applied to fatty areas of the body such as the abdomen and thighs. The hormone is then absorbed transdermally (literally "through the skin") into the system. In addition, I gave Laura some herbal combinations—*Dong quai* and vitex among them—for natural hormone balance.

Lastly, I prescribed DHEA, an adrenal hormone produced by both men and women. It is a precursor of both male and female hormones (testosterone and estrogen) and is useful for weight loss, diabetic control, life extension, and immune function. The level of DHEA in the body reaches a peak in the twenties and then diminishes with age. A likely reason for its lack of general usage in the medical world is that it cannot be manufactured as a drug and thus is not potentially profitable to the pharmaceutical industry.

Laura's response to the program was gratifying. Not only did her PMS resolve, but so did her depression and irritability. The DHEA improved her energy level and her sexual desire, as well. Needless to say, all this had a positive effect on her relationships. Laura's was another case of physical imbalance causing emotional imbalance. Addressing the physical problem had a positive effect on her emotional well-being.

Natural vs. Synthetic Estrogen

Hormone replacement therapy (HRT) is a major issue in women's health today. Many controversies surround the safety of synthetic estrogen, and women are looking for safe and effective alternatives. Laura did not require estrogen replacement therapy, which is generally provided by the pharmaceutical derivative of pregnant mares' urine. The most commonly used drug for HRT is Premarin, which is high in estradiol and proven to promote cancer growth in susceptible individuals. In addition, the hormones from mares are not designed to be metabolized by the human system, and the collection of urine from pregnant mares is one more unnecessary and inhumane abuse of animals. The pregnant mares are kept immobilized and catheterized in cramped stalls for continuous urine collection, and their foals sold for slaughter. The mares are immediately impregnated to repeat the cycle until they are no longer useful for this purpose.

Another important point is that hormone replacement therapy is not necessary to combat osteoporosis. Osteoporosis can be treated very well with natural progesterone, magnesium and calcium in the proper balance, together with other minerals such as boron. Provera, the synthetic progesterone, has numerous side effects. Alternative physicians prescribe natural forms of estrogen, derived from the soybean, that are in a balanced formula of estrogen's three components (estradiol, estrone, and estriol). These natural estrogens are provided to physicians by compounding pharmacies. Estriol is a portion of the estrogen complex that not only does not encourage cancer, but actually protects against it! Estriol, though widely used in Europe for many years, is available in the United States only through compounding pharmacies.

Soy is an excellent source of estrogenlike activity and should be included in the diet of menopausal women. Of note is that in countries such as Japan, where soy is a dietary staple, there is a very low incidence of menopausal symptoms and of breast and uterine cancer. Statistics show that this same population, when exposed to the typical American diet, loses this protection, indicating that this is not a genetic disease.

The combination of natural estrogen, natural progesterone, DHEA, and testosterone (all based on laboratory measures), a healthy diet containing extra soy, plus herbal, vitamin, and mineral supplements more effectively prevents symptoms of menopause, erroneously seen as an inevitable part of aging. Of particular interest are vitamin E (400–800 milligrams daily), which can reduce hot flashes through its estrogen-stimulating properties, and magnesium (200–400 milligrams daily), which together with the trace mineral boron, is as important as calcium in the prevention and treatment of osteoporosis.[6]

Is there a corresponding male menopause? I believe so. Some physicians refer to this phenomenon as male andropause. Men who complain of such problems as fatigue, weight gain, and loss of sexual interest or function may be deficient in male sex hormones, the androgens. Testosterone and DHEA levels can be measured and supplemented, leading to a reversal of these difficult symptoms, thereby giving these men a new lease on life.

Thyroid Imbalance

The following case is yet another example of the mood-hormone connection. Jennifer came to see me, depressed, tired, unable to get up in the morning to attend her college classes, and feeling overwhelmed by her graduate-level course work. Jennifer's history revealed that she was often cold, especially her hands and feet (she even wore socks to bed), had thinning hair, dry skin, constipation, and was losing the outer part of her eyebrows. I suspected an imbalance in her thyroid, the energy-generating gland located below the Adam's apple.

When I asked about thyroid disease, she said that it had been suspected before, but her tests had been normal. I checked her thyroid hormones, including thyroid antibody levels. An underactive thyroid can often hide behind "normal" blood tests. Dr. Broda Barnes's technique of monitoring thyroid function through body temperature is used by many alternative practitioners. If the temperature is consistently low, these physicians treat the patient with thyroid replacement therapy, monitoring progress both by clinical signs and symptoms and by rise in temperature.[7]

Although Jennifer's thyroid hormone levels were normal, she did, in fact, have anti-thyroid antibodies in her bloodstream, confirming a diagnosis of Hashimoto's thyroiditis. This is a common autoimmune disease to which women are more susceptible than men. It is treatable with thyroid hormone, antioxidants, and adrenal support. Her signs were those of hypothyroidism, suggesting that the circulating hormone was being rendered ineffective. With this condition, there are often intermittent signs of hyperthyroidism—overactive thyroid, such as irritability or heart palpitations. I prescribed thyroid hormone from natural sources and asked her to monitor her body temperature so that I could adjust her dosage. She asked whether this would suppress her own thyroid function and whether she would need it for the rest of her life. The answer was no on both counts. The treatment actually supported her own gland, allowing it to heal. She did well. Within ten days of starting the program, she was feeling alive again. Her mood and energy lifted, as did the gloomy fog of her mornings past.

Adrenal Hormones and Hypoglycemia

The adrenal glands, which secrete the stress hormone cortisol, tend to be neglected in most medical diagnoses. However, maintaining healthy adrenal glands is very important as our fast-paced modern lifestyles create stress-laden lives. Alternative physicians tend to treat low-functioning adrenals immediately in order to restore adrenal function and allow people to deal much more effectively with stress, rather than waiting for someone to have complete adrenal failure or Addison's disease, leading to further compromising of their health.

Poor adrenal function is intimately related to a major, generally undiagnosed cause of depression: hypoglycemia, or low blood sugar. This disorder is often related to stress and poor eating habits, both of which affect the adrenal glands. Although doctors may diagnose other glandular deficiencies, low adrenal function, which is related to hypoglycemia, remains a medical orphan. Our tiny, but very important, adrenal glands, located just above the kidneys, prepare us for fight or flight. Many of us live in a continuous state of stress, leading the adrenals to secrete the hormone cortisol, which raises blood sugar temporarily, only to have it plummet over and over again, until these overtaxed glands are exhausted, and so are we. Coffee drinking is often an attempt to boost blood sugar and give a quick shot of energy by stimulating already tired glands. Trying to boost energy with caffeine is like beating a dead horse.

Diagnosing Hypoglycemia

Thea came to me complaining of mood swings. At times, she would fly off the handle for little reason yet at other times be quite calm and capable of dealing with her emotions and behavior—and children. By the time her workday began, she had already packed her ten- and twelve-year-old's school lunches, dropped them off at school, and then prayed that no traffic delays would make her late for work. Her eating habits were the key to discovering the underlying cause for her mood swings. When questioned, she described a typical pattern: breakfast consisted of coffee and doughnuts, grabbed up in the lobby of her office building and gulped down as she dashed up to work. This was followed by coffee and doughnuts again for her 10 A.M. energy slump. Then a quick sandwich at her desk with a Coke, and a cup of coffee within her reach at all times.

She would arrive home in the evening, exhausted, foggy-brained, and wondering how she would get through the evening, help her children with their homework, and tuck them in before she collapsed into bed. The coffee would handle her fatigue during the day, but she did not want to drink it at night, when it would interfere with her sleep. She remarked that she did feel better—more energetic and clearer-headed—after she ate, but time was precious and meals took last place in her order of priorities.

Her diagnosis? Hypoglycemia resulting from poor eating habits, particularly in a person like her, whose family history of hypoglycemia made her genetically predisposed to this condition. The disorder can present itself in a variety of ways: depression, irritability, anxiety, panic attacks, fatigue, "brain fog," headaches including migraines, insomnia, muscular weakness, and tremors, all of which may be relieved by food. Hypoglycemics may crave sweets, coffee, alcohol, or drugs. In fact, many addictions are related to hypoglycemia. Coffee and sugar consumed by recovering addicts only prolongs their problem, though in a less dangerous, more socially acceptable form.

It is interesting to note that large amounts of these substances are consumed at Alcoholics Anonymous meetings and on psychiatric wards. Patients can often overcome coffee, drug, and alcohol addiction through correcting their hypoglycemia, with minimal withdrawal symptoms or later cravings. For example, I recommend that recovering alcoholics follow the hypoglycemic regimen described below and take in addition the amino acid glutamine, which is particularly useful when a craving strikes.

Treating Hypoglycemia

For Thea's hypoglycemia, I prescribed a program designed to both strengthen her adrenals and maintain adequate blood sugar levels. This included:

- Eliminating refined carbohydrates (sugar, white flour), coffee, and alcohol

- Eating small, frequent meals of complex carbohydrates, high fiber, and protein

- Daily supplementation with chromium, manganese, potassium, B vitamins, pantothenic acid (vitamin B_5), and vitamin C

Thea responded well to the nutritional program. Within three months she was feeling like herself again—active, enthusiastic, optimistic, and with stable moods. She continued the hypoglycemic diet and remained on a maintenance dose of supplements. As we can see, Thea had a metabolic disturbance—hypoglycemia—which superficially appeared as psychological in origin. While therapy together with specific stress reduction techniques would have been useful, the underlying imbalance had to be addressed first.

FOOD AND CHEMICAL SENSITIVITIES

Food and chemical sensitivities are often present in individuals with some or all of the above conditions, which can lead or contribute to depression.[8] We generally think of allergies as manifesting by a rash, hives, nasal congestion, or gastrointestinal problems. These reactions are mediated by the classically recognized IgE (immune globulin E) protein component of the immune system. However, food and chemical sensitivities mediated by another component, IgG (immune globulin G), can produce a great variety of symptoms such as depression, anxiety, "brain fog," fatigue, hyperactivity, attention deficit disorder, joint pains, migraines, irritable bowel syndrome, and food cravings, mimicking many other illnesses in the process. This syndrome is often misdiagnosed because it mimics so many other diseases and may even be labeled as psychosomatic or emotional.

Diagnosis and Treatment of Food and Chemical Sensitivities

Rotation and Elimination Diets.

Alternative medical practitioners often recommend specific diagnostic and treatment programs for this food and chemical sensitivity syndrome. A common approach is "rotation and elimination," whereby the patient avoids the offending substance, then gradually reintroduces it until it is tolerated. This food can then be eaten on a rotating basis, no more often than every four days, to avoid further sensitivity. Disadvantages of this technique include nutritional limitations, personal inconvenience, and inability to avoid some common substances, particularly airborne pollutants and allergens.

Nambudripad's Allergy Elimination Technique.

One particularly exciting new technique for permanently desensitizing people to offending foods and chemicals is called NAET (Nambudripad's Allergy Elimination Technique). Diagnosis is by muscle testing (applied kinesiology), using an indicator muscle to determine if a particular substance causes weakness in the individual's energy field.[9] Treatment is with acupuncture or acupressure. After a twenty-five-hour period of avoidance, the patient can often go back on the offending food or be exposed to the chemical with no further problem. While this may sound impossible, just as acupuncture once seemed, the results are compelling. The process may be explained in the same way as acupuncture, in which treating subtle energy channels can affect physical processes.

I treated a woman with a dairy allergy with NAET. Two things happened. First, she noticed that without even trying she no longer went on her nightly ice-cream binge. She had also had a drooping left eyelid since adolescence. At one point, she had even considered cosmetic surgery for it. After the NAET, her eyelid stopped drooping and matched the other one! She brought me an earlier photo, saying, "I can't believe this. It's not happening anymore." Somehow her dairy allergy was connected with her eyelid droop, and when the allergy cleared the eyelid came back up. We see how pervasive yet subtle the effects of a food allergy can be.

AMINO ACID DEFICIENCY

In cases when depression appears unrelated to other metabolic causes, we check the patient's plasma amino acid levels as described in Dr. Priscilla Slagle's book *The Way Up from Down* and *The Healing Nutrients Within* by Drs. Eric Braverman and Carl Pfeiffer.[10] Brain chemicals called neurotransmitters carry messages of stimulation or inhibition between nerve cells. If these messengers are in short supply, depression can result. By loading up on the precursors (the amino acids the body converts to neurotransmitters), it is possible to reverse depression. For example, the amino acid precursors tyrosine and phenylalanine produce norepinephrine and dopamine, and tryptophan is converted to serotonin.

Antidepressant drugs work in a similar way as the amino acid precursors, promoting the formation of neurotransmitters in the brain and thereby elevating mood. If a patient is already on antidepressant medication(s), he can remain on it while we work on balancing his chemistry. He may later discontinue the medication after the amino acid therapy takes effect.

Tryptophan, the low-cost amino acid safely and effectively used for depression and insomnia for many years, unfortunately is no longer available in the United States. It is interesting to note that ever since 1989, when a toxic batch of tryptophan from the Showa Denko company in Japan caused a serious illness called eosinophilia myalgia and a number of deaths, it is no longer available over the counter in the United States. Although it was clear that the illness was due to a contaminant and not to the tryptophan itself, as was stated in an article in the *New England Journal of Medicine*, the ban remains. It is also curious to note that the selective serotonin reuptake inhibitor (SSRI) Prozac, which was being released at the time, has a similar action; that is, it enhances serotonin availability, thereby elevating mood. The competition to the drug companies was wiped out by the prohibition against tryptophan.

Tryptophan is now available, by prescription, at compounding pharmacies. Also, in recent times, 5-hydroxytryptophan (5-HTP), a metabolite that has the same action, has become available over the counter.

Other amino acids that affect mood are tyrosine, L-Glutamine, threonine, and D, L-Phenylalanine. Special laboratory tests can determine deficiencies of specific amino acids, and the treatments are based accordingly.

Vitamin and Mineral Deficiencies

A simple and often overlooked cause of depression is a lack of specific vitamins and minerals that are essential to metabolic processes. The body is run by a myriad of chemical reactions as it digests, absorbs, and utilizes the raw material that we put into it in the form of food. Vitamins and minerals are essential cofactors or chemical helpers in metabolic processes. If, through nutritional deficiency or poor absorption, these are not available, metabolism is impaired, causing symptoms.

For example, a common condition in women, who regularly lose blood in their menstrual cycle, is iron-deficiency anemia. This chronic loss of iron, as seen in our first case with Catherine, impairs the oxygen-carrying capacity of the red blood cells. Her depression and fatigue might have been detected much earlier and treated with iron supplements, thereby aiding her immune system, which was compromised by the low iron.

A similar cause of these symptoms, especially in older individuals, is vitamin B_{12} deficiency, which is easily detected by a blood test and corrected by supplementation. B_{12} is best given by injection, because the problem often results from poor intestinal absorption of this particular vitamin. Women taking birth control pills can have deficiencies of vitamins B_6, B_{12}, folic acid, and vitamin C, leading to depression, fatigue, confusion, and irritability. It is of note that vitamin C can act as a natural tranquilizer. Drs. Abram Hoffer and Humphrey Osmond reported patients' responding to 10 grams of vitamin C daily when tranquilizers had been found ineffective. Magnesium deficiency can produce anxiety, irritability, and hypersensitivity to noise, all of which can be rapidly reversed with magnesium supplementation.

Deficiencies in almost any of the vitamins and minerals can be present with emotional or cognitive symptoms such as depression, anxiety, or impaired memory and concentration—the very symptoms we saw in our case examples. The treatment is either by determining the specific deficiencies through laboratory tests (blood and urine) followed by appropriate supplementation or by taking a combination megavitamin/mineral supplement. Because lab tests can be costly, I most often recommend the latter. The RDA—Required Daily Allowance of vitamins and minerals—advocated by the orthodox dietitians and the FDA is meaningless. The recommended levels are not nearly sufficient for good health maintenance, but only for preventing serious, end-stage deficiency disease, such as scurvy (vitamin C deficiency) or pellagra (vitamin B_1 deficiency). Of interest is that the average American diet is generally deficient even in the RDA!

What causes these deficiencies? We need only consider the high-sugar, low-fiber, additive-preserved foods that many people "live" on, combined with the impaired absorption that accompanies such poor nutrition. It is no wonder that we are a nation of stressed, depressed, fatigued individuals with learning disabilities and degenerative diseases in all the body systems. We are overfed and undernourished. A poorly nourished body contains a malnourished brain.

Malabsorption.

Other causes of nutritional deficiencies are malabsorption and/or poor digestion. If the digestive system is malfunctioning, the port of entry for nutrients will not allow proper absorption. Then, in order to break down foods in the stomach, we need the right amount of hydrochloric acid, secreted by the parietal cells of the stomach lining, and pancreatic enzymes. A number of other factors involved in digestion and absorption, such as bile acids, are deficient in many people. Thus, we can take all kinds of supplements, but they are useless unless they can be absorbed and digested.

Leaky Gut Syndrome.

Another major problem leading to nutritional deficiency is leaky gut syndrome. Certain illnesses such as candida and parasites actually cause leaks in the gut. The gut wall is impaired and molecules of food that have not been broken down to their simplest molecules are absorbed by the body through the intestinal wall. The body does not recognize these molecules as friendly food, but rather as "enemies," and forms antibodies against them, leading to allergic reactions. The individuals suffering from this syndrome may be overweight, but they are not absorbing their food and are not well nourished. In addition, they may be facing serious problems from their allergic reactions.

ST. JOHN'S WORT AND OTHER HERBS

An herb that has become extremely popular for the treatment of depression is St. John's wort. Despite its strange name ("wort" is old English for plant), it has become a lifesaver for many people. It acts similarly to such antidepressants as Prozac, Zoloft, and Paxil, but without the side effects, at a far lower cost, and without a prescription. The recommended dose is 300 milligrams of standardized extract (0.3 percent hypericin), three times daily. In Germany, where herbs are prescribed by medical doctors, the prescriptions for St. John's wort outnumber those for antidepressants twenty to one. In addition, St. John's wort is an excellent treatment for PMS, menopausal symptoms of anxiety and depression, and menstrual cramps. It even stimulates the immune system and is useful in the treatment of chronic viral conditions, such as herpes and Epstein-Barr virus. Unlike the single, magic-bullet approach of Western medicine, nature gives us an array of healing elements in each product.[11]

There are many other herbs that I prescribe for depression, including valerian and hops for sleep, kava for relaxation and sleep, ginseng for energy and immunity, and the other immune-enhancing herbs already mentioned: echinacea, goldenseal, and astragalus.

THE USE OF ANTIDEPRESSANT MEDICATION

Some people experience severe depression who, despite the risks and side effects, may need medication. In my book *St. John's Wort: Nature's Blues Buster*, I give a more complete discussion of the use of the various antidepressants and the research comparing them to this herb. In my research and experience as a medical doctor, I see no reason to take the chemical route unless the natural one fails. In over 85 percent of cases with the correct diagnosis, we can treat depression and its many symptoms by natural means. Depression is not a Prozac deficiency.

Drugs can be very effective in many cases, but the negative consequences such as headache, dizziness, irritability, insomnia, and sexual dysfunction can far outweigh the positive effects. The newest class of antidepressants, the selective serotonin reuptake inhibitors like Prozac (the most popular), Zoloft, and Paxil, work by allowing an accumulation of serotonin in the space between the neurons, thus creating an excess of this "feel-good" neurotransmitter. However, most mild to moderate depression responds as well to St. John's wort, and without the inherent problems of these synthetic antidepressants.

PSYCHOTHERAPY

Despite the strong influence that our biochemistry has on our moods, there is still a place for psychotherapy—in helping us deal with these natural changes and raise our feel-good chemicals naturally. That is, when we start to feel better, our neurotransmitter levels will rise naturally, assuming we have enough of the precursors or raw materials to manufacture them.

In addition, an important role of psychotherapy is getting to know and understand ourselves better. There are some particularly useful techniques that I have incorporated into my practice over the years, including Voice Dialogue and EMDR (Eye Movement Desensitization and Reprocessing), for depressed patients who often suffer from feelings of inadequacy and self-loathing despite their accomplishments.

Voice Dialogue.

Consider the case of Corinne. Although a beautiful and gifted thirty-two-year-old actress, Corinne was sure that she was a fraud. Her greatest fear was that "they'll find out how dumb and incompetent I really am." She was also terrified of getting old and losing her looks, certain that her other attributes were nonexistent. In fact, in addition to her acting career, Corinne had also written and directed a play and was well respected in the theatrical community. She was still not convinced of her worth, however, and insisted, "It was a fluke."

I understood Corinne's fear and loneliness. The frightened child inside, a victim of childhood abuse, still felt that she "must have deserved the mistreatment" that she had received at the hands of her disturbed mother. Our work consisted of helping Corinne find her own inner good mother and nurturing her back to good mental health and a positive self-image through a therapeutic technique called Voice Dialogue.[12]

People who, like Corinne, lack a sense of self-worth seem to have an Inner Critic looking over their shoulder, telling them how stupid, boring, ugly, and useless they are. They expect failure and rejection in whatever they do. When things do not turn out perfectly, they hear their Critic say, "See, I told you you were incompetent (or useless, or worthless)." Depressed people often set impossible standards of performance for themselves. Then, when they can't meet these standards, the vicious cycle of negative self-worth is reinforced. The cycle can continue to build until it envelops the depressed individual in a prison of pessimistic thinking. Voice Dialogue, developed by Drs. Hal Stone and Sidra Stone, consists of the therapist actually addressing this Inner Critic and offering it some understanding.

EMDR.

A number of other psychotherapy methods allow the individual to reverse a dysfunctional pattern that often underlies depression. One that I use successfully in my practice is EMDR, or Eye Movement Desensitization and Reprocessing, developed by psychologist Francine Shapiro. A form of release work, this therapy helps the individual to recall the incident(s) and reexperience the trauma in a safe setting. This allows the mind to finally release the suppressed emotions. After as few as one or two sessions, a patient can complete the unfinished process of long ago, and is able to get on with his or her life.

An analogy for this process is that the incident puts the brain's recorder, like a VCR, on pause, and EMDR, which induces rapid eye movements in the individual, allows the VCR to release and move through the old film into the present. A possible explanation for this is that the rapid eye movement of EMDR is similar to that which occurs during dream sleep. Emotional leftovers of the day are processed neatly by our brains at this time. This technique seems to be a way of producing the same healing function. Preliminary research has indicated that the brain chemistry actually shows corresponding changes as a result of this therapeutic work.[13]

COMING BACK INTO BALANCE

The psychiatrist can be not only a healer, but an educator and facilitator as well, helping people to make choices in lifestyle, diet, supplements, and medications. Rather than curing depression, the goal is to bring balance in body, as well as in mind and spirit. The physical imbalances can run the gamut from hypoglycemia to viral and fungal infections, hormonal imbalances, allergies, sensitivities, toxic chemical or metal overload, and deficiencies of vitamins, minerals, or amino acids. Imbalance in one area is reflected in problems in other areas, and the weakest link shows first.

The ideal treatment for an imbalance such as depression is holistic. This means evaluating the whole person and treating each imbalance accordingly, while being aware that the body/mind seeks homeostasis. When as many areas as possible are addressed on the physical, emotional, and spiritual levels, shifts take place that can move the individual toward wholeness and health.

A Comprehensive Approach to Depression: Nutritional Medicine and Biofeedback

Melvyn R. Werbach, M.D.

Let thy food be thy medicine.
—Hippocrates

BACK TO THE ROOTS: A LOOK AT HIPPOCRATES' VISION OF HEALTH

The teachings of Hippocrates, the ancient Greek physician recognized as the father of Western medicine, provide an excellent framework for a holistic approach to the treatment of depression. It is interesting to note that although physicians still take an oath upon graduation from medical school to practice by the standards set by Hippocrates, these standards are too often forgotten in the practice of modern medicine.

Hippocrates' vision of health was primarily an ecological model that focused on the interrelationship of individuals and their environment, an issue of great relevance in dealing with depression. He looked at a balance between human nature, lifestyle, and the environment in defining health:

Health is the expression of a harmonious balance between the various components of man's nature, the environment, and ways of living.

Hippocrates believed that mind and body are so interconnected that one cannot be considered without the other. Today, there is a split between psychiatry, which deals with mental disorders, and the rest of medicine, which tends to ignore the psychological influences upon health, illness, and healing. Further, Hippocrates believed that it is critical to focus on the individual, not on the disease, allowing a physician to look at the whole person before making a decision:

> *It is more important to know what sort of person has a disease, than to know what sort of disease a person has.*

Hippocrates firmly believed that people had the inherent power to heal themselves and that the physician's role was to suggest rational treatments that encourage the return to "harmonious balance." Safety was of primary importance in all treatments, a value that is often forgotten when antidepressants, despite their potentially serious side effects, are excessively prescribed in contemporary medicine. Natural healing methods took precedence over drugs in the Hippocratic approach:

> *The natural power within us is the greatest force in healing.*

Hippocrates further believed that the physician's job is to be an educator, giving assistance by providing information, care, and companionship, as well as by assisting people in healing themselves. Successful treatment results from a partnership between physician and patient. According to Hippocrates, it is critical that physicians avoid impatience with patients if they want to facilitate healing, as the physician/patient relationship has a strong impact on healing processes:

> *Some patients, though their condition is perilous, recover their health simply through their contentment with the goodness of the physician.*

Finally, Hippocrates believed that the family and caregivers played a key role in the healing process and that the external circumstances must be conducive to the cure. His unique, holistic approach to health and health care offers great insights in addressing our health challenges, particularly depression.

A COMPREHENSIVE MODEL OF DEPRESSION

A comprehensive contemporary medical or ecologic model essentially follows these same principles propounded by Hippocrates. This model emphasizes treatment methods that encourage natural healing processes, have general salutatory effects that extend beyond any of the reductionistic medical specialties, and have minimal risks of adverse effects. The ecologic model looks to see what environmental factors may be influencing a person's illness, evaluates psychosocial influences on the course of every illness, and then employs corrective psychological and behavioral interventions in the treatment process. It is important that health professionals always see themselves, at least in part, as therapists, as they need to be aware of the behavioral and psychological aspects of the whole person in order for their treatments to be therapeutic.

This ecologic model also employs the concept of the body/mind, which views the mind as a part of the body called the brain, and views the body as a stage for the expression of the mind. The mind influences the course of all illness—as in the case of psychological stress, which can cause both physical illness and mental illness.

Depression can be viewed from a comprehensive perspective in three different ways:

1. Depression can be a failure of a body system. It is often the first symptom of a serious disease such as cancer, well before there is any other sign or symptom of the disorder.

2. Depression can be simply a mental/emotional state due to a physical or psychological change within the brain.

3. Depression can be a psychological defense that provides a protective function. For example, by becoming depressed, one can unconsciously protect oneself from dealing with painful issues.

Depression can also be a warning sign, signaling that the body/mind is off course. If it is warning you of something psychological, it could be indicating that your life is not on the right track or that you have made some poor decisions or have not made a decision that you need to make. If it is warning you of something physical, it could be indicating that you need more exercise or a better diet. Depression can be warning you, in a very healthy way, that you need to make some changes. Depression can be as important as pain. We need to have access to feelings of sadness just as we need to have access to feelings of pain.

If we look at depression from this comprehensive perspective, we recognize that there are many underlying root causes. The most important causes—genetic, functional, structural, psychological, nutritional, pollutants, and environmental sensitivities—are discussed in detail in chapters 2 through 4 and 6 through 7.

Formal Criteria for Depression

What are the formal medical criteria for depression? Two primary forms of depression are described in the American Psychiatric Association's *DSM-IV*.[1] The first is *Dysthymic Disorder*, which is characterized by a depressed mood for at least two years as well as specific symptoms that cause significant distress or impairment in functioning but are not due to drug use. At least two of the following six symptoms must be present to be diagnosed as **dysthymic disorder**:

- Poor appetite or overeating
- Insomnia or hypersomnia
- Fatigue or loss of energy
- Low self-esteem
- Poor concentration or difficulty making decisions
- Feelings of hopelessness

This simple checklist provides the basis for differentiating between simple feelings of sadness and symptoms that would qualify as criteria for a depressive syndrome.

The second depressive disorder is called *major depressive episode*, which is marked by a depressed mood or markedly diminished loss of interest or pleasure during a two-week period, as well as specific symptoms that cause significant distress or impairment in functioning but are not due to drug use. At least four of the following seven symptoms must be present to be diagnosed as having a **major depressive episode**:

- Poor appetite or overeating
- Insomnia or hypersomnia
- Fatigue or loss of energy

- Feelings of worthlessness or excessive or inappropriate guilt (more severe than simple low self-esteem)
- Poor concentration or difficulty in making decisions
- Recurrent thoughts of death or suicidal ideation
- Psychomotor agitation or retardation (physical activity associated with mental processes)

We do not know whether dysthymic disorder and major depressive episode are different or if they provide sufficient answers to many of our remaining questions as to the true nature of depression. These diagnostic classifications, however, do offer a common framework and terminology in dealing with depression, making it possible to look at an individual who is feeling depressed and determine whether he or she meets the criteria for a clinical diagnosis of depression. These classifications also help us recognize that depression is not simply a matter of sadness, but a syndrome with numerous aspects.

SELECTING APPROPRIATE TREATMENTS FOR DEPRESSION

There are many approaches to treating depression, ranging from psychological to nutritional and environmental. The following categories cover the primary treatment approaches provided by conventional and alternative/complementary–oriented health professionals. The optimum approach is an integration of the appropriate therapies to suit the specific needs of an individual.

Psychological
- Individual
- Conjoint
- Family

Behavioral

Biochemical
- Drugs
- Herbs

Electrical
- Electroconvulsive
- Electrotherapeutics

Psychophysiological
(mind/body therapies)

Meditative

Somatopsychic
- Movement
- Deep tissue massage

Acupuncture

Homeopathic

Nutritional

Detoxification

Environmental change
- Psychological
- Reduced exposures

Provocative neutralization
(Allergy response testing)

How does one best select the appropriate treatments? The simplest approach is to have criteria for evaluating treatments, such as the following:

Safety: Select the safest of the applicable treatments that might be useful.

Cost: Is the treatment cost-effective?

Efficacy: How effective is the treatment?

Speed: How quickly does the treatment work?

Availability: Is the treatment available locally, or will it be difficult to find?

Patient preference: The patient's feelings about the various approaches are very important, but this is often a forgotten priority. According to Hippocrates, the ideal patient/physician relationship is one of partnership.

Compliance: Is a patient likely to follow the prescribed treatment? Patients frequently fail to comply with their physicians, a major problem that has been verified by surveys. For example, a major proportion of patients fail to take their medication as prescribed. In many instances, however, doctors neglect to evaluate *why* patients are not taking the medication.

Did the physician give the medication in an authoritative, threatening way, or in a manner that encouraged partnership by expressing care and concern? Physicians who discuss treatments with their patients and make decisions together with them very rarely have a problem with compliance. Physicians can tell patients to call them to discuss the medication if they have any questions or problems that arise. If patients are thinking of stopping the medication, physicians can tell them if they agree or disagree. Compliance will always be less of a problem, if the physician/patient relationship is one of partnership.

Ideally, a patient will see a health professional who is knowledgeable about the characteristics and efficacy of a wide variety of treatments and is thus able to more closely match the treatment and the appropriate health practitioner to the patient. Commonly, however, people go directly to health professionals who are knowledgeable in only one or two treatment approaches and who tend to stretch the applications of those treatments in an attempt to include patients within their area of expertise.

This chapter focuses on two of the many treatment approaches to depression: nutritional medicine, a form of natural biological treatment, and biofeedback-assisted relaxation training, a form of psychophysiologic treatment.

NUTRITIONAL TREATMENT OF DEPRESSION

Nutritional medicine is one of the most valuable and yet neglected forms of treatment, at least partly because of the failure of allopathic medical schools to provide students with adequate training in the field. The role of dietary factors, including food sensitivities, as well as the importance of dietary neurotransmitter precursors, vitamin deficiencies, and mineral imbalances are of key importance in the treatment of depression.

There are two primary types of nutritional interventions: *nutrient repletion* and *nutrient pharmacotherapy*. Nutrient repletion refers to identifying specific nutritional deficiencies in an individual and then instituting a corrective diet and/or prescribing dietary supplements. Supplements are intended to supplement a sound diet, not to be taken in lieu of proper basic nutrition. Nutrient pharmacotherapy refers to taking nutrients to nourish the body at pharmacological dosages that often far exceed what we are able to derive from natural substances in the diet. This therapeutic approach can be used to push biochemical reactions in the desired direction.

Dietary Factors and Depression

Depression is often associated with an inadequate diet. On the one hand, depression can lead to malnutrition due to a lack of appetite (anorexia) and, on the other hand, poor eating habits may lead to depression by failing to provide the adequate nutrition for proper functioning. Food sensitivities along with excessive consumption of caffeine, sugar, and alcohol are the main dietary offenders in depression.

Food Sensitivities and Depression

A number of anecdotal reports suggest that reactions to foods can provoke various pathopsychological symptoms, but there is little published research. The most fascinating work in this area is that of Doris

Rapp, M.D., past president of the American Academy of Environmental Medicine. Dr. Rapp videotaped people receiving substances to which they had adverse reactions, including the onset of depression. The subjects were then given a different dosage and the depression disappeared. This technique is called provocative neutralization. Dr. Rapp recorded these dramatic changes repeatedly under double-blind conditions, sometimes with infants and young children. Unfortunately, because this aspect of her work is not in written form, it has gone largely unrecognized.

The best published research study concerning food sensitivities and mood is by David King from the University of Massachusetts Department of Psychology. His double-blind study examining the role of allergens in causing psychological symptoms, including depression, demonstrated that those receiving an allergen (food or chemical substance) would experience greater cognitive/emotional (thinking/feeling) symptoms than those receiving a placebo. King concluded:

> *This clear demonstration of cognitive-emotional symptoms following allergen exposure under double-blind conditions suggests that a link between psychopathology and sensitivity to common environmental substances cannot be overlooked in searching for the etiology of psychiatric symptoms.*[2]

Caffeine

Increased caffeine intake (above 700 milligrams daily) has been found to be associated with higher scores on a depression inventory in both healthy college students[3] and in various psychiatric studies for hospitalized patients.[4] Some clinical or diagnostic clues are particularly helpful in recognizing excessive caffeine intake. For example, in a study among outpatients attending an affective (mood) disorders clinic, high caffeine intake was specifically associated with low energy, hypersomnia (excessive sleeping), and agitated depressions.

Sugar

A high intake of refined sugars also appears to be associated with depression. Do caffeine and sugar cause depression, or do depressives merely ingest more in an attempt to improve their mood? In one study, investigators asked twenty-three people who were experiencing depression without any known cause to consume a caffeine-free and refined sucrose–free diet for one week. Those whose symptoms improved were then given caffeine, a sucrose-sweetened drink, and two corresponding placebos in random order for six consecutive days, under double-blind conditions. Approximately half of the subjects experienced a return of their mood disturbance and symptoms when challenged with caffeine and sucrose, but not when challenged with the placebos, suggesting that both caffeine and sucrose may be frequent contributors to depression and related complaints.[5]

Alcohol

There is mounting evidence that alcohol causes depression by reducing the level of neurotransmitters, such as serotonin, in the brain. In fact, one cause of alcoholism appears to be genetically low brain serotonin levels. Since serotonin is important for mood regulation, low brain serotonin is associated with a tendency toward depression. Alcohol seems to temporarily increase brain serotonin turnover, an effect that improves mood but results in further serotonin depletion. This may explain why an alcoholic feels better after a drink, but is more depressed than ever after sobering up. The result can be a vicious cycle in which the very drug that seems to make the victim feel better causes a gradually deepening depression.[6]

VITAMIN DEFICIENCIES AND DEPRESSION

Deficiencies of vitamin B complex and vitamin C can play a major role in depression. However, if one becomes deficient enough in any of the essential nutrients, depression can be part of the resulting syndrome.

B Vitamins

Deficiencies of certain members of the vitamin B complex will cause depression as part of their respective deficiency syndromes. The efficacy of raising B vitamin levels in a clinically depressed population has been poorly studied. However, there have been studies in which normal volunteers became depressed following diets that were severely restricted in one or more B vitamins.[7]

- **Folic Acid.** Folic acid deficiency is the most common of all vitamin deficiencies, and depression is considered part of the folate deficiency syndrome. Serum (blood) folate levels are inversely correlated with the severity of the depression.[8] In addition to low folate levels causing depression, folate deficiency often occurs secondary to depression because of such factors as poor diet and the use of alcohol and drugs.[9] From a clinical perspective, serum folate levels are frequently reduced and occasionally deficient in depressed patients.[10]

  Depressed patients with folate deficiency whose energy tends to get depleted very quickly are most likely to respond to folate supplementation. This has been supported by the work of M. I. Botez of the Clinical Research Institute of Montreal, who has published widely on neuropsychiatric manifestations of folate deficiency. He found that those folate-deficient patients whose depressions are secondary to easy fatigability are the most likely to respond to folate supplementation.[11]

- **Thiamine and Riboflavin.** Depression is also seen in other B-complex deficiencies, including riboflavin.[12] Depression is also common in the earlier stage of thiamine deficiency, when it manifests as a low-energy syndrome with a variety of complaints.[13,14]

- **Vitamin B_6.** Vitamin B_6 is an important coenzyme in the production of neurotransmitters and is required for the conversion of dietary tryptophan into serotonin. Laboratory evidence of vitamin B_6 deficiency is common in depression.[15] Among hospitalized patients, vitamin B_6 deficiency correlates specifically with endogenous depression, or depression that is unrelated to external events.[16] A diagnostic clue is the presence of mild neurologic symptoms such as numbness, pins and needles, or electric shock sensations.[17]

  Despite a lack of studies investigating the efficacy of vitamin B_6 supplementation, two subgroups with both depression and B_6 deficiency have been shown to be responsive. One group is women with excessive estrogen. Estrogen supplementation can cause depression by blocking B_6 activity and accelerating tryptophan metabolism, which makes it less available to be converted into serotonin. Vitamin B_6 supplementation can benefit a depressed woman with this deficiency caused by estrogen excess.[18]

Women who are on the pill are prime candidates. Patients with celiac disease (the inability to tolerate wheat gluten) constitute the other group responding to B_6 supplementation.[19]

- **Vitamin B_{12}.** Depression may also be due to a vitamin B_{12} deficiency. Although this deficiency is commonly associated with a particular type of anemia called macrocytic, or large red blood cell anemia, it can cause depression without the presence of anemia.[20, 21] Many physicians overlook this and, if patients are not anemic, they assume that they are not B_{12} deficient. However, a marginal B_{12} deficiency can still exist that will not cause anemia but will cause a clinical syndrome; in fact, there is even early evidence that depressed patients with normal vitamin B_{12} serum levels may respond to vitamin B_{12} injections.[22]

  In some cases when people complain of tiredness or fatigue, it is a symptom of depression. Psychiatrists often see people who come in with a variety of symptoms that are part of the depressive syndrome including fatigue but who do not consider themselves to be depressed. In one double-blind crossover study, a group of people who complained of tiredness noticed a significant improvement in their general well-being following a course of B_{12} injections but reported no improvement following a course of placebo injections.[23]

Vitamin C

Depression is the first clinical symptom of scurvy, the vitamin C deficiency disease,[24] which usually is a result of a poor diet. If a person is slowly becoming depleted in vitamin C, the first observable sign is depression. A state of vitamin C deficiency that has not developed into a full clinical syndrome of scurvy is marked by chronic depression, tiredness, irritability, and vague ill health.

On the other hand, if you examine a group of people who are depressed, how often do you find this state of vitamin C deficiency? Is it very rare, or is it very common? The prevalence of ascorbic acid deficiency among various populations of depressives has not been fully explored; however, in one study of a large group of hospitalized psychiatric patients, plasma vitamin C levels were significantly lower than in those of healthy controls, and one-third had levels below the threshold, which has been associated with detrimental effects on behavior.[25]

In another instance, the diets of twelve depressed women who subsequently attempted suicide were compared to twelve other women who were not depressed and had no history of suicide attempts. The only significant difference found was a lower intake of ascorbic acid.[26]

Studies suggest that the mood of patients with marginal vitamin C deficiency may improve with ascorbate supplementation. For example, forty marginally vitamin C–deficient male chronic psychiatric patients, most of whom were schizophrenic, randomly received either ascorbic acid or placebo under double-blind conditions.[27] Three weeks later, only the supplemented group showed a significant decline in a standardized measure of depression (the depression scale of the MMPI).

MINERAL IMBALANCES AND DEPRESSION

The minerals that seem to be the most important in terms of depression include iron, calcium, magnesium, and potassium.

Iron

Iron deficiency is believed to be the most prevalent worldwide nutrient deficiency. It is foremost among the minerals implicated in depression and characterized by fatigue and microcytic, or small cell anemia. Patients generally respond to iron supplementation. One point that is not well known, however, is that even after iron supplementation has normalized hemoglobin levels, the depression may take months to resolve.[28]

Calcium

There is evidence to suggest that serum calcium concentrations may be elevated in depression[29] and lowered following successful electroshock therapy.[30] Such elevation is commonly due to a pathologic process such as hyperparathyroidism, which causes excessive loss of calcium from the bones. Other data, however, suggest that plasma calcium tends to be reduced in patients with depression.[29,31] Differences between plasma and serum calcium in relation to depression may represent a change in a calcium-binding factor that is present in the plasma but not in serum, which reflects biological factors of affective disease.[29]

In evaluating depression, we are most interested in the nutrient level in the brain but have to settle for other findings that do not necessarily correlate with this measure. However, calcium concentrations in the blood serum, which is easy to measure, appear to be elevated in depression much like calcium concentrations in the cerebrospinal fluid that bathes the brain,[32] and it may decline after depressed patients are given electroconvulsive therapy.[30,33]

In regard to treatment, the results of two double-blind studies suggest that calcium, along with vitamin D, may be of some benefit in improving mood.[34] However, calcium supplementation has yet to be tested in the treatment of clinical depressions.

Magnesium

Serum and plasma magnesium levels may be either increased[29] or decreased[35] in seriously depressed patients. The literature is conflicting in this regard, although, among a group of hospitalized psychiatric patients, both high and low plasma magnesium levels were noted in the more disturbed, excitable patients,[36] suggesting that either end of the scale is associated with similar psychiatric changes. Cerebrospinal fluid magnesium may be decreased in hospitalized depressed patients, especially those who are suicidal.[37] Magnesium deficiency is the cause of hypocalcemia (low calcium levels) in about one out of five patients.[38] In these cases magnesium supplementation should normalize the calcium levels.

Depression may also be part of the magnesium deficiency syndrome. Magnesium deficiency should be suspected when irritability and agitation are present.[35] This is a high-energy, agitated, irritable type of depression. Evidence of magnesium deficiency requires determining the cause and providing adequate supplementation until the underlying problem is corrected.

Potassium

Hypokalemia, or low blood potassium, is found in perhaps 20 percent of medically hospitalized patients, and it is frequently associated with a dysphoric mood (exaggerated feeling of depression and unrest without apparent cause). A patient with depression and potassium deficiency will tend to show fatigue, weakness, and perhaps an organic

Nutritional Evaluation

The following nutritional evaluation lists the various types of clinical and laboratory testing that may be helpful in completing a truly complete comprehensive nutritional evaluation. Every patient does not require such an extensive and elaborate evaluation; a health professional should carefully select which tests are most useful for the individual patient.

1. Dietary history (caffeine; refined sugars; alcohol)
2. Physical exam (Look for signs of vitamin B complex and vitamin C deficiencies.)
3. Rule out food sensitivities.
4. CBC (Complete Blood Count) with red cell indices (nutritional anemias)
5. Neutrophil segmentation (Hypersegmentation may be due to either folate or B_{12} deficiency.)
6. Folic acid serum folate; 24-hour urine for formiminoglutamic acid (FIGLU)
7. Riboflavin: glutathione reductase activity in erythrocytes and its stimulation in vitro by flavin adenine dinucleotide (expressed as "activity coefficient" or percentage stimulation)
8. Thiamine: RBC transketolase activity and its stimulation in vitro by thiamine pyrophosphate (thiamine pyrophosphate effect)
9. Vitamin B_6: Serum pyridoxine and RBC glutamic oxaloacetic transaminase activity
10. Vitamin B_{12}: urinary methylmalonic acid level; serum vitamin B_{12} level by microbiological assay
11. Vitamin C: ascorbic acid loading test
12. Calcium serum and plasma calcium
13. Iron: serum ferritin
14. Magnesium: magnesium loading test; serum, RBC and WBC magnesium
15. Potassium: serum potassium
16. Phenylalanine: plasma and 24-hour urine
17. Tryptophan: plasma and 24-hour urine
18. Tyrosine: plasma and 24-hour urine
19. Phenylacetic acid: plasma and 24-hour urine
20. Hydrochloric acid: baseline and poststimulation gastric acidity

brain syndrome like difficulty in thinking clearly.[39] Hypokalemic patients may also have reduced serum magnesium levels, which was the case of 42 percent of a group in one study.[38] Among an unselected group of depressed patients, serum and plasma potassium levels are likely to be normal. Intracellular potassium levels of depressed patients may be low,[40] however, which raises the unanswered question of whether some of these people would respond to an increased potassium intake. Autopsies have found reduced cerebral potassium in suicide victims,[39] a finding that certainly raises the suspicion that low brain potassium may be important in suicidal depressions.

NEUROTRANSMITTER PRECURSORS

Serotonin and norepinephrine are two chemical substances that function as neurotransmitters in the brain and exert a major influence on brain function. Since both of these major neurotransmitters are derived from biochemical precursors present in the diet, there has been a great deal of interest in investigating the effect of increasing the intake of their dietary precursors.

Tryptophan: A Serotonin Precursor

L-Tryptophan is an essential amino acid found in dietary protein that produces the important neurotransmitter serotonin. In order to be converted into serotonin (5-Hydroxytryptamine), tryptophan must first be converted into 5-Hydroxytryptophan (5-HTP), the immediate precursor to serotonin.

Tryptophan is in a group of several large neutral amino acids with which it must compete in order to be transported across the blood-brain barrier. As tryptophan tends to have the lowest concentration in foods among these amino acids, it has a difficult time crossing the blood-brain barrier in adequate quantities. One way to help it to get across is to avoid ingesting protein for ninety minutes before or after a tryptophan supplement. Another way is to eat a carbohydrate to stimulate insulin release, thereby lowering the peripheral levels of the other competing large neutral amino acids. Because the most common side effects of tryptophan supplementation are gastrointestinal, it should be taken at mealtimes.

There is a good deal of evidence that a cause and effect relationship exists between tryptophan and depression. There is some doubt in the scientific literature, however, about its efficacy.[41] One possibility is that there may be a therapeutic window (a floor and a ceiling) in the dosage range. If it gets above that ceiling level, it may not work, and if it is too low, it may not work. Negative studies regarding tryptophan have tended to use daily doses above 6 grams, a very high dose.[42]

The FDA removed L-Tryptophan from the market a few years ago because of a sudden occurrence of numerous cases of an often fatal illness, EMS (eosinophilia myalgia syndrome). Almost all the evidence suggests that the cause was the introduction of a contaminant due to a change in the manufacturing process by one of the major world suppliers in Japan. However, the FDA has yet to release tryptophan for unrestricted sale.

5-Hydroxytryptophan (5-HTP)

Supplementation with 5-Hydroxytryptophan, a metabolite of tryptophan and the immediate precursor of serotonin, also appears to be a promising treatment. There is even reason to believe that 5-Hydroxytryptophan may be superior to tryptophan.[43] Both substances enter serotonergic neurons; in other words, neurons that depend on serotonin to transmit the impulse from their ending to the start of the next neuron. However, 5-Hydroxytryptophan also enters the catecholaminergic neurons before it is converted into serotonin. Therefore, it may foster the release of the catecholamines, or other substances that are important in terms of mood. For this reason, you may get a greater therapeutic effect with 5-Hydroxytryptophan than with tryptophan.

Both serotonin precursors, L-Tryptophan and 5-Hydroxytryptophan, seem most effective for acute endogenous depressions (depressions coming from within), especially those marked by anxiety, agitation, or aggression.[44,45]

L-Phenylalanine: A Norepinephrine Precursor

The neurotransmitter norepinephrine is formed from L-Phenylalanine, which like L-Tryptophan is an essential amino acid found in dietary protein. While tryptophan tends to be sedating, phenylalanine tends to have a stimulating effect and can occasionally cause anxiety, headaches, or even hypertension. It is contraindicated in phenylketonuria (a hereditary disease caused by the body's failure to oxidize phenylalanine to tyrosine), patients receiving a monoamine oxidase inhibitor, and women who are pregnant or lactating.[46]

With the aid of vitamin B_6, L-Phenylalanine can also be converted to phenylethylamine (PEA), an amphetamine-like neurotransmitter that is abundant in chocolate and that may affect both mood and attention.[47,48] A deficit of phenylethylamine in the brain is believed to lead to certain forms of depression. Phenylacidic acid is a metabolite of phenylethylamine, so plasma and urinary phenylacidic acid levels are used as a measure of brain phenylethylamine. Phenylacidic acid levels are reduced in depression and, the more severe the depression, the lower the levels.

In studies of antidepressant drugs, phenylacidic acid levels rise toward normal when the drug is effective. In a study that was reported in the *Journal of Clinical Psychiatry*, Dr. Hector Sabelli and his associates at Rush Presbyterian St. Luke's Medical Center in Chicago found that their patients with major depression had significantly lower than normal plasma and twenty-four-hour urinary phenylacidic acid levels. Seventy-five percent of the patients who were supplemented with L-Phenylalanine improved almost immediately as their phenylacidic acid levels rose. Side effects consisted of slight transient headaches, constipation, transient nausea, insomnia, and increased anxiety.[47]

Because of a lack of placebo-controlled studies, the efficacy of all the forms of phenylalanine on the market remains to be proven. Anecdotal case reports show it to be effective, but there are no good placebo studies at present.

Tyrosine

The results of small double-blind studies have suggested that tyrosine supplementation may be effective for some unipolar depressives (people who have lows but not highs).[49,50] Like tryptophan, tyrosine is a large neutral amino acid and should be given with a carbohydrate. No protein should be eaten for ninety minutes before or after its ingestion.

S-adenosylmethionine (SAMe)

S-adenosylmethionine is an important methyl group donor whose metabolism is closely related to folic acid. In depressive states, the activity of this enzyme may be reduced. Supplementation with this substance has been found to be effective in a number of studies, and there is some experimental evidence of its efficacy.[51] Side effects are mild and transient; however, SAMe is contraindicated in bipolar depressives as it can induce mania.[52]

HYDROCHLORIC ACID DEFICIENCY

A deficiency in hydrochloric acid may reduce the intestinal absorption of many of the nutrients discussed earlier. Current evidence shows that both B_6 and folic acid should be well absorbed because of compensatory bacterial overgrowth in the small intestine. However, there are several mechanisms by which vitamin B_{12} deficiency can occur when the level of hydrochloric acid in the stomach is low, and there is evidence that suggests the possibility that niacin, riboflavin, and thiamine deficiencies can develop as well. The situation regarding mineral absorption is not entirely clear.

A deficiency of stomach acid may also cause increased putrefactive breakdown of amino acids, particularly of tryptophan, phenylalanine, and tyrosine. The results can be a lower ratio of tryptophan and tyrosine to the other large neutral amino acids with which they compete to cross the blood-brain barrier. This leads to reduced brain levels of these amino acids, a condition known to be associated with depression.[53]

The efficacy of hydrochloric acid supplementation in treating depression with accompanying hydrochloric acid deficiency remains to be studied scientifically. Clinicians have reported cases, however, where hydrochloric acid supplementation along with vitamin B complex seemed to be effective. One report was of a patient who had a seventeen-year history of endogenous depression and clinical signs of a vitamin deficiency. This individual improved dramatically following supplementation with hydrochloric acid before meals along with vitamin B complex.[54]

In another report, a thirty-six-year-old woman who suffered from depression for many years and who was resistant to antidepressant medications as well as tranquilizers and psychotherapy, reported excess gas and chronic constipation. Lab testing suggested low stomach acid and reactive hypoglycemia along with deficient mineral absorption. Her serum vitamin B_{12} was in the normal range, although it was on the low side.

Summary of Nutritional Treatment

To summarize the nutritional treatment of depression:

1. Avoid caffeine and refined sugars.
2. Rule out food sensitivities.
3. Replete deficiencies of B complex, vitamin C, iron and magnesium, potassium, and hydrochloric acid.
4. Consider neurotransmitter precursor therapy.
5. Consider supplementation with S-adenosylmethionine (SAMe).

She was treated with injections of vitamin B_{12} and folic acid along with oral hydrochloric acid and pancreatic enzymes. The injections gave dramatic relief within twenty-four hours, and it lasted for two or three days. Eventually, the injections were successfully tapered off.[55]

Nutritional Influences on Depression: A Guide to Treatment Options

This chart is a summary of specific nutritional factors regarding depression, including the dosages and trial periods that appear to be relevant. The various nutritional treatments have been ranked according to the level of scientific validation.

Ratings of Clinical Efficacy

* – ***	Efficacy proven by placebo-controlled studies
+	Efficacy noted in open trials
–	Efficacy postulated based on indirect data

Dietary Factors
* Avoid caffeine
* Avoid refined sugars
* Rule out food sensitivities
+ Avoid alcohol

Nutritional Factors

** S-adenosylmethionine (SAMe): 800 mg twice daily (14-day trial)

** L-Tryptophan: 2 gm three times daily (14-day trial)

* L-Tyrosine: 100 mg/kilograms of body weight daily in three divided doses (14-day trial)

* Vitamin C: supplement if deficient: 1 gm daily (3-week trial)

+ Folic Acid: supplement if deficient: 1 mg daily

+ 5-Hydroxytryptophan: start with 25 mg daily and increase as tolerated over 10–14 days to 75 mg three times daily with meals (14-day trial)

+ Iron: supplement if deficient: ferrous sulfate 300 mg three times daily

+ Magnesium: supplement if deficient: 500 mg daily

+ L-Phenylalanine: 500 mg upon arising and at noon; increase by 500 mg daily to about 1.5–2 gm twice daily as tolerated. Combine each dose with pyridoxine 50 mg (D-Phenylalanine may be substituted) (14-day trial)

+ Potassium: supplement if deficient: 4–6 gm daily in excess of losses

+ Riboflavin: supplement if deficient: 50 mg daily

+ Thiamine: supplement if deficient: 50 mg daily

+ Vitamin B_6: supplement if deficient: pyridoxine 100 mg daily

+ Vitamin B_{12}: supplement if deficient: 1,000 mcg IM two to four times per week until hematologic correction; then once monthly or as needed

Other Factors

+ rule out Hydrochloric Acid Deficiency

© Melvyn R. Werbach, M.D.

BIOFEEDBACK AND DEPRESSION

We now move from the physical modality of nutritional medicine to a psychophysiologic modality called biofeedback. I was particularly focused on the biofeedback field for many years and continue to find it a very exciting and effective way of treating a variety of both physical and emotional symptoms.

Biofeedback is a training procedure in which physiologic activities are utilized to provide a person with information concerning the functional state of his or her body. Mastery is gained by establishing connections with the internal cues that relate to changes in these activities. It is often used to train a normalization of overactivation of the sympathetic branch of the autonomic nervous system—the so-called fight or flight syndrome. Someone who is overly "geared up" or "uptight" can be taught to relax through biofeedback.

The instruments most commonly used are the electromyograph (EMG), to measure muscle tension; the GSR, to measure skin conductance (which relates to the activity of sweat glands); the skin surface temperature monitor; and the electroencephalograph (EEG), to measure brain waves. Nowadays, the instrumentation is commonly hooked up to a computer display.

Relaxation Response Training

Biofeedback incorporates well into a regimen that is best called *relaxation response training*, which is a procedure that usually takes about three-quarters of an hour at least once or twice a week in the office using biofeedback instrumentation to assist in its mastery. In my clinical practice I provide biofeedback and also teach diaphragmatic breathing, progressive muscle relaxation, autogenic training, guided imagery, and meditative mantras. People practice twenty minutes twice a day at home. I also provide psychological support and suggestions for stress management. I have been integrating this package into my practice for almost twenty-five years and find it very helpful for appropriate patients.

What I particularly like about relaxation response training is that when people learn to train their inner workings to normalize a psychophysiologic problem, they have a new skill that can be utilized for the rest of their lives. All they need to do is to maintain some allegiance to it, practice it, and reinforce it as often as necessary. Some people do not need to formally practice, whereas others find that it only works if they continue to practice regularly.

Where does relaxation training fit into the treatment of depression? It reduces symptoms related to heightened activation and focuses on normalizing functions regardless of the underlying cause. Because relaxation training produces a calming affect, it is indicated for agitated or anxious depressions.

Biofeedback can also be effective in helping individuals move toward healing, regardless of what caused them to get into a hyperdepressed state. Even if the cause is not known at the beginning, progress can still be made in calming the body down. This calm state can then make the cause become more apparent.

For example, if a person becomes depressed over a physical symptom, once the symptom abates with relaxation training, the depression sometimes, instead of lessening, actually worsens, suggesting that the symptom was serving to distract that person from the underlying depression. In other words, a whole variety of physical symptoms can actually be substitutes for depression, and the underlying depression often needs to become conscious in order to move toward healing.

This situation is called somatization, a process that occurs when a psychological scenario is being acted out in the soma. It disrupts the functioning of a body that is structurally normal and causes it to behave abnormally. A medical practitioner may examine the body without recognizing how the presenting problem is being influenced by mental processes. Biofeedback is very useful for somatization because it tends to move the body more toward normal regulation and therefore will convert the distress back into emotions where one can become aware of underlying feelings and conflicts.

Relaxation training can also facilitate other modalities, such as psychodynamic psychotherapy, which is not as intense a procedure as psychoanalysis. With relaxation training, people can be brought to a state of calmness in which they are more self-aware and able to take in new information. This allows them to have an increased awareness of inner information so that they are more capable of interacting successfully with the therapist in a therapeutic manner.

A COMPREHENSIVE APPROACH TO DEPRESSION: A CASE STUDY

A patient I worked with a number of years ago demonstrates this comprehensive model of treating depression. This case combined fairly traditional psychotherapy with the use of biofeedback and relaxation training and illustrates some of the complexities in dealing with depressed patients.

The patient was a fifty-year-old housewife who was referred by a psychiatrist whom she had consulted regarding insomnia. Sixteen years earlier she had begun to note difficulty in staying asleep and felt exhausted and agitated. At the time she was caring for her six-year-old son, who had developed a dramatic fever. She had been instructed to keep the boy inactive, and that was quite stressful to her. Initially she was placed on phenobarbital for sleep and agitation. Although she was given the diagnosis of hyperthyroidism and developed hypothyroidism following treatment for the disorder, her sleep did not improve.

When I initially saw her, she reported that she would stay up until two in the morning and then take 10 milligrams of Valium and 100 milligrams of Tuinol (a barbiturate sleeping pill). Then she would wait until she became drowsy, go to bed, and sleep for two and one-half hours. Because it was not strong enough she would then have to repeat the medication, and get another two and one-half hours of sleep. Strangely enough, she did not feel tired during the day and was able to function well despite this unusual regimen.

Seven years earlier she had first sought psychiatric care for her insomnia and for her husband's impotence. She noted that she and her husband tended to upset each other, and she hid her insomnia from him as he would harass her about it. Nine months earlier she had developed a spastic colon after being placed on bed rest for a neck injury. She would awaken with abdominal cramps and diarrhea and could have as many as fifteen bowel movements in a day.

She described herself as intense, dogmatic, and dependent on drugs. She noted that when she was anxious, she would break out in a cold, clammy sweat. This anxiety reaction could be triggered by almost any situation that was even slightly out of the ordinary.

We initially placed her in a series of biofeedback training sessions in order to give her the ability to calm down and increase her self-awareness. Between the ninth and tenth sessions, she had herself admitted to a medical hospital to be withdrawn from all medications. The biofeedback counselor found her to be enthusiastic and a pleasure to work with. He noted she became increasingly depressed as she made progress in establishing the relaxation response, an example of the phenomenon I referred to earlier. His impression was that she had denied and repressed her personal needs for many years and had dealt with her stress by drugging herself. He recommended that she enter psychotherapy and continue biofeedback.

The patient chose not to see me for the ten-session reevaluation that I normally do, and she terminated treatment after completing thirteen biofeedback training sessions. She returned, however, three months later after experiencing increased anxiety and depression. She said that she was exhausted during the day and could nap two or three hours at a time but was unable to sleep. She and her husband also continued to have considerable difficulty with their relationship. We agreed that she would return to biofeedback for an additional seven sessions, and that she would see a therapist regularly.

In her therapy sessions, she noted that, since discontinuing her medication, she had become more dependent on her husband because of her increased anxiety. He was unable to tolerate this, and thus was increasingly distancing himself from her. The following month her husband separated from her, which precipitated a real crisis. She felt overwhelmingly helpless and anxious without him, despite the support from her therapist. She did find some relief from her insomnia by taking 400 milligrams of Thorazine, a major tranquilizer, although she was not happy with the side effects of the medication.

The next month she made a suicide gesture by swallowing six 200-milligram tablets of Tuinol. I was contacted by her husband and hospitalized her. The psychiatric hospital provided the intensive support she needed, and she did well. While there, she worked frequently with the GSR (one of the biofeedback instruments mentioned on page 112) in order to establish control over her anxiety. The GSR is psychologically the deepest of all the biofeedback instruments and is amazingly perceptive as to changes in the inner state.

She became so adept at utilizing the GSR that she was able to sleep through the night, despite loud noises in the hospital. She involved herself in new activities and resolved much of the marital conflict. She also participated in individual and conjoint psychotherapy sessions. All anti-anxiety and sleeping medications were gradually withdrawn, and she became increasingly able to function despite moderately high anxiety levels.

Following discharge from the hospital she continued to improve. Her marriage also improved, and she began to work on getting her real-estate license and developing a career. She also reported that she was finally enjoying going to sleep, rather than preparing for battle at bedtime. We decided to end our work together with the understanding that she would return if and when she needed my assistance. She subsequently made contact with me on a few occasions simply to tell me that she was doing well. A few months later another crisis occurred: Her husband suddenly died. She dealt with his death quite well, and since that time she has pursued her career in real estate.

This is an example of how several treatment approaches were tried and successfully integrated. The more comprehensive our model for understanding depression, the greater the variety of possible treatments from which to select and the more each treatment can be tailored to help resolve the imbalance of a specific individual. Basing treatment on the individual rather than on the diagnosis greatly enhances the ability to heal depression.

The Natural Pharmacy:
Herbal Medicine for Depression

Janet Zand, O.M.D., L.Ac.

The physician is nature's assistant.
—*Galen, second century* A.D.

Depression has come more and more to the forefront in health care in recent years. A great percentage of ailments that individuals present to their doctors today seem to have some form of mental/emotional complication that can be perceived as depression. The millions of individuals suffering clinical or symptomatic depression can experience great benefit from some specific attention to their own health as well as guidance from a health professional who understands the basic tenets of natural medicine.

Natural medicine, including herbs, diet, and other noninvasive therapies, is particularly appropriate in treating the underlying causes and symptoms associated with depression. Unlike conventional, allopathic medicine, natural medicine works in a gradual manner, is humanly comprehensible, and may even be considered to be ordinary—like ordinary magic. Natural medicine is consistent with the rhythms of nature and the ways in which nature is organized. Historically, there has been a commitment in medicine to do no harm, and when you are using natural substances such as herbs and working at a gradual pace, the likelihood of doing harm is almost completely eliminated.

UNDERLYING CAUSES AND SYMPTOMS OF DEPRESSION: A MIRROR IMAGE

A fundamental principle of natural medicine is that physiology and psychology are intimately related. In examining the medical literature, it is fascinating to note that the symptoms and causes of depression can often be interchanged. For example, some of the symptoms associated with depression include chronic fatigue syndrome, insomnia, excessive sleep, loss of appetite, excessive appetite, headaches, backaches, joint aches, bowel disorders, as well as feelings of worthlessness and inadequacy. On the other hand, the causes of depression read like a mirror image: tension, stress, chronic headaches, chronic stomachaches, bowel problems, chronic nutritional deficiencies, chronic allergies, chronic physical disorder, poor diet, excessive sugar and caffeine intake, endocrine disorder such as hypothyroidism, endometriosis, lack of sun exposure, and assaults from the environment such as toxic metals.

In effectively dealing with the underlying causes and symptoms of depression, I have found that it is important to discover the individual's weakest physical link. The weakness may be a nutritional problem, undiagnosed hypothyroidism, chronic yeast or viral infection, intestinal parasites, seasonal affective disorder (SAD), or something as basic as dehydration (often seen in professional athletes) or lack of potassium. I try to determine these potential problems before prescribing dietary changes, exercise, nutritional supplements, homeopathy, and/or specific herbs or herbal combinations for treating depression or its associated symptoms. The following are some examples of common causes I have observed to be underlying my patients' depression.

Hypothyroidism, for example, often has numerous associated mental symptoms. Patients suffering from hypothyroidism very often feel that they cannot cope, that life is simply too much, and find themselves withdrawing from the world. Typically, patients experience a tremendous mental shift after appropriate treatment for hypothyroidism.

To test yourself at home for an underactive thyroid, keep a thermometer by your bed at night. In the morning, when you wake, immediately place the thermometer under your arm and hold it there for fifteen minutes. This may seem like an eternity, but it is important to be still. Any motion may give a false reading. Do this for five consecutive days. If the reading is consistently 97.6 degrees Fahrenheit or lower, you may have an underactive thyroid, and you should consult with your physician.

Certain nutrients are used to enhance thyroid activity. Kelp, a seaweed that contains iodine, is often useful in supplementing thyroid function. L-Tyrosine, an amino acid, is also effective in stimulating proper thyroid function and fighting depression associated with depressed thyroid function. A naturally oriented health care practitioner may also prescribe a thyroid glandular. The B vitamins are also very important to improve energy and assure proper glandular function.

Adaptogenic herbs, specifically *Eleutherococcus senticosus*, better known as Siberian ginseng, may also be considered in cases of hypothyroidism. This herb helps to regulate the entire endocrine system, including the thyroid and adrenal function.

As for dietary considerations, sufficient protein is necessary to prevent hypothyroidism. Raw cruciferous vegetables such as broccoli, cabbage, and kale may suppress thyroid function. These vegetables in their cooked state are not problematic but should only be used in small amounts in their raw state.

Our diet also has a tremendous impact on our moods. Since the dawn of civilization people have used food to alter their mood. Alcohol, sugar, and stimulants such as coffee have been utilized for this purpose. Until recently scientists were not convinced of the effect of food upon mood, but in the last ten years they have finally acknowledged that food can affect how you feel, think, and act. I find that poor dietary habits are not the exception but the rule among my depressed patients. Most people suffering from depression usually have marginal nutritional deficiencies associated with changes in mood and even altered brain waves, including deficiencies in B vitamins, selenium, potassium, and amino acids. Memory loss, confusion, depression, irritability, and anxiety have all been linked to dietary indiscretion.

Potassium deficiency, in particular, is another common cause of depression. Women who are particularly low in potassium can have acute episodes of depression accompanied by fits of crying with seemingly no cause. One woman who came in to see me began crying within sixty seconds although we were not discussing anything particularly emotional. When I asked her what was wrong, she said, "I don't know. All of a sudden I just start crying." I gave her an old naturopathic remedy—apple cider vinegar, honey, and water—and within a few sips, she started calming down and feeling better. She took that simple formula with her meals for a month or so and the crying stopped.

L-Tryptophan, an essential amino acid, is the precursor to one of the most important neurotransmitters, serotonin. Tryptophan helps to raise the levels of serotonin in the brain. Serotonin is needed to regulate sleep, secrete pituitary hormones, and perceive pain. Serotonin is most often abnormally low in depressed people. After a carbohydrate-rich meal, insulin causes competing amino acids such as tyrosine, phenylala-nine, and leucine, to leave the blood and enter muscle tissue. With fewer amino acids thus vying for entry, more tryptophan can enter the brain and be converted into serotonin. Increased serotonin levels result in increased relaxation and drowsiness. You can try this out on yourself. Try eating a meal high in carbohydrates, such as pasta with a fruit dessert, and see how you feel compared with after a high-protein lunch, such as fish with vegetables.

Eating higher-protein meals will increase the amount of the amino acid tyrosine in the blood. Through research it has been demonstrated that for tyrosine to be effective therapeutically, it is best taken in sup-plement form with a small amount of carbohydrate. The carbohydrate stimulates insulin secretion, which reduces the levels of other competing amino acids, and allows easy entry of tyrosine into the brain. An increase in brain tyrosine will ultimately increase the levels of cate-cholamines, particularly dopamine. Clinically, tyrosine is effective in treating depression associated with fatigue due to low thyroid and/or adrenal function.

Feelings of gloom and doom are often associated with a serious infes-tation of intestinal parasites. Patients suffering from parasites often feel that their world is coming to an end. I once treated a couple who had con-tracted an unusual disease while traveling in Africa. They were diagnosed at UCLA Medical Center with Ross River disease. The man was also diagnosed with an unusual intestinal parasite. Both of them were sur-vivalists who were extremely paranoid and felt that the world was com-ing to an end. They periodically traveled to the wilderness with their guns and camouflage gear. After treatment with an herbal milk thistle extract combination and two nutritional supplements, lipoic acid and pine bark extract, their physiology improved and the digestive symptoms associated with the parasitic infection cleared up, so that they had an extreme shift in mental outlook. Soon they began to store their guns in the basement, made fewer trips to the wilderness, and the woman decided to burn the camouflage gear.

Candidiasis, a chronic infection by the yeast *Candida albicans*, also has associated mental symptoms including feelings of disorientation, confusion, and being out of control. On the physical level one may experience joint and muscle ache and pain, as well as bodily pain that is not associated with any apparent cause. Several years ago a professional wrestler came to see me suffering from apparent arthritis and depression. He had been around the medical block, seeing orthopedic surgeons, internists, and endocrinologists. Finally, he came to my office bringing in stacks of blood work. I examined him and gave him an extensive questionnaire. Nearly two-thirds of his answers pointed to candidiasis, and one of his primary symptoms was depression. We began treating him with pau d'arco, bifidus—a two-thousand-year-old Chinese herbal formula for joint pain—and a series of homeopathics. Within ten weeks all of his pain disappeared and his depression lifted simultaneously.

HERBAL MEDICINE: A NATURAL APPROACH

Herbal medicine has a long and respected history and holds a valuable place in the treatment of mental/emotional disorders such as anxiety and depression as well as the vast majority of health problems. When using the leaves, flowers, stems, berries, and roots of plants to both prevent and treat illness, herbal medicine not only helps to alleviate symptoms but also helps treat the underlying problem, as well as strengthen the overall functioning of a particular organ or body system.

Throughout history, herbs have been used for medicinal purposes in traditional cultures worldwide. Asia, Europe, the Middle East, Africa, and the Americas all have a rich history of herbal healing. In China, authoritative texts on herbal medicine compiled over four thousand years ago are still used today. Texts from the ancient cultures of India, Egypt, and Mesopotamia describe and illustrate the use of many medicinal plants. Ancient Ayurvedic medical treatises discuss herbs that are being researched today for their therapeutic properties such as turmeric, gotu kola, neem, *ashwagandha*, and ginger. Traditional cultures in Europe prior to the Roman conquest also relied on herbs for medicine. In Europe, homegrown botanicals were the only medicines readily available from early Christian times through the Middle Ages.

THE RISE OF MODERN MEDICINE AND THE DECLINE OF HERBALISM

As in Europe, the early American colonists relied upon herbs for medicine, and this reliance continued until the early twentieth century.

The first *U.S. Pharmacopeia*, published in 1820, included an authoritative listing of herbal drugs, with descriptions of their properties, uses, dosages, and tests of purity. Following periodic revisions, the *U.S. Pharmacopeia* became the legal standard for medical compounds in 1906.

In the early twentieth century, however, the science of pharmacology began to focus on capturing the patentable active properties of plants by identifying, isolating, extracting, and synthesizing individual plant components, rather than studying and using the medicinal properties of the whole plant.

Pharmaceutical laboratories began to replace the herbal apothecaries as the providers of drugs protected by patents. The use of herbs in the United States, previously considered mainstream medical practice, began to be considered unconventional and unscientific; it fell into relative obscurity. With the progression of modern medicine in the twentieth century, most physicians have come to rely on the *Physician's Desk Reference* (PDR), an extensive listing of chemically manufactured drugs, as opposed to the *U.S. Pharmacopeia*, with its reliance on herbal compounds.

MODERN RESURGENCE OF HERBAL MEDICINE

Today, there is an amazing resurgence among both consumers and the medical community in the medicinal use of herbs. Many reasons account for this phenomenon.

First, the current crisis in health care calls for more cost-effective remedies, as well as an emphasis on prevention. Second, the rise in popularity of alternative medicine has brought herbal medicine to the attention of millions of consumers and health professionals. Third, the enormous body of research from around the world has finally shown the medical community that herbal medicine has moved beyond folk medicine and anecdotal reports.

Finally, consumers are looking for safer remedies that do not have the dangerous and troubling side effects of many conventional drugs. For example, Prozac, the most popular SSRI (selective serotonin reuptake inhibitor) antidepressant drug in the United States, has had a controversial history of serious side effects, whereas the herb St. John's wort, which research has demonstrated to be as effective as Prozac, has few known side effects.

The larger percentage of current research validating herbal medicine has been conducted abroad, particularly in Germany, Japan, China, Taiwan, France, and Russia, with the *German Commission E Monographs*[1] being probably the single most powerful collection of herbal research. As a result, we are now able to identify some of the specific properties and interactions of botanical constituents, as well as to better understand why certain traditionally used herbs are effective in treating specific conditions. Still, only about 5,000 of the estimated 250,000 to 500,000 plants (variation due to including or excluding subspecies) on the earth today have been extensively studied for their medicinal applications.

HERBS FOR TREATING DEPRESSION

Depression is an illness that involves the entire body. In naturopathic medicine as well as Chinese Medicine, herbs and herbal combinations may be used to bring balance back to the body, as well as counter fatigue and debility often associated with depression. In using herbs for depression, I recommend, however, that a person not stop or alter any currently prescribed antidepressants or medications without consulting with the physician.

Chinese Medicine has long believed that certain physiological imbalances may lead to psychological depression. For example, if the energy of the liver is "stuck," you will more likely be chronically irritated and often depressed. If herbals are taken to "release" this block, then according to Traditional Chinese Medicine, it is believed that you will feel better physically as well as psychologically.

In my own practice of twenty years, I have seen this proven time and again. Not too long ago, John, a thirty-six-year-old male who had been on the antidepressant drug Paxil for two and a half years, came to see me. He said that he had felt relief from the depression for the first year and a half, but now it had returned, and his sex drive, which historically had been strong, had ceased for the last three years. John was also suffering from digestive problems. He was fearful of going off the Paxil because of his rage and what he called his "rager fits." In the past, he experienced such intense anger, anxiety, and agitation that he scared himself. After much discussion about going off the drug, his psychiatrist agreed to wean him slowly off the Paxil. As John decreased his dosage, he also began taking herbal and nutritional supplements.

When the day came for his last dose of Paxil, John came into my office angry and frightened, announcing: "Look at me, all six foot four and 225 pounds of me—when I get angry, I cannot only be a horrible sight but dangerous, truly dangerous." In Chinese Medicine the diagnosis for John was "stuck liver Qi" leading to agitation, irritability, and anger, accompanied by a variety of digestive problems. He was given an herbal combination to "quiet and rebalance his liver Qi." Although this treatment plan may sound strange, Traditional Chinese Medicine has successfully used this methodology for over two thousand years.

After three weeks he came bouncing into my office and asked, "I feel better than ever, but is this going to last?" I placed him on a maintenance program for three months and saw him once a month during that time. By his own admission, he claimed he was a "new man." John not only recovered his desire to live and his sex drive, he lost his chronic agitation and negativity and went from chronic digestive problems to occasional discomfort when he overate.

Herbal medicine is perhaps one of the most respected of the ancient natural therapies that has stood the test of time. Today there is an enormous interest in medicinal plants and a rediscovery of many traditional applications of therapeutic herbs. The World Health Organization reports that 85 percent of the world's population use herbs as their main form of medical treatment. Here in the United States we are fortunate to be able to combine the best of modern medicine with the folklore of ancient herbal therapies.

Herbs are very much like the foods we eat, and in fact some of what we eat, such as parsley, ginger, garlic, onion, thyme, and rosemary, are actually herbs and can be used therapeutically. Like food, herbs contain different therapeutic substances such as vitamins, minerals, trace minerals, and active ingredients such as volatile oils, alkaloids, flavonoids, bitters, mucilage, saponins, anthraquinones, and tannins. Herbs may be used in many forms such as teas, tinctures, capsules, tablets, caplets, lozenges, syrups, compresses, poultices, sprays, liniments, and oils.

It is important to remember that herbal preparations, whether they are intended for the common cold or depression, cannot stand alone in their effectiveness as a treatment. Herbs are a piece of the puzzle, which includes a balanced diet suitable to one's lifestyle and body type, exercise, and designated periods of rest in whatever form that may take (i.e., meditation, yoga, breathing exercises, sitting and reading a book, etc.)

Herbs are frequently divided into four main categories: *relaxants/sedatives, antidepressants, restoratives,* and *stimulants.* Some herbs may be easily grouped into more than one category because of their broad effectiveness. The following herbs are successfully used in treating various forms of depression.

RELAXANT/SEDATIVE HERBS

Within the herbal kingdom there are many nervous system relaxants/sedatives primarily used for their anti-anxiety effect, including kava kava, valerian, passion flower, skullcap, chamomile, hops, and linden blossom. It is believed that herbs, which contain volatile oils, can directly affect the limbic system of the brain and induce a more relaxed state.

Kava Kava (*Piper methysticum*)

Native to the South Pacific islands, kava has been used in ceremonial beverages for centuries. The active principles in the root are a number of lactones known as kava pyrones. Through its relaxing effect on the central nervous system, kava is beneficial in reducing anxiety, tension, and restlessness. Kava kava is generally used not to treat clinical depression but to mitigate common stress-related anxieties.

Kava is excellent for helping to relax because with it there is no loss of mental clarity. It is also helpful in dealing with insomnia, as it promotes restful sleep. What is most remarkable about kava, however, is that it does not produce toxic side effects or symptoms of withdrawal, such as found with drugs like benzodiazepine.

For example, several years ago, Elizabeth, a thirty-eight-year-old female, came into my office complaining of anxiety and difficulty in calming her mind, and also reported bouts of insomnia. She was a successful Hollywood talent agent and would often keep late hours. "I'm not crazy, like I don't feel I need psycho meds, I just need to be toned down a notch." After a week of 37.5 milligrams of kava in the morning and 75 milligrams at night, Elizabeth phoned and said she was considerably more relaxed and her sleep was normal. She continued this dosage of kava for three more weeks and then decreased it until she was only using it once in a while when she felt she needed it.

How does kava affect brain chemistry? Well, we know for example that the drug benzodiazepine increases the activity of gamma-aminobutyric acid, or GABA, in the limbic system, producing a sense of calmness. The amygdala, a small organ the size of a large pea in the temporal lobe of the brain, regulates sensations of anxiety, and is also a site for benzodiazepenes. In 1991 a study was done that identified amygdala as the preferential site for kavalactones, the active ingredient in kava.

It is recommended to avoid using kava with alcohol, antidepressants, or other drugs that can affect the central nervous system. In Germany, kava extracts are approved for use with nervous anxiety, stress, and unrest, but not to be used in cases of pregnancy or while a mother is lactating.

Valerian Root (*Valeriana officinalis*)

With a long history of use in European traditional medicine, valerian root is a strong calmative that exerts a mild sedative effect on the central nervous system. The active ingredients of valerian, valepotriates, and its sedative properties were discovered in 1966 and quickly became the subject of a large amount of scientific research in Germany.

Valerian root is most helpful for insomnia, restlessness, and anxiety. It helps one to fall asleep faster and provides a deeper, more restful sleep. In Germany, valerian root is approved as an over-the-counter medicine for "states of excitation" and insomnia due to nervousness.[2] A scientific team representing the European Community has reviewed the research on valerian and concluded that it is a safe nighttime sleep aid. These scientists also found that there are no major adverse reactions associated with its use, and unlike barbiturates and other conventional drugs used for insomnia, valerian does not have an adverse reaction with alcohol and is not addictive like some conventional benzodiazepine medications.[3]

Approximately one-third of the adult population suffers with some kind of sleep disorder. I have found valerian to be very useful for helping to gently regulate sleep. In fact, I have a very personal story about valerian. When I first met my husband, I noticed that he had a bottle of Xanax and one of Valium in his bathroom. I asked him what he did with these and he said, "What do you think?" I explained to him that if he was thinking about being my husband, I didn't think it was acceptable for him to be taking Valium at bedtime. "Are you serious?" he responded. "Yes," I answered. Well, to make a long argument and story short, it has been ten years and my husband sleeps regularly with the occasional help from a valerian herbal combination, and on the rare evening when he is very stressed he may add a kava combination as well. What he most likes about not using Xanax and Valium is the fact that he wakes up feeling fresh instead of drugged or confused.

Passion Flower (*Passiflora incarnata*)

Passion flower has a long tradition of use for its mildly sedative properties. This herb has been approved in Germany as an over-the-counter drug for states of nervous unrest.[4] Passion flower is very often combined with other calmatives, including chamomile, skullcap, and valerian. These calmatives are even more effective when they are combined with calcium and magnesium. Research also shows that passion flower extract has antispasmodic and hypotensive properties.[5]

Skullcap (*Scutellaria lateriflora*)

Skullcap is a calmative that has traditionally been used to relieve tension headaches, anxiety, insomnia, and premenstrual tension. Skullcap's effectiveness is enhanced when combined with such herbs as valerian, chamomile, passion flower, and/or vervain. The herb also has a tonifying effect on the liver, helps regulate cholesterol, and has been shown to increase the high-density lipoproteins (HDL), or good cholesterol.

Chamomile (*Matricaria recutita*)

Chamomile is an important sedative herb and nerve tonic. In Europe, it is widely used as a digestive aid in the treatment of heartburn, nausea, and flatulence; as a mild sedative helpful with insomnia; and as an anti-inflammatory. Chamomile is licensed in Germany as an over-the-counter drug for gastrointestinal spasms and inflammatory diseases of the gastrointestinal tract often associated with nervous disorders.

Hops (*Humulus lupulus*)

Hops, with both calming and sleep-inducing properties, is used in Europe for nervous tension, restlessness, and excitability, as well as sleep disturbances. This helpful herb has also been licensed in Germany for sleep disorders and states of unrest and anxiety. However, unlike other sedatives, hops does not lead to dependence or withdrawal symptoms, and there are no reports of adverse side effects.[6]

Linden Blossom (*Tilia europea*)

Linden blossom has been used for centuries by Europeans in the treatment of nervous tension. It is also believed to reduce hardening of the arteries. Linden blossom is commonly prescribed throughout Europe for patients with anxiety and cardiovascular history.

ANTIDEPRESSANT HERBS

St. John's wort is the best known of the antidepressant herbs, although many Chinese, Ayurvedic, and Native American herbal combination remedies can also sustain antidepressant effects. These combination remedies, however, are best prescribed by a health professional who is knowledgeable of herbal medicine.

St. John's Wort (*Hypericum perforatum*)

This is an effective nervine tonic with an antidepressive action that has been used by Europeans as an anti-anxiety remedy for centuries. It actually has a 2400-year history of safe and effective use, and, in fact, Hippocrates himself used St. John's wort. In Germany, more than 50 percent of depression, anxiety, and sleep disorders are treated with Hypericum. This herb also has antiviral properties and is commonly used for PMS, menstrual cramps, and menopausal stress that triggers irritability, anxiety, and depression.

St. John's wort has traditionally been taken internally to treat neuralgia, anxiety, tension, and depression. Indeed, convincing research has demonstrated that St. John's wort is an effective remedy for mild to moderate depression. The therapeutic effectiveness has been shown to often be similar to that of the SSRI antidepressant drugs Prozac, Zoloft, and Paxil. St. John's wort, however, has far fewer side effects than these antidepressant drugs, and is available over the counter for a fraction of the cost of prescription antidepressants.

Depression is believed to stem from a chemical imbalance in the brain. Depressed levels of the three neurotransmitters, serotonin, norepinephrine, and dopamine lead to what we know as depression. Conventional, allopathic medicine has solutions for low levels of serotonin and norepineph-rine, but dopamine deficiency is still not clearly resolved. Recent research has implied that Hypericum acts somewhat like a combination of sero-tonin, norephinephrine, and dopamine. Currently there are psychiatrists who are actually using St. John's wort conjunctively with serotonin reup-take inhibitors such as Prozac, Paxil, and Zoloft and weaning their patients off the prescription drug. Hypericum should not be mixed with any MAO inhibitor prescription drugs. This could possibly result in elevated blood pressure, increased anxiety, muscle tension, fever, and mental confusion. If you want to try St. John's wort, please do not stop or alter any currently prescribed medication without consulting with your physician.

It should be noted that St. John's wort must normally be taken for two to ten weeks before the herb takes hold and works to regulate and balance mood. I have seen it work as quickly as three days, but like con-ventional mood regulators it is best to give it some time to be substan-tially effective.

The common dosage for St. John's wort is 300–400 milligrams two to three times daily, depending upon the severity of the depression. I have begun treatment with as little as 150 milligrams three times daily, depend-ing upon the sensitivity and body weight of the patient. Obviously, seri-ous, chronic depression should not be self-diagnosed or self-treated.

RESTORATIVE HERBS

Restorative herbs help to renew the vitality of the nervous system and are thus commonly used in treating depression and its associated symptoms. Nervous system restoratives include St. John's wort (dis-cussed above); Siberian, American, and Chinese ginseng; *Ginkgo biloba*; *Dong quai*; *Fo ti*; borage; lemon balm; oatstraw; rosemary; vervain.

Siberian Ginseng (*Eleutherococcus sentiocosus*)

I have used Siberian ginseng in my practice for many years for a wide range of physiological and psychological problems. Although it is not a true form of ginseng, it has many of the properties of ginseng and is such a powerful adaptogen that it was given the name "Siberian" or "Russian" ginseng. Siberian ginseng has been used extensively in Russia to improve performance and resistance to disease. Russian cosmonauts used Siberian ginseng prior to and during their space flights to help them stay awake and alert. Russian Olympic athletes were required to take Siberian ginseng during training as well as during the Olympic Games.

Siberian ginseng is known to affect kidney function, adrenal function, and thyroid function. It helps to increase the good (HDL) cholesterol and is a blood pressure regulator. It has also been shown to increase biological resistance and has a tremendous capacity to reduce side effects of numerous allopathic medications, including chemotherapeutic agents. In my own practice I have found this herb in conjunction with milk thistle seed and pycnogenol to be very effective in reducing the side effects of cortisone—weight gain, swollen face, depression, and swelling throughout the body—as well as the side effects of chemotherapy and radiation.

Siberian ginseng is also specifically used to control stress. This herb can reduce the activation of the adrenal cortex in response to stress as well as prevent stress-induced lymphatic congestion. Siberian ginseng is an effective herb for chronic fatigue, as many people suffering from this syndrome have a good deal of lymphatic congestion in addition to being depressed. It is also useful when fatigue is associated with insomnia, agitated depression, and nervous exhaustion.

The most extensive research on Siberian ginseng, however, relates to its brilliant ability to regulate blood sugar. I have observed people in my practice with serious hypoglycemia, a common cause of depression, make tremendous strides with the use of this herb, especially when combined with small amounts of the trace mineral chromium.

American Ginseng (*Panax quinquefolius*)

American ginseng, a true form of ginseng native to the United States, contains significant amounts of trace minerals that are increasingly difficult to obtain today in our mineral-depleted soil. This herb is effective in enhancing physical and mental performance as well as mood. Any long-term use of this herb should be supervised by a knowledgeable health professional.

Chinese Ginseng (*Panax Ginseng*)

Ginseng has a long history of use and a wide range of possible therapeutic applications. Thus, the term "Panax," which derives from the Latin word *panacea*, meaning "cure all." A powerful adaptogen, Panax ginseng helps the body to cope with stress through its effects upon the functioning of the adrenal gland.[7] Other important properties include antioxidant, antihepatotoxic (liver protecting), and hypoglycemic effects.[8,9]

Panax ginseng is very effective in small doses, especially in men over forty-five who may be experiencing mild depression due to a drop in hormone levels. However, some people who take Chinese ginseng for depression become anxious and irritable because of its stimulating nature. Proper dosage for an individual must be determined as side effects, including headaches, skin problems, and other reactions, can occur if ginseng is abused. Any long-term use of this herb should be supervised by a knowledgeable health professional.

Ginkgo (*Ginkgo biloba*)

Ginkgo trees are the oldest living trees on earth, first appearing about 200 million years ago. The leaves of the ginkgo tree contain several compounds called ginkgolides that have unique therapeutic properties. A standardized ginkgo extract has been developed in Germany to treat cerebral dysfunction with the accompanying symptoms of memory loss: dizziness, tinnitus, headaches, and emotional instability coupled with anxiety.

It has been commonly found that older individuals who are suffering from insufficient blood flow to the brain are especially susceptible to depression. In fact, many individuals over the age of fifty who are diagnosed as suffering from depression but are not responding to antidepressant medication may be suffering from cerebrovascular insufficiency.[10] One study reported that older patients suffering from depression who received 240 milligrams of *Ginkgo biloba* extract daily experienced significant improvements in mood, motivation, and memory after only four weeks and even more marked improvement by the conclusion of the eight-week study.[11]

Dong Quai (*Angelica sinensis*)

Dong quai is an adaptogenic Chinese herb that is excellent in treating numerous female health problems. In China, women begin taking *Dong quai* when they start menstruating and often continue taking it for the rest of their life, often incorporating it into their diet. *Dong quai* is normally taken in combination with other herbs, as it is a strong herb.

Dong quai has a sedative-like effect on the central nervous system and can be useful in influencing mood. This herb is also helpful in depression, as it has a protective effect on the liver, and in Chinese Medicine depression results when the liver becomes toxic or overburdened. For example, I have observed many patients suffering from acne whose dermatologists have prescribed Acutane, which often has a negative effect on the liver. Acutane causes an elevation of liver enzymes, which in turn causes the individual to become very depressed. People with hepatitis also have elevated liver enzymes, often leading to feelings of depression. The treatment plan in Chinese Medicine for such cases is to detoxify and strengthen the liver, and *Dong quai* can be effective as part of this treatment and alleviating depression.

Fo Ti (*Polygonum multiflorum*)

Fo ti is a rejuvenative herb that, according to Chinese Medicine, helps to normalize or strengthen the Earth (pancreas and stomach), Water (kidney), and Wood (liver) elements. According to Chinese Medicine *Fo ti* is also a "blood builder," helping to fortify the blood. A good deal of depression is due to what Chinese Medicine refers to as "blood deficiency," a condition that is significant not only for women, as it is possible for men to have "weak blood." *Fo ti* is also used in Chinese Medicine to stimulate vital energy (*Qi*), promote fertility, enhance longevity, and increase overall vigor; it is beneficial for neurasthenia, insomnia, dizziness, and hypertension.

Borage (*Borago officinalis*)

Rich in minerals, especially potassium, borage has historically been used as a tonic, as it gently improves energy. Long ago I worked in an herb room with a master herbalist. People would visit, and I would watch the herbalist prescribe various herbal preparations. I cannot remember one prescription for fatigue and depression that did not include borage. And each time he would prescribe it he would say, "I love borage."

Lemon Balm (*Melissa officinalis*)

Lemon balm is known to be antibacterial, antidepressant, antihistaminic, antiviral, carminative, and mildly sedating. Traditionally, it has been used for anxiety and depression as well as the common cold, indigestion, headache, flu, insomnia, and nervousness.

Oatstraw (*Avena sativa*)

Oatstraw has been shown to be very effective as a sedative and has proven useful for some kinds of insomnia and nervous disorders. Oatstraw is especially effective for debilitation associated with anxiety or depression. In Europe it has been used for centuries to treat nervous exhaustion. This herb is used clinically in cases of drug withdrawal from stimulants, narcotics, tranquilizers, coffee, nicotine, and alcohol. It is especially effective for depression associated with drug withdrawal. Oatstraw is high in silica and helps to enhance calcium absorption, which along with magnesium is very important in mood.

Several years ago, I treated a twenty-six-year-old male named Patrick. He was a strong yet nervous professional athlete. He came to see me complaining about his nervousness before games and reported with embarrassment a disinterest in sexual relations with his wife. The primary issue at hand was Patrick's excessive nervousness prior to game time. The solution was not an easy one, because I couldn't prescribe anything that might make him sluggish or interfere at all with his physical and mental acuity. I chose oatstraw and prescribed two capsules two times daily. One month later Patrick came into my office beaming from ear to ear. "I have to tell you, I'm smooth as silk before a game, and my wife and I are having sex again. I couldn't ask for anything more."

Rosemary (*Rosmarinus officinalis*)

Rosemary is known to be antibacterial, antidepressant, antifungal, antispasmodic, cardiotonic, carminative, circulatory stimulant, tranquilizing, and sedating. This herb has been used historically for anorexia, anesthenia, depression, headache, insomnia, painful menstruation, and nervous exhaustion.

Vervain (*Verbena officinalis*)

Vervain is known to be antidepressant, antihypertensive, antispasmodic, and mildly sedating. It has been used historically for depression, headache, hypertension, insomnia, melancholy, menopausal symptoms, and nervous exhaustion.

Herbs for Depression and Related Symptoms

Herb	Medicinal Use	Part Used	How Taken	Possible Side Effects
American ginseng	Helps to strengthen overall constitution; helps to relieve debilitation after an illness	Root	Tincture, tea, capsule, tablet, extract, whole root	Nervousness, insomnia, diarrhea
Borage	Adrenal restorative; tonic; nervine	Leaves	Tincture, capsule, infusion	None known
Chamomile	Relaxes; induces sleep; soothes upset stomach	Flower	Tincture, tea, capsule, dried flowers	Possible allergic reactions in sensitive individuals
Dong quai	Regulates menstrual cycle; good for PMS and other discomforts of menstruation; promotes circulation; enhances immunity; liver tonic; analgesic	Root	Tincture, capsule, tablets, whole root (often used in combination)	Rare, mild. Some may be allergic to *Dong quai.*
Fo ti	Invigorates liver and kidneys; promotes longevity; fertility and vigor; neurasthenia; insomnia; dizziness	Root	Tincture, capsule, tablet, whole root	Rare. Large dose may result in numbness of extremities and skin rashes.

Herb	Medicinal Use	Part Used	How Taken	Possible Side Effects
Gingko biloba	Age-associated memory loss; poor circulation to extremities; hearing loss; early stages of Alzheimer's	Leaves of young trees	Tincture, capsule	Rare. Mild gastrointestinal upset in less than 1 percent of people.
Kava kava	Calms anxiety, tension, conditions of restlessness	Rhizome	Tincture, capsule, tablet	Mild gastrointestinal upset
Lemon balm	Insomnia; nervous disorders; sedative spasm relief	Leaf	Capsule, dried leaf	None known
Linden blossom	Nervous tension; antispasmodic	Dried flowers	Tincture, infusion, tea	None known
Oatstraw	Insomnia; nervous disorders; depression associated with drug withdrawal	Whole plant	Tea, extract, capsule	None known
Panax ginseng	Adrenal support from stress; revitalizes those suffering from fatigue and debility; endurance for athletes; assists recovery from surgery	Root	Tincture, capsule, tablet, extract, whole root	Rare at recommended dosage; rare insomnia or overstimulation

Herb	Medicinal Use	Part Used	How Taken	Possible Side Effects
Passion Flower	Sedative for excess nervousness and anxiety; can induce sleep; dysmenorrhea; high blood pressure; antispasmodic	Whole plant	Tea, tincture, extract	None known
Rosemary	Antidepressive; circulatory and nervine stimulant	Leaves, twigs	Tincture, infusion	None known
Skullcap	Sedative; nerve tonic	Leaf	Tincture, tea, capsule	Possible giddiness, irregular heartbeat
St. John's wort	Mild to moderate depression	Flowering tops	Tincture, capsule, tablet, extract, tea	May make skin more light-sensitive in fair-skinned people
Valerian root	Insomnia; mild anxiety; restlessness	Root	Tincture, capsule, tablet, extract, dried root, tea	May cause mild upset stomach in small percentage of people
Vervain	Depression; tension, stress; strengthens nervous system	Aerial parts	Tincture, infusion	None known

Nervous System Stimulants

Nervous system stimulants such as coffee, black tea, green tea, kola nut, guarana, gotu kola, and yerba mate can be very effectively used in short-term situations to "spark" the nervous system. They are all caffeine-containing plants, and in large amounts caffeine has been shown to produce nervousness, insomnia, elevated blood sugar, elevated cholesterol levels, heartburn, and irregular heartbeat. Amounts of caffeine can vary widely, even within the same product such as coffee, but the following are approximations of the amount of caffeine in commonly used food products:

8-oz cup of coffee	50–100 mg
8-oz cup of black tea	40–80 mg
8-oz cup of green tea	20–40 mg
800 mg of guarana	30 mg
6-oz cup of mate	25–50 mg
12-oz can of cola-type beverage	50 mg
6-oz cup of cocoa	15 mg
1-oz bar of milk chocolate	6 mg

Coffee beans contain approximately 1 to 2 percent caffeine. With the popularity of coffee and coffeehouses, most Americans will be hard-pressed not to admit to knowing the effects of a cup of coffee. When used sparingly as an herbal remedy, it is considered a very effective mental stimulant.

Tea and green tea (both are *Camellia sinensis*) have also long been used as beverages before, during, and between meals throughout the world. More recently green tea has been especially associated with a variety of benefits related to its antioxidant properties. As for mood, many people report feeling an emotional lift without the harshness of coffee when they drink tea.

A popular Chinese mixture of kola nut, gotu kola, and *Polygonum multiflorum* is believed to prolong life and enhance mood and sense of well-being. In India there is an old adage concerning gotu kola: "two leaves a day will keep old age away." It is believed that gotu kola will help to resolve various types of mental anxiety and nervous disorders.

DIFFERENT FORMS OF HERBS

Herbs and prepared herbal compounds are available in different forms such as raw, whole herbs, tinctures, extracts, capsules, tablets, lozenges, and ointments. Both individual herbs as well as complex herbal formulations can be found at your local health food store or pharmacy and in many grocery stores.

Raw, Whole Herbs

The use of raw, whole herbs involves drying and then cutting or powdering plants or plant parts, to be used for teas or cooking.

Tinctures

In a tincture, alcohol is employed to extract and concentrate the active properties of the herb as well as to act as an effective natural preservative. A tincture is a very effective way to administer herbal compounds, as the body easily assimilates it and the herb is in a concentrated form. For the same reasons, tinctures are also cost-effective; however, the full taste of the herb comes through very strongly and some may find the taste to be bitter and unpleasant. Another concern when using tinctures is the presence of the alcohol. If you wish to lessen the amount of alcohol in a tincture, mix the appropriate dose with one-quarter cup of very hot water. After about five minutes, most of the taste of the alcohol will have evaporated away, and the mixture should be cool enough to drink.

Extracts

Extracts can be made with alcohol (like tinctures), or the essence of the herb can be leached out with water. When purchasing a liquid extract of an herb, the only way to be certain of the extraction process (alcohol or water) is to read the label. Extracts offer essentially the same advantages and disadvantages as tinctures. They are the most concentrated form of herbal treatment and therefore the most cost-effective and have a virtually indefinite shelf life. They are also easy to administer but have a strong herbal taste.

Capsules and Tablets

Capsules and tablets contain a ground or powdered form of the raw, whole herb. They are considered the most convenient way to take an herb, and one can avoid the unpleasant taste of the raw, whole form. Clinically speaking, there does not appear to be much difference between the capsules and tablets in terms of therapeutic results. As finely milled herbs tend to degrade quickly, it is important that herbs be promptly encapsulated or tableted within twenty-four hours of being powdered. When buying herbs, read the labels to make sure fresh herbs have been used in the product. Capsules and tablets are not as strong and potent as tinctures and extracts, with the exception of certain herbal concentrates in capsule form.

Teas

Many delicious blends of herbal teas are now available to the public. You will find loose herbs that are ready for steeping, herbal formulations for specific health conditions, and convenient prebagged teas. Some teas such as spearmint, rosehip, or lemongrass are generally intended for sipping or accompanying a meal. Other teas are consumed for their medicinal properties. For example, linden blossom, St. John's wort, or oatstraw tea can be used to enhance your mood; peppermint tea for indigestion; or chamomile, valerian, or hops tea to aid sleep. Steeping in boiled water for a few minutes will release the fragrant, aromatic flavor as well as the herbs' medicinal properties.

Essential Oils

In most cases, essential oils are distilled from various parts of medicinal and aromatic plants. Essential oils are typically extremely concentrated, and one or two drops of the oil often provide a sufficient dosage. Some oils can be safely applied directly to the skin, but most essential oils can irritate the skin so it is recommended to dilute them in fatty oils or water prior to topical application.

Essential Oils for Depression

The following essential oils can be used in an aromatherapy room diffuser to reduce depression, anxiety, and stress and to enhance mood. Follow the instructions on your diffuser, but one or two drops should be sufficient for a small room, and five to ten drops for a larger room.

- **Bergamot (*Citrus bergamia*):** Helps to balance the emotions and is excellent for reducing depression, anxiety, and insomnia.

- **Geranium (*Pelargonium graveolens*):** Useful for relieving anxiety, stress, discontentment, and depression.

- **German chamomile (*Matricaria recutita*):** An excellent antidepressant for individuals who are subject to stress, anxiety, oversensitivity, suppressed anger, or insomnia.

- **Lavender (*Lavandula angustifolia*):** Helpful for problems of the central nervous system, including nervousness, irritability, exhaustion, insomnia, and depression.

- **Rosemary (*Rosmarinus officinalis*):** A stimulating herb that acts as an antidepressant, also enhances memory and balances the body and mind.

Therapeutic Massage with Essential Oils for Depression, Stress, and Insomnia

A powerful aromatherapy recipe for relieving stress, depression, and insomnia is to combine two drops of lavender and one drop of chamomile essential oils in three ounces of almond, olive, or your favorite massage oil. Massage up and down each side of the spine from the neck to the sacrum, before retiring to bed. Another recipe that is more stimulating, and therefore should be done during the day, is a combination of lavender, rosemary, or peppermint essential oils. Combine one drop of each oil to three ounces of massage oil and massage up and down the spine.

ARE HERBAL REMEDIES SAFE FOR TREATING DEPRESSION?

If herbal remedies are used in the recommended doses, adverse reactions or side effects are unusual. Problems are more likely to occur if an herb is overused when the dosage is too high or if it is taken continuously for too long a period of time. Chamomile, for example, if given on a daily basis for too long, may cause an allergy to ragweed, and the prolonged use of licorice can lead to high blood pressure.

Herbs should be used for set periods of time or alternated with another remedy or remedies. For example, if an individual has taken St. John's wort for three months and is still feeling depressed, he should discontinue using the herb and try to find an appropriate alternate herb or herbal formula. On the other hand, even if an individual is doing well on St. John's wort after four to six months he should still stop using the herb and try another herb or herbal formula to deal with any other symptoms. For example, if the predominant remaining symptom is fatigue, one may want to take Siberian ginseng; if the symptom is agitation, kava may be called for; if insomnia is the major complaint, valerian is the appropriate herb.

Moderation is the key when using herbs for therapeutic purposes. Consult with a qualified herbalist or health care professional if you have questions about the use of a particular herb or herbal formula.

Today, herbal medicine is enjoying a renaissance in the United States, and almost 50 percent of the American population use dietary and herbal supplements to improve their health. Consumers are becoming more and more informed about their health choices and are looking to utilize the best that conventional medicine and natural medicine have to offer. Based on current trends, the twenty-first century has the potential of becoming the "healthiest" century in human history.

Homeopathy and Depression

Jacquelyn J. Wilson, M.D.

The highest ideal of cure is the speedy, gentle, and enduring restora-
tion of health by the most trustworthy and least harmful way.
—Dr. Samuel Hahnemann (1755–1843),
founder of homeopathy

As more antidepressant prescription drugs have become available in the
United States over the past twenty years, the diagnosis and treatment of
depression in both children and adults have continued to rise. In 1996 the
sales of the popular antidepressant Prozac exceeded $2.36 billion, and
sales were running even higher in 1997.[1] Still, many believe that depression is far underdiagnosed in our American society.

THE NEED FOR CHOICE

Americans have become accustomed to receiving an exclusive regimen of antidepressant drugs, psychotherapy, or electroshock therapy
from their medical doctors to treat depression. Historically, doctors in
the United States have rarely recommended other treatments such as
herbs, homeopathic medicines, acupuncture, or low-dose, battery-pow-
ered transcranial electrostimulation. In Europe, however, therapeutic
choices for treatment of depression have been much broader. Patients
with mild to moderate depression are often treated with herbs or with
homeopathic medicines before prescription psychotropic chemical drugs
are used.

Results from one recent research study of twelve patients has suggested that the homeopathic treatment of depression and anxiety using single medicines can benefit the patient who requests homeopathy or whose physician recommends homeopathy after partial or poor response to traditional antidepressant prescription drugs.[2] This research showed no adverse effects of using homeopathic medicines along with prescription antidepressants. Unfortunately, there are very few research studies like this, even in Europe where homeopathic treatment is more widely used.

Patients need more treatment choices for depression, whether antidepressants or homeopathy, as one approach will not work all the time. For example, if a woman who is breast-feeding has been prescribed Lithium for manic-depression, the medication must be discontinued because the Lithium comes out in the breast milk and can cause neurodevelopmental problems in the baby. In fact, most chemical antidepressant drugs have not been tested for their effects on nursing infants or children, so doctors are reluctant to prescribe them in these cases. Older individuals are also more susceptible to the adverse effects of traditional prescription antidepressant chemical drugs because of age-related physiologic changes in vital organs. Further, coexisting medical problems may contraindicate the use of traditional prescription drugs.

Much more research needs to be done both with chemical antidepressant drugs and with other natural methods, including homeopathic medicines, to find more safe and effective ways of stimulating and balancing the mind and body. The prescription standard drug treatments and the homeopathic over-the-counter medicines for depression may not provide the magic solution, but they both can be lifesaving. By including the option of homeopathic medicines, there is hope for those patients who have not responded to or tolerated prescription antidepressant drugs. Homeopathy, a well-established, extremely safe therapeutic system, is also beneficial for individuals who want to try natural treatments before taking antidepressants.

WHAT IS DEPRESSION AND WHAT TRIGGERS IT?

Depression is a mood disorder of the central nervous system (the brain). It can suddenly appear for no apparent reason, signaling that the body is out of balance. For many people, feeling depressed usually means feeling sad over a certain situation such as a death, divorce, or loss of a job. Most of these depressions that are triggered by a known loss heal over time by themselves. The process, however, can be speeded up with very safe homeopathic medicines.

A major depression can be like a life-threatening illness, as more serious depression can persist or culminate in suicide. Once a major depression becomes established, it tends to recur and get worse, and the treatment becomes more difficult and complicated. For this reason adequate diagnosis, safe treatment, and careful monitoring needs to be done before depression becomes more serious. Being under treatment by a psychiatrist or other health professional when you have a serious depression is no guarantee that suicide will not occur, but it does decrease the odds. The health professional needs to know the seriousness of the depression he or she is treating and feel certain that the treatment works.

Children and Depression

Extreme sadness in children is not rare, and depression can begin at any age. In fact, the National Institute of Mental Health estimates that 5 percent of children (four million) under age eighteen are depressed. Others believe that as many as one-fourth of children have at least one serious depressive episode by age eighteen. Many of these children are already taking antidepressant medication. In 1997 nearly 600,000 youngsters in the United States, including 275,000 under age twelve, were prescribed Prozac or another of the selective serotonin reuptake inhibitors (SSRIs) for depression.[3]

Children's depression generally stems from an external source such as an infection or serious emotional shock, which creates an imbalance in the brain that then leads to depression. We do not fully know the real triggers of depression, but there is more evidence now that shows many behavioral changes come from common infectious diseases such as strep throat. For example group A Beta-hemolytic Streptococcal infection, a very common contagious disease, can upset the mind's balance through autoimmune-mediated relationships, resulting in recurrent depression and obsessions.[4] Blood tests can measure autoimmune proteins that the body makes as antineural antibodies that attack the caudate nucleus and basal ganglia of the brain and cause behavioral changes like tics and chorea (a nervous condition marked by involuntary muscular twitching of limbs or facial muscles).

Conventional medicine is just researching and looking at this new association of mental illness related to infectious diseases. For children who have strep-induced brain antibodies and changes in their behavior, new treatments are impressive. One dose of gamma globulin or one plasmaphoresis session are two of the new experimental treatments that have been effective in restoring normal behavior for six to eight weeks in children with tics, chorea, or obsessive-compulsive behaviors that often accompany depression.

SYMPTOMS AND CAUSES OF DEPRESSION AND STANDARD TREATMENTS

Research has shown that in clinical depression the level of serotonin, a chemical in your body, may decline. Because of this imbalance and probably others not yet identified, there is a feeling of irritability or sadness, inability to sleep, lack of concentration, loss of appetite, lack of energy, and trouble in feeling pleasure. These are some of the symptoms that can point to depression, especially if they last for more than two weeks, and if normal, everyday life feels like too much to handle.

Depressed feelings are often associated with chronic illness like cancer. Hormonal disorders like low thyroid can cause depression, and the hormonal functions such as menstruation, menopause, childbearing, sexual desire, and fertility can all affect mental health and mood. It is probably a complex set of interactions and imbalances that results in depression, and these imbalances increase with age. Often treating the underlying disorder effectively will improve the depression as the body restores its balance, making other therapy unnecessary.

To bring serotonin levels to normal, doctors usually prescribe SSRIs such as Prozac. Prescription antidepressant drugs can be effective for eight out of ten moderate to severe depressions, but they are usually costly and have potentially severe drug interactions. They can cause side effects like upset stomach, headaches, difficulty sleeping, drowsiness, nervousness, and anxiety. These SSRI prescription chemical drugs work for many to relieve depression symptoms, but for others do not help and/or cause too many unpleasant side effects. As a result, traditional tricyclic antidepressants, or MAO inhibitors, are then used, but they seem to have even more side effects. In some extreme cases, electroshock therapy is used as treatment for severe suicidal types of depression with no obvious triggers. This is less commonly done now than earlier as more medicines are now available to treat depression.

Patients who are not benefiting from the standard depression treatments, who experience unpleasant or dangerous side effects, or who simply want to try a natural approach may benefit from homeopathic medicines.

HOMEOPATHY AND HOMEOPATHIC MEDICINES

Herbal plants and flowers have been used for thousands of years to treat mood disorders. From this background, homeopathy emerged in Europe in the early 1800s through the work of Samuel Hahnemann, a German general physician. Today, homeopathy is the second most widely used medical system in the world, following Traditional Chinese Medicine and acupuncture.

Hahnemann discovered that plants and other natural substances could be prepared through special homeopathic procedures in order to release their healing power and render them the safest medicines known. This was a big change from the traditional use of herbs taken in the form of teas or dried plants pressed into pills or capsules.

Hahnemann found that serial shaking and diluting of herbs, as well as other plants and minerals, rendered them more effective and less toxic, thereby eliminating unpleasant side effects. He diluted the original substances over thirty times and shook them vigorously between dilutions, adding a great deal of kinetic energy to the medicinal solutions, which were often prepared and preserved in alcohol. He tested these specially prepared homeopathic medicines on people who were well first before giving them to sick people. When given a homeopathic medicine, well people develop symptoms and changes in their body and mind known as *provings*. These symptoms are carefully recorded, and the pattern noted for each medicine in the homeopathic *Materia Medicas* used by homeopathic practitioners. When a sick person exhibits the same or a similar symptom pattern, she is then given the similar homeopathic drug in order to stop the pattern and stimulate healing. This treatment approach is called "likes cure likes" (the Law of Similars) and is the basis of homeopathy.

Because of Hahnemann's ground-breaking work, there is now the *Homeopathic Pharmacopoeia of the United States* (HPUS). It has monographs on over 1200 official homeopathic drugs, giving directions for making them into safe drug products for over-the-counter or prescription use. Each homeopathic drug monograph provides very detailed methods of preparation as well as safety measures in identifying and manufacturing the drug.

The United States Food and Drug Administration consults the convention of HPUS to regulate homeopathic drugs. The HPUS lists the

Definition of Homeopathy from the *Homeopathic Pharmacopoeia of the United States*[5]

"Homeopathy is the art and the science of healing the sick by using substances capable of causing the same symptoms, syndromes and conditions when administered to healthy people.

"Any substance may be considered a homeopathic medicine if it has known 'homeopathic provings' and/or known effects which mimic the symptoms, syndromes or conditions which it is administered to treat, and is manufactured according to the specifications of the *Homeopathic Pharmacopoeia of the United States* (HPUS).

"Official homeopathic drugs are those that have been monographed and accepted for inclusion in the HPUS.

"Central to all homeopathy is the determination of the effect of substances on healthy volunteers and the use of the developed 'drug picture' by the consumer and/or trained healthcare practitioner according to the homeopathic principle of *similia similibus curentur*—Let likes be cured by likes. (Ed. The ability to prove new homeopathic medicines on healthy volunteers who can report subtle mind and mood changes opens the door to discovering many new drugs for depression. This possibility has caused the ever widening choice of drugs available in the *Homeopathic Pharmacopoeia of the United States*.)

"Historically, homeopathy has been practiced by medical doctors, and has been used for self-care by the general public.

"The issuance of the book, *The Homeopathic Domestic Physician* by Constantine Hering, M.D. (1835) opened this healthcare modality to the public.

"Homeopathy is an ideal therapeutic medium for self-medication of symptoms usually associated with self-limiting conditions since the selection of the proper remedy for the case is dependent on the symptoms that the body exhibits in its reaction to the illness.

"In the use of homeopathy for conditions which are other than self-limiting, the consumer is advised to use the services of a healthcare provider."

name, manufacturing method, and potencies of homeopathic drugs available over-the-counter as well as by prescription, particularly if certain potencies are toxic or if indications or the route of administration, such as injection, require a prescription. All homeopathic drugs are named in Latin. Labels on homeopathic drugs optionally list the expiration dates and National Drug Codes. There are various homeopathic drug methods of delivery, but the most common is sublingual in liquid or sucrose form, or in lactose pellet, tablet, or lozenge.

PREPARATION OF HOMEOPATHIC MEDICINES

Homeopathic medicines are prepared mainly from natural substances, primarily of botanical origin including plants and herbs, as well as from animal/human substances and minerals. Homeopathic medicines undergo a special form of preparation that involves shaking or grinding during serial dilutions, increasing the potency in direct proportion to the amount of shaking/grinding and diluting that is done. During preparation, the raw material is diluted by putting one part of raw material in nine parts of pure water (known as "X" potency) and vigorously shaken. This X potency process is repeated 6, 12, 30, 200, or 1,000 times. Another potency process, called the "C" potency, is based on one part raw material with ninety-nine parts of water. The increase in potency may be due to the kinetic energy applied to the medicine during the shaking or grinding.

THE PHYSICS OF HOMEOPATHIC MEDICINES

Recent physics experiments have shown that the special processing and preparation method used to make homeopathic drugs from raw natural materials acts to eliminate any poisonous qualities of substances and creates special electric crystals in water after the 6X dilution[6] that transfers information and energy to the person in some unknown way.[7]

The basic method of how and why homeopathic medicines work is still unknown, but they probably target the immune system in a certain manner, acting in the antibody/antigen arena, as this requires some individualization for effectiveness. Homeopathy stimulates change in the body at a very complex level of cellular chemistry that also includes the very dilute arena of hormones. Hormones are present in the blood at very low levels of concentration, similar to the low number of molecules in low-potency homeopathic dilutions. This similarity in concentrations may be why homeopathic medicines act so gently in the body.

THE HOMEOPATHIC PERSPECTIVE ON DEPRESSION

Homeopathy views each person individually, even though one may have received a diagnosis identical to others who have depression. In order for homeopathy to be most effective, people need homeopathic medicines chosen for their individual types or constitutions. From the homeopathic perspective each person's depression is unique, like a fingerprint. In making the patient's diagnosis, not only are the signs and symptoms considered important, but also factors such as the patient's mental and constitutional features, general physical patterns of likes and dislikes, and other seemingly unimportant physical details or conditions that might influence any of these manifestations, for better or worse.[8]

Many factors in addition to the seriousness of the depression contribute to an individualized treatment in homeopathy, including the time of day, even the hour when depression is experienced; appetite; sex drive; and nighttime dreams. Individualization also considers all of the symptoms accompanying depression, like rashes, constipation, diarrhea, arthritis, asthma, and female disorders. The presence of a triggering cause, such as the loss of a loved one, may suggest three or four homeopathic medicines that could be helpful. The possible combinations of symptoms or diseases are endless, which makes every patient with depression unique, but they also have similar common characteristics that form a pattern that can be recognized by those trained in the use of homeopathic medicines.

The homeopathic perspective views depression as a syndrome that includes the changes in the mind, as well as a collection of imbalances in different parts of the body. Because all past medical history and current symptoms are interrelated, they are used together to find the homeopathic treatment that matches the individual's pattern. This intense individualization of treatment is rarely seen in conventional medicine except in two areas: genetic profiling of disease that can identify which patients will respond to a particular drug even with the same diagnosis and allergy desensitization therapy for patients with individual allergies.

The Two Major Ways of Prescribing Homeopathic Medicines

Since homeopathy's inception over two hundred years ago, there have been two major paths of prescribing: classical, single-medicine prescribing; and combination prescribing (using two or more homeopathic medicines simultaneously). When looking at the scant research performed in single medicine or combination homeopathy, both ways are just about equally effective in research outcomes, and are the preferred methods.[9]

Classical, Single-Medicine Homeopathic Prescribing

The daily or intermittent use of single medicines, or a series of individual medicine treatments over a period of days to months or even years, is the classical homeopathic approach, used for both acute and chronic disease including depression. The unique group of signs and symptoms each depressed person exhibits is sorted out in classical homeopathic case taking, which can take one or two hours of interview and examination time. Depending on the pattern that the homeopathic practitioner sees, the similar medicine will be chosen. With over 1,200 homeopathic drugs in the *Homeopathic Pharmacopoeia of the United States*, many homeopathic doctors use computer-aided searches looking for homeopathic drugs similar to their client's disease expression pattern. This pattern may also include factoring in any relevant data gathered from the extensive current and past medical history, physical exam, or lab data.

Over one thousand hours of homeopathic training are needed to develop the skills required to find single homeopathic medicines helpful for patients with chronic illness, including those chronically depressed patients. If a patient has unusual symptoms or presents a rare pattern without the common triggering causes, more practitioner homeopathic skills may be needed.

Today, the limiting problem with single-medicine homeopathy is the time and skills needed to find the most similar medicine to effect change in a chronically ill person. Fortunately for single-medicine prescribers, many patients with easily recognized homeopathic depression patterns respond to commonly used homeopathic medicines such as *Ignatia amara*, a homeopathic medicine often found in homeopathic first-aid kits or health food stores. Many of the homeo-pathic drugs referenced for depression will only benefit a very small subset of depressed patients. Currently, a prescription chemical drug that only has a 5 percent therapeutic response rate would rarely come to market except as an orphan drug or a drug for obesity. The homeo-pathic pharmacopoeia, however, is filled with drugs with less than a 5 percent response rate, which is beneficial for the depressed patient who fits into that response group and needs an individualized homeo-pathic medicine.

Knowing how to prescribe homeopathic medicines widens the ther-apeutic choice of medicines for depression to 250, in addition to the twenty-three general chemical antidepressant prescription drugs listed for depression in the 1997 *Physicians' Desk Reference*. Outcomes for depressed patients will certainly be improved with more therapeutic choices.

The benefits of single-medicine prescribing are:

1. Restores the health of patients safely and quickly

2. Advances the detailed knowledge about individual homeopathic medicines

3. Uses less raw materials for medicine preparation, thus lowering the cost of manufacturing

4. Theoretical potential of less side effects

5. Less suppression of symptoms

The drawbacks of single medicine prescribing are:

1. The immense homeopathic knowledge and homeopathic skill needed by the practitioner for successful prescribing in chronic disease like depression

2. The increased time needed to individualize to one medicine

3. Necessity of expensive homeopathic software data bases, com-puter equipment, and training for the health professional

4. Problems with choosing the correct potency

5. The follow-up visits are each longer

6. Healing crises or aggravation of symptoms before a return to balance and health

7. The increased chance of therapeutic error by having wrongly chosen a dissimilar medicine that does not work

8. Longer time for healing to begin if the wrong medicine is chosen

In addition, the medical data generated by modern diagnostic medical tests in the laboratory, radiology, and pathology that is collected by many health care providers are barely integrated into the classical homeopathic schema and are for all practical purposes wasted. Because single-medicine prescribing is so time-intensive, after one to two hours there is much less time and energy available to encourage empowerment of the patient, or for patient self-care.

The Combination Homeopathic or Complex Homeopathic Approach

The combination homeopathic approach involves giving two or more homeopathic medicines at the same time. These medicines are often combined in one pill. Other times, different single or combination medicines are given at different times in the day or week.

Provings of combination homeopathic drugs to elicit symptoms of the drug combination have rarely been done. Most homeopathic pharmaceutical companies market their own favorite combinations in oral form, with indications on the label. The trade name of the combination will be protected, but the ingredients are mostly generic homeopathic drugs in single or multiple potencies. Many have been marketed safely for over one hundred years and are presumed to be clinically effective.

Many companies have extensive combination products that cover a myriad of diagnostic categories, including disorders of the mind like depression. Product literature explains the holistic methodology to be used in treating chronic disease. Less consultation of the generic homeopathic data base is needed when using proprietary combination prescribing, which saves time. Most combination prescribing for depression can be done holistically in thirty to forty-five minutes compared to one to two hours for single-medicine prescribing.

The advantages of combination prescribing are:

1. A health care provider with few homeopathic skills is more likely to prescribe the similar medicine in a much shorter time and have it be effective.

2. Less healing crises.

3. No need to individualize the potency when several are included in the combination.

4. More familiar tablet size and dosing schedules.

Combinations are often formulated from knowledge derived from successful clinical practice experience that integrates the relevant lab, past medical infectious diagnoses, and clinical diagnoses that health care providers recognize. These diagnostic tests also characterize and individualize the patient in a more holistic manner.

Success with combination homeopathic medicines provides incentive to study individual homeopathic medicines in more detail than simply knowing their major pathologic scope of action required for acute combination prescribing. Health care providers then become more familiar with the myriad of individual medicines that commonly benefit major diagnoses of chronic disease. This makes it even easier for them to choose combinations that will be more effective for each patient.

The disadvantages of combination prescribing are:

1. It is not possible to know which medicine caused what changes or if a side effect or allergy develops which medicine in the combination was involved.

2. Prescribers will not be able to increase their knowledge of each individual medicine when patients get better.

3. Mild side effects may be more frequent.

4. Because more medicines are used, drug preparation is costlier.

5. It is easier to ignore the total holistic individualized approach if pathologic diagnoses are the only thing used to choose homeopathic medicines.

6. If different potencies are needed that are not in the combination, then it will be difficult to choose the correct next potency needed without biofeedback assistance.

Theoretically, more suppression of symptoms is possible with combinations, just based on a diagnosis. However, using combinations holistically, after deriving a systematic overview and an understanding of the individual's pathological relationships, can be effective for chronic disease. Clinical efficacy may also be reflected in the homeopathic research, and by the millions of doses of homeopathic combinations sold worldwide during the past 150 years.

CASE STUDIES OF DEPRESSED PATIENTS TREATED WITH HOMEOPATHIC MEDICINES

Sixty-Five-Year-Old Widow with Hypothyroidism, Osteoarthritis, and Severe Depression

After the death of her husband of forty years, this woman continues to live alone on their ranch in California. She is accompanied to our session by her son, who lives nearby. He says that he has never seen his mother so depressed and attributes her depression to his father's sudden death three years ago.

She agrees that she feels depressed and that the six different antidepressants she received from the psychiatrist have not helped. She does not want to receive electroshock therapy. She has lost her enthusiasm for life and does not care if she dies. Her hypothyroidism, which was diagnosed one year earlier, has not responded to the medication Synthroid. The drug makes her too nervous regardless of the dose, and she has also lost weight.

She is taking herbs, vitamins, and aspirin for her arthritis pains in her toes, feet, and knees. She is no longer sexually active, has no sex drive, and is on estrogen replacement therapy.

She now wants to try natural homeopathic treatment for her problems. She likes the idea of an individualized homeopathic medicine to help her pains, hormone troubles, depression, and appetite. She feels she has grieved for her husband, is not suicidal, and is ready to get on with her life on the farm as soon as the depression lifts.

Her physical exam shows a well-developed, slightly thin woman who looks sad and depressed. Her toes are slightly swollen and warm to the touch, and their movement causes pain. Lab tests from her other doctors show high TSH and low T_4 (thyroid hormones), with slight elevation of her sedimentation rate. After a two-hour consultation using biofeedback and computer-aided homeopathic data base searches, the homeopathic medicine made from gold, *Aurum metallicum,* is prescribed in a 30C potency (two pellets a day), along with Thyroid USP one-half grain by mouth daily. Aurum is an over-the-counter homeopathic medicine prescribed for her moderately severe depression with loss of appetite, osteoarthritis of her toes, and secondary hypothyroidism.

A one-week follow-up shows much improvement. Her mood and appetite are better and she has stopped losing weight. Her toes and knees are less painful. She is able to tolerate the thyroid medication without feeling she is speeded up or that her heart is racing. Her biofeedback readings on her electro-acupuncture points on her hands and feet are improved. I feel that the homeopathic medicine *Aurum metallicum* 30C is helping restore her health. The prescription thyroid medicine is agreeing with her. Her son comments that she is getting back to her old self.

A three-week follow-up shows that she is still improving and that her feet and knees have stopped hurting. She can do more on the farm and has reached out to the community to help others learn to read. I tell her to continue the thyroid pill daily and to take the *Aurum metallicum* as needed. She is to check back in a few weeks.

On the seven-week follow-up visit she is no longer feeling depressed and her sedimentation rate, T_4 and TSH are now normal on the Thyroid USP one-half grain a day by mouth. She has taken the *Aurum metallicum* 30C about once or twice a week as needed for her mood. She feels she is on the road to recovery and will check back with me as needed.

Four months later she comes back, saying she is starting to feel depressed again and that the *Aurum metallicum* 30C is not helping. It seems like the same imbalance of the mind is returning, so I continue with the same medicine, *Aurum metallicum,* but change the potency to 200C to be taken for three days, one pellet by mouth and then as needed. She is to save the *Aurum metallicum* 30C and call me to report in five days.

She phones in five days and says her mood is improved and that she feels better. I tell her to take the Aurum as needed and to continue the thyroid medication and check back in a couple of months.

Several months later she calls to say she is fine and does not need to come in. One year later she calls to say the Aurum 200C that she used from time to time for her depressed feelings is no longer working. She is beginning to feel more depressed. We have another visit in which I feel that the nature of her depression has not changed. Therefore, according to homeopathic methodology, I raise the potency of *Aurum metallicum* to 1M, a 1,000 potency. This new potency of the same Aurum acts well, and she regains her health within several weeks.

Several years have gone by, and she takes her thyroid pill daily, but no other medicine. Her depression seems to have disappeared, and she is no longer using the Aurum but keeps it on hand just in case. It is possible that her hypothyroidism will be cured too, but that may take several years to happen and will be tested by gradually decreasing the prescription Thyroid USP and checking the TSH.

Thirty-Five-Year-Old Woman in Shock After Husband Kills Himself with Gun

I am called by the police to pronounce a man dead who had shot himself in the stomach in his garage. His wife is crying hysterically in the bathroom. She cannot believe that he is dead. Her sobs are audible, and she looks like a wreck. She is a healthy woman who has recently come to the United States from Colómbia. Her two young children are still sleeping.

Because the cause of her hysterical crying and sadness is the emotional shock from the sudden death of her husband, the first-aid homeopathic grief medicine *Ignatia amara* is indicated, or the prescription chemical drug tranquilizer Valium.

She opts for the homeopathic medicine, *Ignatia amara*, having heard about homeopathy in her native Colómbia. I have *Ignatia amara* 30X potency in my black bag and give her two tablets to take sublingually (under her tongue) immediately and pour twelve more into a drug envelope for her to use as needed. She is instructed to add two pills of *Ignatia amara* 30X to her pint-sized drinking water bottle and shake it up to dissolve it. She can sip from this bottle over the next few days as frequently as every five minutes, or whenever she feels she needs to calm down and center herself, or whenever the grief overwhelms her. By doing this, she is able to care for her children and attend her husband's funeral without feeling drugged.

Homeopathic medicines can help the person with both mild and severe types of depression get well faster without the side effects of chemical drugs. Getting over a depression quickly may prevent the brain from getting stuck in the rut of depression and having reoccurring episodes of deeper depression.

THE HOMEOPATHIC TREATMENT OF PATIENTS WITH DEPRESSION

Homeopathic medicines, usually given by mouth in very small doses that do not require a prescription, are individualized for each person's depression based upon the characteristic symptoms of the depressed person, including the cause. This form of prescribing on the basis of similars is the essence of homeopathy.

Individualization in homeopathy means sorting through 250-plus homeopathic drugs that have been used for various forms of depression and finding the best one or ones that match the individual symptoms a given patient exhibits. Matching the drug to the individual's symptoms takes considerably more time than writing a prescription for an antidepressant chemical drug. To help in the individualization process, practitioners may use several computer programs that help them choose the most similar homeopathic medicine from the comprehensive homeopathic medicine data base.

Unfortunately there have been no large clinical trials showing that treatment with homeopathic medicines is effective for clinical depression. However, homeopathy does have many individual case reports from doctors' practices that describe marked improvement in the depression and other symptoms after homeopathic treatment. Surely some of the successes with homeopathic medicines could be purely placebo responses, but not all. There are research studies that show homeopathic medicines are more than a placebo. Patients must have the freedom to choose the therapy that they believe will help them despite there being no existing randomized controlled clinical trials.

As homeopathy moves beyond being an emerging field with no Ph.D. programs, to a science with graduate degrees and the requisite research that accompanies such development, the prescribing of homeopathic medicines will become easier, clearer, and more widespread.

Major Depression

It is important to realize that some forms of depression are more serious and may end in suicide. A major depression is defined as recurrent suicidal feelings or thoughts of death, loss of interest in work, and markedly diminished pleasure in almost all activities in life. Other common symptoms of a severe major depression are significant weight loss or gain, trouble sleeping or too much sleeping, slowness or speediness, fatigue or loss of energy, feelings of worthlessness, and diminished ability to think or concentrate. Severely depressed people need the care of a medical doctor, and at times a specialist psychiatrist.

Suicide risk is higher if depression or suicide runs in the family or if the person is a substance abuser or impulsive with aggressive behavior. Any mention of suicide must be taken very seriously, even in children. Determine whether the child or adult has developed a detailed plan. Ask direct, straightforward questions: "Frequently, when a boy (or girl) feels so sad and has these worries, he feels like hurting himself. Have you ever felt like that? Have you ever felt like killing yourself? Have you tried it?"

If an attempt was made, get an idea of its seriousness. Ask "What prevented you from following through?" Ask if there are guns or weapons in the house that could be used for suicide and insist that they be removed.

If you feel a person may kill herself, and she already has a detailed plan, then you must immediately refer her to a psychiatrist or an emergency room.

Current research on depression and heart disease indicates that people who experienced episodes of major depression were more than four times as likely to have a heart attack as those who were not depressed. Patients who developed depression following a heart attack were shown to have a 3.5 times greater risk of dying from heart disease in the next six months than those not diagnosed as depressed.[10] Depressed women who are lethargic and have low levels of awareness are at a higher risk of heart disease.

Women have a higher incidence of depression during their reproductive years. Regular chemical drugs for depression can be effective for many but are often not well tolerated because of the side effects or are forbidden because of breast feeding.

Homeopathic treatment may be effective for a serious episode of depression. A skilled homeopathic practitioner should be consulted to work with the psychiatrist or family doctor. Although the cause for a serious depression may not be known, it may be that the mild depressions in the past were not treated properly and damaged the emotions, which led to the development of a serious depression that tends to be recurrent.

Mild Depression

Mild depressions may be treated with self-care using common homeopathic medicines such as Bach Flower remedies, tissue or cell salts, or *Ignatia amara*. When there is a mild depression and the cause is known, then the choice of which homeopathic medicines to pick for self-help is simplified. For example, if there has been a recent death of a loved one and the person cannot cry or is crying too much, then *Ignatia amara* 6X or 30X or 6C or 30C should help the person sleep and express the grief. Relief can be expected within the day if the homeopathic medicine is matched correctly. The following homeopathic medicines have also been successful in treating mild depression.

THE COMMONLY USED HOMEOPATHIC MEDICINES FOR DEPRESSION

Ignatia amara (St. Ignatius Bean).

Ignatia is the most commonly used homeopathic medicine for emotional problems. It is prepared from a seed of the fruit that grows on a tree native to the Philippines, whose natives wore the seeds as amulets. This homeopathic medicine is for emotional trauma, great disappointment, ill effects of bad news, jealousy, shame or mortification, sudden grief or disappointment such as death of a loved one, stillbirth, a romantic breakup, or loss of job.

Ignatia is indicated for the person who cries and sobs, is sad, and has trouble sleeping. This person may start laughing from grief or get a convulsion or facial muscle spasms. The emotional trauma may cause sudden loss of function in any organ, such as inability to move an arm. The person may sigh a lot or seem hysterical. There may be mental and physical exhaustion from grief. Stress may be felt as a lump in the throat when not swallowing or trembling of the hands or jerking of the legs during sleep. Eating seems to help. The person may be chilly, very sensitive, and touchy. Tobacco smoke may not be tolerated and can make a headache worse. The grief may not be expressed except through sobs. *Ignatia amara* is used in several potencies, traditionally the 6X or 30X or 30C, and is found in many combinations and homeopathic first-aid kits. It acts quickly, often best taken in the morning, and can be repeated as needed.

Pulsatilla (Wind Flower or Anemone).

This homeopathic medicine is prepared from a flower that grows in the open fields in Europe, the United States, and elsewhere. People who will respond to *Pulsatilla* cry when talking about their symptoms, are usually mild-mannered, and are more of a slower thinker than the Ignatia type. They are needy and clingy. Women and children who are the Pulsatilla type express sadness, like to be held, are affectionate, respond positively to sympathy, and are not thirsty. Their sadness often begins in puberty and worsens around the changes in hormones at the menstrual period, childbirth, or menopause. Often the person tends to be on the overweight side and a bit timid, but very emotional, laughing and weeping very easily. They are also chilly, but like open air, which makes them feel better. They need fresh, cool air and cannot sleep in a warm, stuffy room. They sleep with their hands over their head and often elevate the head on pillows.

Their symptoms are ever-changing or alternating. Their moods shift. They can be mild and pleasant, then irritable and tearful, especially in the evening. Pains can appear suddenly and disappear gradually, or the intensity increases until it reaches its climax and all of a sudden the pains disappear. Infectious diseases such as mumps, measles, cystitis, otitis media, or gonorrhea can precipitate the ill health and depression. This type can have suicidal thoughts or commit suicide by drowning or shooting.

Sepia (Inky brown juice of the marine mollusk cuttlefish).

Sepia is for those who are depressed and tired from working too hard or raising a family; have lost their sex drive; or experience menstrual, PMS, or menopause problems. They feel sick and tired of being around their loved ones. A person who needs Sepia hates to be consoled or given sympathy, withdraws, is weepy, a screamer, tends to have brown spots on his or her face, a yellowish complexion, sluggish circulation, feels cold, and improves with a lot of exercise, such as aerobics or running miles a day. They may experience depression or sadness with tears and irritability, indifference to friends and family, including spouse and children, and can be very sad during menses. Sepia may be very helpful in postpartum depression when the mother does not bond with the baby and gains weight rapidly. The Sepia type is usually a woman who is exhausted and chilly, weeps when asked about her symptoms, is critical, and faints easily. Her ailments disappear after intense exercise or being in a warm bed. There may be dropping down of the uterus, vagina, and eyelids. She can have milky or yellow discharges or a history of gonorrhea or venereal warts. Sepia is often useful for hot flashes and perspiration on the head from menopause and the accompanying depression with weeping.

Natrum muriaticum (Table salt or sea salt).

This mineral-based medicine is often used for depression and sadness or deep grief, especially after Ignatia has been helpful earlier for an emotional loss. The person who responds to *Natrum muriaticum* is usually a very private type who does not cry in public, has shut down emotionally, and does not like to be consoled. Consolation makes these people angry. They desire to withdraw from friends and family and do not like company. They often fall in love with people who are already taken, so that the relationship never works out, or they get trapped in a no-win situation. Love losses like divorces or deaths of loved ones can cause the depression to begin. They may laugh so hard that tears come to their eyes. Their dreams are often frightening, such as dreams of robbers in the house or of fire. They can crave salt or salty foods like chips, popcorn, and pretzels and dislike being in the sun too long, as it weakens them. They are chilly types but like the outdoors, the seaside, and music.

The *Natrum muriaticum* type can be more depressed at night and especially in bed. They ruminate over and have difficulty expressing their losses and often cannot weep. Instead of tears, the nose will run watery, the skin will weep from an eczematous itchy skin rash, or they will get heart palpitations or feel nervous. The eyes can be too dry, the nose too wet or dry, the vagina too dry, and the skin dry and cracked in the fingertips and around the nails. They can lose or gain weight. The neck and body can be thin, but the face looks normal and may be greasy. The tongue may be mapped and lips cracked in the middle. There can be edema, anemia, herpes, and headaches. If the person had a history of malaria, especially with a very long continued chill and a craving for salt, then *Natrum muriaticum* is strongly indicated. Rarely is suicide a reality.

Aurum metallicum (Gold).

Before 1800, Arabian doctors used gold as a medicine for depression, foul breath, and pain in the heart with palpitation. Homeopathically prepared gold, made from the metal found in mines, is *Aurum metallicum*. Aurum is used for severe depression, often in serious business types who may have chronic hepatitis or liver or testicular disorders, or enlarged lymph glands. This is a remedy that often suits people who are very intense, idealistic, and want to be the best and set high goals.[11] Life for this type is a constant burden, and there is the desire to commit suicide by jumping from a height or by shooting. The thought of death alone gives pleasure. The depression may be associated with a business failure or loss of a loved one. This could also be related to a postpartum depression, especially when the woman gives birth during winter months, or if she has had a tendency to suffer depression in the past, during the short daylight days of winter.[12]

Such people are very self-critical and may have weakness of memory or mind. They can feel hurried and imagine that they neglected their duties and deserve blame. They are very irritable and can talk continuously without waiting for replies. Often the bones are painful, and there may be shortness of breath from heart disease and extremely bad breath, especially in teenagers, or sinusitis.

The person may be chilly, and the depression and illnesses worsen at night. There may be headaches, hypertension, inguinal hernias, ulcers of skin or bones, fetid discharges, exophthalmic goiter, and redness of the face, with a knobby red nose. There also may be very strong symptoms, such as violent palpitations at puberty, or painful headaches that are accompanied by wanting to kill oneself for relief. At times, music gives relief, but the person may do excessive meditation or abuse drugs or alcohol. Aurum is used for this type, which also has the strongest desire for suicide.

Natrum sulphuricum (Sodium and sulfur).

The remedy *Natrum sulphuricum* is another mineral medicine made from sodium and sulphur and is one of the twelve homeopathic tissue salts. It may be used for depression and asthma or depression and a head injury. At times, the person who responds to *Natrum sulphuricum* may have ideas of suicide by hanging or shooting. The illnesses, especially depression or epilepsy, may have started after a head injury, from a divorce, or the death of a loved one. These people are warm-blooded, but feel bad in damp or hot, humid weather. There may be asthma in children or after grief, which worsens at four A.M., in damp weather or with exertion. There may also be chest infections like bronchitis or pneumonia and a history of venereal diseases like gonorrhea, venereal warts, or plain warts. A strange symptom is that lively music makes one sad. Gallstones and ringworm are often associated with this type.

SPECIALIZED HOMEOPATHIC TREATMENTS FOR DEPRESSION

Homeopathy has long recognized the association of the past medical history of infectious illnesses and disturbances to the health of a person in mind or body. There are many effective and very safe homeopathic treatment possibilities for illnesses related to infections gone awry in the body. One specific group of homeopathic medicines, called nosodes, are prepared from the infectious agents (germs) that cause disease or from diseased products of the body. These homeopathic medicines are sterilized so that they cannot cause infections. Examples of those homeopathic medicines used for depression are Medorhinnum, made from the gonorrheal urethral discharge; Syphilinum, from the sore of syphilis; and Psorinum, from the sore of scabies, the itch mite. Other nosodes, prepared from common infectious materials from diseases like toxoplasmosis, have long been used in homeopathy to restore mental health, especially depression.[13]

BACH FLOWER HOMEOPATHIC REMEDIES: SELF-CARE

Bach Flower Homeopathic Remedies are official homeopathic medicines made from flowers. A person can self-prescribe up to six of these medicines out of thirty-eight possibilities and combine them in a bottle for self-care. The following Bach Flower Homeopathic Remedies are used for various forms and symptoms of depression:

Agrimonia eupatoria, Flos. (Agrimony).

For those not wishing to burden others with their troubles, and who cover up their suffering behind a cheerful facade. They are distressed by argument or quarrel and may seek escape from pain and worry through the use of drugs and alcohol.

Ulex europaeus, Flos. (Gorse).

For feelings of hopelessness and futility, and little hope of relief.

Sinapsis arvensis, Flos. (Mustard).

For deep gloom that comes on for apparently no known reason, sudden melancholia, or heavy sadness. Will lift just as suddenly.

Ornithogalum umbellatum, Flos. (Star of Bethlehem).

For grief, trauma, loss. Used for the mental and emotional effect during and after a trauma.

Castanea sativa, Flos. (Sweet Chestnut).

For those who feel they have reached the limits of their endurance. Used for those moments of deep despair when anguish seems to be unbearable.

THE BIOCHEMIC TISSUE SALTS

The twelve biochemic tissue salts listed in the homeopathic pharmacopoeia are mineral medicines composed of the inorganic parts of cells. Many years of clinical experience and observed results have led to the introduction of skillfully formulated combined remedies for use in certain groups of ailments.[14]

The main combination of biochemic tissue salts used for mental depression, insomnia and neurasthenic conditions is a mixture of *Ferrum phosphoricum*, *Kali phosphoricum*, and *Magnesia phosphorica*. The cell salts are usually used in low "X" potencies of 3X, 6X, 12X. The *Biochemic Handbook* lists in its repertory of symptoms and corresponding remedies, the following individual cell salts:

- **For depressed spirits:** *Kali phos., Calc. phos., Nat. mur.*

- **For despondent moods:** *Nat. mur., Nat. sulph.,* Silica (called Silicea in the HPUS)

- **For melancholy:** *Nat. mur., Kali phos.*

- **Hopeless with dejected mental spirits:** *Nat. mur.*

- **Fits of crying:** *Kali phos.*

Conclusion

Homeopathy is a well-established and extremely safe therapeutic system, but like conventional medicine, it is not a perfect treatment system. Both systems need to have further outcomes research with collaboration and sharing of information that will improve the therapeutic possibilities for all individuals needing treatment for depression.

Ayurveda and Yoga for Depression and Promoting Mental Health

Shri Kant Mishra, M.D., M.S., Doctor of Ayurveda

The mind is the source of bondage and the mind is the source of liberation.

—The Bhagavad Gita

Ayurveda and yoga have been utilized for promoting physical, mental, and spiritual health for thousands of years. Ayurveda, India's traditional system of natural medicine, dates back to 3500 B.C. and originates from the Hindu scripture *Atharva Veda*. The literal meaning of Ayurveda is the "Science of Life," *ayur* meaning "life" and *veda* meaning "knowledge" or "science." Yoga, a system of psychophysiological and spiritual healing developed in India, derives from the word *yukti*, meaning "to unite" or integrate the individual soul with the Universal soul, and has also been continuously practiced for over five thousand years.

The World Health Organization officially began promoting "traditional" medicine such as Ayurveda, yoga, and Chinese Medicine in developing countries in 1978. Since that time there have been increasing efforts, especially by Western countries, to incorporate the world's traditional medicine with modern medicine in their national health care systems.

In recent years Ayurveda and yoga have stimulated a great deal of interest worldwide. Public awareness of Ayurveda and demand for Ayurvedic herbs and services have grown tremendously in the past few years in the United States. Hatha yoga, a form of physical yoga, has become so popular here that for many it has become the exercise of choice or a regular part of many people's exercise programs. Many forms of hatha yoga are being taught across the country in YMCAs, fitness centers, gyms, yoga studios, and private homes. Numerous physicians, health practitioners, and psychotherapists are now recommending hatha yoga as well as meditation, another form of yoga, to their patients.

The major goals of Ayurveda and yoga are to provide optimum physical, mental, and spiritual health, through the integration of body, mind, and spirit. They also play a strong role in dealing with depression, anxiety, and mental disorders. Ayurveda utilizes dietary therapy, herbal compounds, lifestyle modifications, cleansing and purification processes, as well as spiritual practices to successfully address depression and mental illness. Yoga as an integrated system including moral/ethical codes, breathing exercises, postures, and meditation has been successfully used to reduce stress, anxiety, depression, and substance abuse. A great deal of work has been done to establish the benefits of yoga in health promotion, disease prevention, and treatment of large numbers of psychiatric disorders.

BASIC PRINCIPLES OF AYURVEDA

Ayurveda is a comprehensive and natural approach to healthy living, based on the understanding of factors helpful and harmful to life. The principal goal is the preservation and promotion of health with emphasis on the enhancement of natural immunity to prevent illness. The secondary goal is the treatment of physical, mental, and spiritual illnesses. Ayurveda employs a holistic concept of the individual, integrating all aspects of life: nutrition, hygiene, sleep, weather, lifestyle, and physical, mental, and sexual activities—with each of these aspects contributing to one's overall health.

Ayurveda maintains health and prevents disease by stressing the importance of simple, everyday acts of proper eating, sleeping, and exercising. It also emphasizes the importance of maintaining emotional balance and not giving in to excess anger, fear, or anxiety in order to achieve harmony of the body, mind, and spirit. These factors make up the foundation of a healthy body, without which no amount or type of medicine can effectively and permanently combat a disease state.

As a complete system of medicine, Ayurveda consists of the following eight branches:

- Internal Medicine *(Kaya Chikitsa)*
- Surgery *(Shalya)*
- Ophthalmology, Otolaryngology, and Dentistry *(Shalakya)*
- Toxicology *(Agad Tantra)*
- Psychology and Psychiatry *(Bhoot Vidya)*
- Pediatrics, Obstetrics, and Gynecology *(Komar Bhritya)*
- Geriatrics, Rejuvenation *(Rasayana)*
- Sexology, Aphrodisiacs *(Bajikaran)*

The areas most applied to mental health and treating mental disorders such as depression and anxiety include psychology and psychiatry, internal medicine, and geriatrics and rejuvenation.

THEORIES OF HEALTH AND DISEASE IN AYURVEDA

Ayurveda is derived from the ancient *Sankhya* philosophy of India that claims all living organisms are a microcosm that reflects the macrocosm of the entire cosmos. The five "elements" *(mahabhoota)*—earth, ether, air, fire, and water—form the basis of Ayurveda and are considered to be the basis of all living and nonliving entities of the universe. These five elements are similar to those in Traditional Chinese Medicine (TCM), with air and ether in place of TCM's Metal and Wood (see page 197 in "Qigong, Chinese Medicine, and Depression").

The Three *Doshas* and Your Constitutional Profile

From the five elements originate the three humors or *doshas: vata, pitta,* and *kapha,* which are collectively called the *tridosha.* According to Ayurveda, each living being possesses a unique psychophysiological or constitutional profile formed at the union of ovum and sperm that determines the specific manifestation of the three *doshas*. The three *doshas* function at both the tissue and the cellular (macro) level as well as at the subcellular (micro) level. At the subcellular level they manifest as neural, electrical, energetic *(vata)*, metabolism *(pitta)*, and fluid dynamics *(kapha)*.

Each of the *doshas* is associated with specific functions and areas in the body. *Vata* represents motion and the activity that allows us to breathe and the blood to circulate. It is seated in the bones, large intestine, pelvic cavity, skin, ears, and thighs. *Pitta* represents metabolism and is seated in the small intestine, stomach, sweat glands, blood, skin, and eyes. *Kapha* represents structure and is seated in the chest, lungs, and spinal fluid around the spinal cord.

Vata.

Vata is the lightest of the *doshas*, representing the elements of air and ether and characterized by changeability, unpredictability, and movement. It indicates neural energy, and represents the physiological aspects of the central and peripheral nervous systems. *Vata* governs the movement of the subcellular elements within the cells, fluids and other materials throughout the body, activity of the organs and muscles, motor and sensory functions, as well as movement of thoughts through the mind. A *vata*-type person tends to be slender, tall, energetic, talkative, anxious, alert, restless, active, and eats and sleeps erratically. *Vata* people tend to disperse their money easily and waste energy.

Pitta.

Pitta, associated with transformative energy, represents a combination of the elements fire and water and is reflected in the metabolic processes at the cellular and subcellular levels. *Pitta* people are generally of medium build and have stable weight and fair skin. Digestion and metabolism, or transformation of food into energy, is a *pitta* function. Governed by fire, *pitta*-type persons are more emotional than are the other *doshas*. They may have a fiery personality and be more apt to exhibit anger and irritability, aggressiveness, and competitiveness as well as have a sharp, biting intelligence and a short, explosive temper. Daily habits are moderate and efficient, with regular patterns of eating and sleeping. *Pitta* people are good organizers and leaders. Their characteristic quality of sharpness manifests in sharp facial features, sharp eyes, and sharp mind and memory. Oily qualities are associated with *pitta* types, including soft, oily, warm skin and straight, oily hair with a tendency to early graying and hair loss. They perspire heavily and have a strong, sulfurous body smell and tend to get inflammatory diseases, acne, ulcers, hemorrhoids, and stomach ailments. *Pitta* girls have early onset of menstruation. Lightness is a *pitta* quality in terms of both color and weight.

Kapha.

Kapha is the densest of the *doshas*, representing a combination of water and earth. *Kapha* is associated with the accumulation and formation of dense structure and corresponds to the physical structure and fluid contents of the body. It maintains fluid dynamics at the intracellular and extracellular levels. *Kapha*-type people have cool, damp, pale skin and a heavy build with a tendency to become overweight. They tend to be slow moving and solid and have great muscular strength. They are emotionally balanced and have easy sleep. Slowness characterizes *kapha*. They are slow to anger and action. They eat slowly and sleep long and deeply. They also have a slow metabolism and digestion with a strong appetite. *Kapha* people tend to procrastinate and be stubborn, with a tendency to hold on to money. They are stable and grounded, with a steady, tranquil personality.

Determining and understanding the individual constitutional profile is important for the diagnosis and treatment of specific diseases. Seven general combinations of the *doshas* are possible and can be ascertained by an experienced Ayurvedic practitioner. Some individuals demonstrate a clear predominance of a single *dosha* (*vata, pitta,* or *kapha*). Others have equal influences of two *doshas*, identified as the dual types *vata-pitta, pitta-kapha,* or *vata-kapha*. Finally, there is a *vata-pitta-kapha* combination, with the three *doshas* in equal proportion. Each person's constitutional profile is characterized by which *doshas* are naturally predominant and which are least influential in the person's overall functioning.

When the *doshas* are in balance according to the individual's inborn constitution, health and vitality abound. Imbalance among the *doshas* is a sign that mind and body are not well coordinated. Once individuals understand the characteristics that go with their specific constitutional types, they can take the measures to restore balance among the *doshas* by making changes in their lifestyle and environment that will also help prevent disease.

Characteristics of the Three *Doshas*

	Vata	Pitta	Kapha
Elements	*Ether and air*	*Fire and water*	*Earth and water*
Build	*Tall and slender*	*Medium, stable weight*	*Heavy, strong, overweight*
Physiological function	*Motion, activity*	*Metabolism*	*Physical structure*
Activity and habits	*Movement, activity restless, wasteful*	*Moderate, efficient, organized*	*Tendency to accumulate fluid*
Sleep and digestion	*Erratic sleep, fast digestion*	*Regular*	*Slow digestion; strong appetite; easy, deep sleep*
Emotional/ mental	*Anxious, unpredictable, alert, restless*	*Fiery, angry, aggressive, sharp, explosive*	*Slow, tranquil, stubborn, procrastinating, stable, grounded*
Organs	*Large intestine, pelvic cavity, skin, ears, thighs*	*Small intestine, stomach, sweat glands, blood, skin, eyes*	*Chest, lungs, spinal fluid*
Cyclic	*Evening; summer; early old age*	*Midday; autumn and late spring; adulthood*	*Morning; winter and spring; youth*

The *vata* type is disturbed by eating raw vegetables, excessive traveling, sleeplessness, excessive exercise, drink, and too much sexual activity. These qualities and behavioral patterns seem to manifest most in those who have the *vata* constitution. The *pitta* type is disturbed by eating excessive hot foods, tea, coffee, alcohol, and too much exposure to heat and sun. The *kapha* type is agitated by eating excessive sweets, or fatty and cold foods, including dairy products. Excessive daytime sleep and an inactive life disturbs *kapha* and produces illnesses. The individual with a specific constitutional profile (e.g. *vata*) is more vulnerable to the type of imbalances and illnesses related to that *dosha*. For example, *vata*-increasing factors are more likely to disturb an individual of the *vata dosha* type and result in a *vata*-related illness.

In addition to an individual's constitutional profile, other factors increase or decrease the strength of a *dosha* such as diurnal, seasonal, and age changes in *doshas*. For example, *kapha* qualities increase in the morning, in the winter season, and at a young age. *Pitta* qualities increase at noon, during the fall season, and during adulthood. *Vata* qualities increase in the evening, the summer season, and in old age. There are continual seasonal changes of the *doshas*: *Vata* is aggravated in the spring season and then manifests as illness in summer. *Pitta* is irritated during the summer, and symptoms or disease manifests during winter. *Kapha* is aggravated during the winter and manifests as illness during the spring.

The Three *Gunas*: Your Psychospiritual Profile

The mind plays a very important role in both health and disease. According to Ayurveda, every living being possesses a psychospiritual profile (*guna prakriti*), in addition to the constitutional profile (*dosha prakriti*). The three *gunas*, or mental/emotional characteristics and habits—*sattva*, *rajas*, and *tamas*—represent our psychospiritual profile.

Sattva guna refers to the good virtues. These people are knowledgeable, religious, dedicated, and hardworking; they have control of their senses and are devoid of emotional factors such as anger, greed, or selfishness. *Rajas* denotes luxurious habits. These people are emotionally changeable, interested in eating and drinking and excessive sexual activities. *Tamas* signifies laziness and inertia. These individuals demonstrate excessive sleeping, substance abuse, indulgence in sexual activities, and are lethargic, quarrelsome, and lacking in knowledge.

Based on these profiles, the person with *sattva guna* has the strongest mental makeup, is able to control the mind, and is free of any impurities. The *rajasic* person has a number of impurities and difficulties in controlling the mind, and the person with *tamasic* has the most impurities and challenging mental makeup.

Similar to the three *doshas*, the *rajasic* and *tamasic gunas* can be brought into balance through lifestyle practices, spiritual enhancement, meditation, and yoga, as well as disciplining the mind. There is a close

Characteristics of the Three *Gunas*

	Sattva	Rajas	Tamas
Emotional/ mental profile	*Knowledgeable, devoid of emotional factors, i.e., anger, selfishness, etc.*	*Very emotionally changeable*	*Quarrelsome, lazy, devoid of knowledge*
Activity and habits	*Religious, dedicated, hardworking, possess total control of the senses*	*Interested in eating, drinking, excessive sexual activities*	*Excessive sleep; indulge in excessive sexual activities; substance abusers*

interaction between *gunas* and *doshas*. Various psychological problems alter the *gunas*, which affect mind and emotions, and subsequently affect *doshas*, producing different types of psychiatric disorders, including depression.

HEALTH PROMOTION AND DISEASE PREVENTION IN AYURVEDA

Because Ayurveda's main focus is on health promotion and disease prevention, it advocates healthy lifestyle, nutrition, exercise, and following strict yearly and seasonal routines. With the adaptation of these practices (i.e., avoidance of harmful practices) and utilization of good habits, optimal mental and physical health can be obtained.

The principles of health promotion and disease prevention are divided into four main disciplines:

- Personal hygiene (*Swasthya vritta*)

- Purification (*Panchakarma*)

- Rejuvenation (*Rasayana*)

- Yoga

Personal Hygiene and Lifestyle Practices (*Swasthya Vritta*)

Personal hygiene consists of proper daily, seasonal, and yearly routines. Various physical, mental, ethical, and spiritual plans are included here, such as exercise, nutrition, sleep, prayer, and meditation. Seasonal routines, however, are based on constitutional profile. The avoidance of certain foods and drinks during a particular season to avoid imbalance of a particular *dosha* can minimize the onset of illness. If routines are conscientiously followed, the *doshas* can remain in balance, and good health can be maintained even into old age.

Ayurveda places a strong emphasis on an individualized approach to nutrition based on an individual's body constitution, *vata*, *pitta*, and *kapha*. An improper diet that is not based on the quality and quantity of food and compatible to one's constitution can cause illness. For example, a person with a *vata* constitution who eats legumes, drinks excess alcohol, and is sleep deprived is more likely to develop mental illness. A person with a *pitta* constitution who eats very hot, spicy food and sweats profusely can develop *pitta* mental disorders. An individual with a *kapha* constitution who eats sour milk products such as yogurt, buttermilk, etc., will experience a lack of energy, excessive sleepiness, and may develop *kapha* mental disorders.

Internal Purification (*Panchakarma*)

Panchakarma, a purification technique, is one of the major procedures of Ayurvedic medicine and is widely used throughout India and the United States. Utilized to eliminate excess *doshas* from the body and to normalize *gunas*, *panchakarma* practice is based on an individual's constitution, disorder, age, and other factors. It consists of the following five processes:

- Vomiting therapy (*Vaman*): Used to remove excess *kapha* impurities or mucus from the body.

- Therapeutic purgation with laxatives (*Virechan*): Used to remove *pitta* or bile.

- Medicated oil and nonoily enema (*Basti*): Used to address *vata* disorders, whose predominant site is the colon.

- Elimination of toxins through the nose (*Nasya*): Nasal administration of herbal preparations and medicated oils into the nose to
purify *prana*, or breath, mind, and consciousness. Introducing
herbs through the nasal passage ensures that their properties are
not destroyed by enzymes in the stomach. Using this route also
helps to increase mental clarity.

- Detoxification of the blood (*Raktamokshan*): Normally accomplished through various forms of bloodletting, it is not routinely
performed in Ayurveda and is illegal in the United States.

In addition to these cleansing techniques, *panchakarma* also
includes diet and lifestyle guidelines, such as getting plenty of rest and
avoiding strenuous exercise, sexual activity, or other stimulation. It is
preceded ten days earlier by *poorvakarma*, which includes procedures
such as sweating induced by a steam treatment with a medicated herbal
decoction and therapeutic massage with medicated oil and paste.

Panchakarma is a very special Ayurvedic procedure that requires
close supervision from a skilled practitioner. It must be individually
prescribed based on an individual's specific constitution and medical
problems. Preferably, it is performed during the transitional period
between two seasons.

Rejuvenation (*Rasayana*)

Following the cleansing regimen of *panchakarma* is a tonifying program, called *rasayana*, established to beneficially affect nutrition, digestion, metabolism, and microcirculation. Treatments include special herbal
and mineral preparations, yoga, and breathing regimens. These practices
are believed to help rejuvenate the individual, slow the aging process,
extend the longevity of life, and restore vitality to the reproductive system.

Yoga

The goal of yoga is attainment of physical, mental, and spiritual
well-being through mastery of the body and mind. It is achieved
through the practice of specific postures, regulated breathing, as well as
awareness and meditation. Yoga and postures beneficial for depression
will be discussed in greater detail beginning on page 186.

Mental Habits to Promote and Preserve Mental Health

In order to maintain proper mental health, the various emotional factors such as anger and greed must be controlled. This can be achieved through practice of proper mental habits and avoidance of unfavorable ones:

- Pursue happiness; avoid anger, jealousy, and bitter words.
- Avoid anxiety, abuse of sexual functions, ego, and animosity.

There are also other social, religious, individual, personal, and physical types of good habits that should be practiced. According to Ayurveda, only through the integration of *doshas* and *gunas* can optimum mental and physical health be achieved.

THE ORIGIN OF DISEASE AND MENTAL ILLNESS ACCORDING TO AYURVEDA

According to Ayurveda, balance of the *doshas* (*vata, pitta,* or *kapha*) is the most fundamental and immediate factor contributing to health and prevention of disease. The first stage in the manifestation of the disease state is an imbalance of these doshas, and in the case of mental illness, an imbalance of *rajas* and *tamas gunas*. These imbalances in turn lead to abnormalities and internal disorders in the bodily tissues and fluids, the excretory system, as well as the metabolic processes such as the digestive and enzymatic systems, resulting in an accumulation of toxins. When these toxins circulate in the blood and clog the channels (*srotas*) in various tissues (*dhatus*), illness arises.

If the pathogenesis and correct stage of a disease is not recognized early on and treated, it may disseminate into the many tissues, creating secondary effects upon the *doshas* and ultimately leading to serious consequences.

An imbalance of *doshas* and *gunas*, as well as external factors, can also lead to abnormalities in the seat of cognition within the brain, resulting in anxiety, depression, and other psychological and psychiatric disorders. Mental disorders can be produced by abnormalities of *gunas* that can lead to abnormalities of *doshas*. Similarly, abnormalities of *doshas* can lead to abnormalities of *gunas* that can produce mental illness. The preliminary phases of mental disorders are easier to treat and are generally characterized by anxiety, palpitation, and confusion, followed by a full-blown disease process.

Depression Due to *Dosha* Imbalances (Endogenous Depression)

According to Ayurveda, depression as well as other mental illnesses may be due to both endogenous and exogenous factors. Endogenous factors include those internal to the body, such as mineral imbalances or slow metabolism. Exogenous factors are those due to circumstances existing outside the body, like a death in the family, divorce, loss of a job, or living in a toxic environment. Although depression and mental disorders can stem from the imbalances of *vata, pitta*, or *kapha doshas* or a combination of the three, most are caused by a *vata* imbalance.

Vata depression is caused by a *vata*-promoting diet, insufficient nutrition, anxiety, and other *vata*-deranging activities. The symptoms for a *vata*-depressed person include insomnia, undereating, weight loss, euphoria, hallucination, and crying spells followed by a loss of speech. The *vata*-depressed individual's diminished interest in eating can result in further *vata* imbalance.

Pitta depression can be caused by excessive hot foods, hot temperatures of the summer season, or excessive sweating. The symptoms of *pitta* depression include sleeplessness, frustration, resentment, and excessive anger as well as homicidal or suicidal ideation.

Kapha depression is caused by a *kapha*-promoting diet, inactivity, and excessive sleep, particularly sleep in the daytime. Symptoms for *kapha* depression include sluggishness, lethargy, feelings of isolation, and problems with speech as well as excessive eating and sleeping. Overeating and excessive sleeping can result in a further exacerbation of *kapha* imbalance.

Depression produced by a combination of the three *doshas* is a very serious form of depression. A person may have a combination of symptoms, usually uncontrollable urges as well as suicidal and homicidal tendencies. It is very difficult to treat.

Depression Due to External Factors

In Ayurvedic medicine, exogenous depression is produced by an imbalance of the mental *gunas*, toxins, drugs, extraterrestrial influences, or evil spirits. A person suffering from the imbalance of mental *gunas* due to excessive fear, loss of a loved one, or the failure of a love affair can experience excessive crying, laughing, or insomnia. Individuals with depression caused by exogenous toxic factors suffer from associated skin problems, confusion, and loss of consciousness. Extraterrestrial and evil spirit–induced depression is produced by curses, astrological influences, and other demigod influences. These factors cause anxiety, grief, and other negative emotions, leading to abnormalities in the mind and *gunas* causing depression.

DIAGNOSIS IN AYURVEDA

The diagnosis of a disease state in Ayurveda is based on eight types of evaluation: history, physical examination, inspection, percussion (tapping with fingers), palpation of specific areas, pulse diagnosis, and examination of urine and stool. There are two additional types of evaluation for psychological and mental functions: the assessment of the psychospiritual profile (*guna*) and the determination of one's mental strength or endurance. There are three classifications of mental endurance:

- High (*Uttama*): Individuals who have a great deal of mental endurance and are very committed

- Intermediate (*Madhyam*): Individuals possessing a lower mental endurance

- Lower (*Heen*): People who lack any mental endurance

The evaluation of mental health also includes a detailed examination of mental factors including speech, intelligence, and memory. Psychological, social, sexual, and physical profiles (such as sleep, sexual function, habits, etc.) are also evaluated.

The physician first takes a detailed evaluation of the present condition, including family, social, personal, nutritional, environmental, and historical information. A written questionnaire with questions about physical attributes, metabolism, sleep, habits, self-image, preferences, interests, and emotions is given to the patient. A comprehensive physical examination of the entire body, including eye, tongue, skin, and pulse diagnosis is performed to identify *dosha* abnormalities, specific disease entities, and any complications. Pulse diagnosis is an important diagnostic tool, especially in determining various abnormalities. It is performed by the right index, middle, and ring fingers, with the index finger being placed closest to the patient's wrist. The characteristics of an individual's *vata dosha* is felt by the index finger, *pitta* by the middle finger, and *kapha* by the ring finger.

TREATMENT OF DEPRESSION IN AYURVEDA

Treatment for depression in Ayurveda is based not only on symptoms, but on a proper diagnosis and elimination of the root cause(s). This is accomplished by normalizing *doshas*, tissues, and the excretory system, as well as the promotion of a healthy state of mind, sensory organs, and consciousness. The treatments for both endogenous and exogenous depression, as well as mental disorders, are threefold: medicinal, mental hygiene and spiritual healing, and nonmedicinal.

- **Medicinal Treatment** (*Yuktivyapashraya*): This treatment includes internal and external cleansing, and medicinal substances. The two primary procedures for internal cleansing are palliation (*shaman*) and internal purification (*panchakarma*). Medicated butters, herbs, and inorganic products are used in this type of cleansing as well as metals to help suppress aggravated *doshas*. External cleansing utilizes massage with medicated oils, nasal inhalation, aromatherapy, and bathing in herbal compounds. The medicinal treatment also includes *rasayana*, or rejuvenation, which employs a program utilizing tonics, breathing exercises, and yoga to help increase the level of general health.

- **Mental Hygiene and Spiritual Healing** (*Satvajaya*): Part of the psychology and psychiatry (*bhoot vidya*) treatment in Ayurveda utilizes meditation, yoga, and *mantra*, as well as a specific form of psychotherapy to bring the mind to a higher level of mental and spiritual functioning.

- **Nonmedicinal Treatment to Counter Extraterrestrial Causes** (*Daivavyapashraya*): This treatment involves the use of practices such as mantras, precious gemstones, auspicious works (service dedicated to God), repentance, worship, meditation, and various rituals to counter astrological influences as well as other extraterrestrial factors.

Medicinal Treatment of Depression

The major elements in the medicinal treatment of depression in Ayurveda include palliation, internal purification, rejuvenation, and the use of medicinal substances to treat the specific illness or imbalance.

Palliation (Shaman).

Palliation means a gradual balancing or pacification of aggravated *doshas*, as opposed to eliminating excess *doshas* as in *panchakarma*. Palliation methods are slower than *panchakarma* and focus more on the spiritual dimension of healing. Palliation is appropriate for people who do not have sufficient strength to undergo the rigors of *panchakarma*. There are seven methods of palliation: light diet, fluid restriction, exercise, sunlight, fresh air, increasing digestive power, and elimination of toxins.

There are specific palliation methods in Ayurveda for *vata*, *pitta*, and *kapha* depression. Treatment for *vata* depression includes proper nutrition, fasting, and avoiding excessive amounts of *vata*-increasing foods such as dry foods and beans, substituting with smooth, sweet preparations such as milk-based drinks. For *pitta* depression one should avoid irritating, hot food and substitute with cold and soothing food like *lassi* (cold curd). In *kapha* depression one should avoid cold curd or stale food and consume more food with astringent and bitter qualities such as bitter melon and black pepper. Other methods like relaxation and exercise can be used in palliation treatment. Herbal oil massage can also be helpful for all types of depression: warm oil for *kapha*, cold oil for *pitta*, and nonirritating oil for the *vata* type.

Internal Purification (Panchakarma).

Panchakarma, discussed earlier on page 174–175, is a treatment program to balance the *doshas* and *gunas* and is the most important form of internal cleansing in Ayurveda. *Panchakarma* is also used to treat all types of depression and mental disorders. In the case of a particular type of depression based on a specific *dosha* imbalance, the herbal medications used in the *panchakarma* may be modified. Specific portions of the *panchakarma* may also be emphasized to address a *dosha* imbalance. For example, vomiting therapy is useful for *kapha* imbalance, purgation for *pitta* imbalance, and medicated enemas for *vata*-type conditions, including depression.

Rejuvenation (Rasayana).

Following *panchakarma*, a program of rejuvenation, or *rasayana*, tailored to the individual's specific form of depression is established to help tonify the body and build general health. *Chyavanprash* and *amrita bindu* are two excellent rejuvenating agents for building general health, the health of the nervous system and dealing with stress-related fatigue. These *rasayanas* are used as adaptogens, or substances that increase the body's resistance to stress. *Chyavanprash,* a well-known tonic that helps to calm and strengthen the mind, is a compound consisting primarily of *amala*, a highly potent source of vitamin C, and other vitamins and minerals. *Amrita bindu* is an herbal food supplement that functions both as a tonic and an antioxidant and is very beneficial for stress management and healthy aging.

In Ayurvedic medicine certain types of *rasayanas* are used for specific *dosha* imbalances, during certain seasons and for specific climates. For example, *vata* types can benefit from garlic and *shilajit rasayanas*, *pitta* types from turmeric *rasayanas*, and *kapha* types from *bhallatak rasayanas*.

Medicinal Substances (Draya Guna).

The Ayurvedic science of medicinal substances utilizes a vast *materia medica* of herbs, minerals (such as pearl, coral, and calcium), and animal products. This science also provides methods for identifying the compound processes used for health promotion, disease prevention, and treatment of physical and mental disorders. Various branches include pharmacology, pharmaceutics, and therapeutics.

Pharmacological compounds and human bodies share basic similarities because they have the same five elements, but in different proportions. Since the imbalance of *doshas* originates from an imbalance of these elements, the ultimate goal is to bring balance by using medicinal compounds with the opposite effects. For example, if an individual is suffering from a *vata* imbalance, he could utilize anti-*vata* compounds containing garlic or *hing* (asafetida).

Certain herbs have the potential to pacify, purify, aggravate, or maintain optimal health of the *doshas*, such as *vata*-aggravating, *vata*-reducing, or *pitta*- and *kapha*-aggravating and reducing. The herbs are divided into fifty groups based upon their therapeutic actions, such as vitalizing agents, heart tonics, and pain relievers. Some of the primary herbs in treating depression and mental illness include:

Ashwagandha (Withania somnifera). Also known as Indian ginseng, this herb is an adaptogen and an agent for health promotion. It is particularly useful for general weakness, exhaustion, and stress-induced fatigue, symptoms that often accompany depression. Various alkaloids from *ashwagandha* act to stimulate the immune system. *Ashwagandha* is useful in *vata* and *kapha* forms of depression.

Brahmi (Bacopa monniera). Used as a "brain tonic" and a potent antioxidant, *brahmi* is the main rejuvenating herb used for the nerves and brain cells. It has been shown to increase intelligence, mental clarity, memory, and longevity. *Brahmi* is highly valued in treating two symptoms that often accompany depression: anxiety and insomnia. It can be helpful in *vata* depression.

Gotu kola *(Centella asiatica)*. This herb has been shown to have positive effects on enhancing memory, which is often adversely affected in certain cases of depression. Gotu kola can be particularly helpful in cases of *vata* or *pitta* depression.

Rauwolfia *(Rauwolfia serpentina)*. This herb is the source of the anti-hypertensive and tranquilizing drug called reserpine. In India this herb is used in combination to treat various psychiatric illnesses such as anxiety, paranoid schizophrenia, and psychosis. Since reserpine, the active ingredient of *rauwolfia*, can produce depression, extreme care must be given in prescribing the dosage of this herb, particularly for long-term use.

Medicated butters, which may be used for external massage or taken internally under supervision by an Ayurvedic practitioner, are also helpful in treating different types of depression. Asafetida-medicated butter is useful in *pitta* depression, garlic-medicated butter in *vata* depression, and aged butter in *kapha* depression.

Mental Hygiene and Spiritual Healing (*Satvajaya*)

A final element of Ayurvedic treatment is *satvajaya*, or practices that release stress, emotional disturbances, and negative habits of thinking in order to help the mind reach a higher level of mental and spiritual functioning. These practices include meditation, yoga, *mantra* (use of sound to change vibratory patterns in the mind), *yantra* (use of geometric figures as a focus of attention), and *tantra*, the practice of directing life-energy in the body. The practice of yoga is described in "Yoga and Mental Health" beginning on page 186. That section gives instructions for alternate nostril breathing and meditation.)

Satvajaya also utilizes a specific form of psychotherapy to normalize the mind, intelligence, and memory. This technique involves applying a contradictory or opposite technique, such as giving psychological assurance to an individual who is suffering from anxiety and delirium over an external cause, like death or loss. For *vata* depression, reassurance and psychological counseling are used to deal with the predisposing factors such as mental trauma and anxiety-promoting issues. For cases of *pitta* depression, soothing and relaxing psychological counseling as well as adequate rest and relaxation are used to address the factors responsible for anger and excessive desire. For *kapha* depression, soothing, affectionate, and pleasure-provoking psychological counseling is very helpful.

Nonmedicinal Treatment to Counter Extraterrestrial Cause (*Daivavyapashraya*)

If the cause of depression is primarily due to astrological influence, the use of astrology, based on the rising sign, position of stars, and the combination of stars, particularly Saturn and Mars, may be helpful in Ayurvedic treatment. The use of precious gemstones, mantras, and worship, such as visiting holy places or engaging in philanthropic and spiritual activities, can help to ameliorate astrological problems. For example, *vata* imbalance can be caused by the influence of the planet Saturn, *pitta* imbalance by Mars, and *kapha* imbalance by Jupiter. The gemstone blue sapphire is useful in balancing the effects of Saturn, coral for balancing the influence of Mars, and yellow sapphire for the influence of Jupiter. There are also several specific mantras and *tantra* practices (based on the union of polar energies) to help an individual recover from mental and physical disorders caused by extraterrestrial influence.

A CASE OF *VATA* DEPRESSION

As described earlier, Ayurveda has different categories of depression based on the balance of *doshas* and *gunas* and an individual's constitutional and psychospiritual profile. A person with *vata* constitution is more likely to develop *vata* depression. The following case illustrates a *vata* type of depression.

A thirty-three-year-old college student came to me complaining of anxiety and depression. Upon examination it was determined that he had a typical *vata* constitution and personality. He was tall, with dark complexion and dry skin. He was very intense, talked continuously, and was almost delirious at times. His pulse diagnosis confirmed an increased *vata* humor. I learned that he had started drinking alcohol excessively about five months before and was eating predominantly dry foods, including potato chips. He also began engaging in excessive sexual activities and was suffering from loss of sleep.

I started the patient on a comprehensive treatment program. He was given an anti-*vata* diet, instructed to avoid alcohol and to engage in an exercise, rest, and relaxation regime. He was taught *pranayama* (yogic breathing exercises), meditation, and specific yoga *asanas* (physical exercises).

He then was started on a palliation program for *vata* depression, receiving anti-*vata* herbal preparations of asafetida and garlic. He also received *ashwagandha rasayana* twice daily, as well as a twice-weekly psychotherapy or *satvajaya* therapy for *vata* depression.

After six weeks of treatment the patient felt better. At that time he also underwent a *panchakarma* treatment preceded by *snehan* (oleation) oil massage. After three months the patient improved significantly and by that time was only taking *rasayana* while strictly following the anti-*vata* diet, along with the rest and relaxation program. As his condition got better, he was able to focus on his studies, and his grades improved.

A CASE OF PITTA DEPRESSION

A forty-five-year-old male executive of a managed care company came to see me complaining of emotional instability and mood swings. He showed strong signs of aggressive behavior and had a *pitta* personality or constitutional profile. He had been under intense pressure to maintain and increase his quota at work, and there was discussion of a possible merger of his company with another managed care entity. At that time he had been eating out at mostly Asian restaurants with very hot and spicy foods and was drinking a lot of alcohol. His mood swings and aggressive behavior seemed to get worse during hot weather. His sleep became erratic, and he continued to be irritable and angry, with increased verbal output and agitated body movements, particularly in his arms and legs. He later developed homicidal and suicidal thoughts.

The examination showed a classical *pitta* psychophysiological profile and his pulse diagnosis showed a strong *pitta* pulse. The patient agreed to use Ayurvedic management of his condition and started on an anti-*pitta* diet, i.e., cold drinks, etc., and was instructed to stop or decrease the intake of alcohol. He was taught yoga, *pranayama*, *asanas*, and rest and relaxation techniques.

He was started on a specific *pitta* palliation program and received *ashwagandha rasayana* and turmeric preparations to counter increased *pitta dosha*. He received *satvajaya* therapy for *pitta* depression. He also underwent *panchakarma* with anti-*pitta* herbal massage.

After two months the patient improved significantly and was able to stay with and succeed in his company. He stopped drinking alcohol, stayed on an anti-*pitta* diet, and continued to practice yoga and relaxation.

A CASE OF *KAPHA* DEPRESSION

A sixty-year-old public servant who had a long history of being emotionally balanced and easygoing came to see me complaining of depression. There had been some downsizing in his government agency, and his wife had been recently diagnosed with breast cancer. He started eating more and gained twenty pounds in one month. He noticed some erratic behavior, a decrease in his verbal expression, and slowed movements of the body, particularly in his arms and legs. He admitted that he had had thoughts of ending his life. He tried to dissociate from his friends and became a "couch potato." He was brought in by his son for evaluation.

On examination the patient showed a classical psychophysiological *kapha* profile. His pulse showed increased *kapha* humor. The patient began an anti-*kapha* diet using astringent and bitter compounds. He began using *triphala rasayana* and was given *trikatu* (black pepper, long pepper). He was advised to exercise, practice relaxation, and avoid excessive sleeping. He was taught yoga *asanas* (exercises) and *pranayama* (breathing exercises).

He was started on palliation treatment and anti-*kapha* herbal preparation *ashwagandha rasayana*. He was provided with *satvajaya* therapy specific for *kapha* depression. He was also put on *panchkarma*, using specific anti-*kapha* herbal compounds, such as ginger, honey, and black pepper. The patient was also given a specific mantra and was asked to wear a yellow sapphire ring.

Each time the patient came back, he showed signs of improvement, and after six months under this health regimen, he said he was returning to his old self again. His social interactions improved, and he was able to maintain his job. At the same time, his wife's cancer went into remission, with no reoccurrence to date. He was advised to keep up an anti-*kapha* diet, yoga, and an exercise program on an ongoing basis.

YOGA AND MENTAL HEALTH

Yoga, practiced in India for thousands of years, is a discipline that focuses on the body's musculature posture, breathing mechanisms, and consciousness. The goal of yoga is attainment of physical, mental, and spiritual well-being through mastery of the body and mind and is achieved through exercise, holding of postures, proper breathing, and meditation. The major emphasis in yoga practice has been upon healthy living, but it has been used extensively for the treatment of many physical, mental, and spiritual illnesses.

Yoga is by far the best known and most popular meditative exercise regimen. It is estimated that over six million Americans currently practice yoga, and it has become a regular activity and way of life among many, including celebrities, business entrepreneurs, and academicians. More importantly, for the last forty years, the medical value of yoga has been recognized in the Western world. Thousands of studies have been done in India and in the West to explore the scientific basis and validity of yoga in health promotion, disease prevention, and treatment of various illnesses. The studies have shown that specific yogic practices can improve one's physiological, psychological, and spiritual well-being.

The Eight Limbs of Raja Yoga

Raja yoga (the eight-limbed yoga) is the classical and most comprehensive form of yoga, first recorded in the *Yoga Sutras* by the ancient Indian sage Patanjali. It is the science of physical and mental control, and literally means "royal yoga." The first five limbs of raja yoga are *yama* (avoidance of unethical societal and moral behavior); *niyama* (observance of societal, ethical, and moral rules); *asanas* (physical exercises and postures); *pranayama* (breathing exercises); and *pratyahara* (minimizing one's needs). These five limbs lay the necessary foundation for the final three—*dharana, dhyana,* and *samadhi*—which are involved with the stages of meditation: concentration, contemplation, and deep contemplation.

The *Yoga Sutras* describe eighty-four *asanas,* or basic physical postures, which when practiced with regularity and discipline can strengthen the limbs, nerves, circulation, and organs, bringing a harmony and energetic balance to the entire body.

Pranayama comes from the word *prana,* which has the literal meaning of "life-energy," and the word *ayam,* meaning "controlling" or "regulating." *Pranayama,* therefore, is controlling life-energy through the breath. A basic principle of yoga is that when the breath, or *prana,* is steady, the mind will be steady and when the mind is steady, the *prana* will be steady. *Pranayama* is a necessary step prior to successful meditation and mind/body control, and essential to meditative exercise. For an individual suffering from depression, *pranayama* can be a valuable tool for helping to generate and balance energy.

Exercise: Alternate Nostril Breathing

Pranayama, or breathing exercises, can provide relaxation and relief of anxiety for those dealing with depression. Alternate nostril breathing helps to balance the flow of *prana,* or life-energy, throughout the body. It is an excellent prelude to meditation.

Sit comfortably in a chair with your feet firmly on the floor. Allow your spine to lengthen, the neck muscles to relax, and the head to balance effortlessly on the spine.

Observe your breathing. Is your breathing rapid and shallow, or is it relaxed? Is the in-breath longer than the out-breath, or are they about the same? Are you breathing from the chest or the diaphragm? Do you pause between breaths? Now, breathe from your diaphragm (just above the belly) in a relaxed fashion for three or four breaths. Do you notice a difference in your breathing pattern?

To begin the exercise, exhale completely through both nostrils and then close your left nostril with your right index finger. Breathing from the diaphragm in a relaxed manner, inhale to a count of ten through your right (open) nostril.

Now, close your right nostril with your right thumb, pause for a few moments, and open your left nostril, exhaling to a count of ten.

> *Pause a few seconds and then inhale to a count of ten through the left nostril, still keeping your right nostril closed with your right thumb.*
>
> *Close the left nostril with your right index finger, pause a few seconds, remove your thumb from your right nostril, and exhale to a count of ten.*
>
> *This constitutes one round of alternate nostril breathing. Continue for three full rounds, always maintaining an equal rate of inhalation and exhalation.*
>
> After you are comfortable with this exercise, you can extend the period of breath retention between each inhalation and exhalation from a few seconds to ten seconds, and then to twenty or thirty seconds. The length of inhalation and exhalation can increase with practice. The keys to achieving full benefit from this exercise are breathing from the diaphragm in a relaxed manner and maintaining an equal rate of inhalation and exhalation as well as a longer rate of breath retention. The ability to breathe in a regulated manner and to retain the breath between inhalation and exhalation has a powerful effect on the body, mind, emotions, and one's level of vitality. This practice provides a calming, energizing, and healing effect on the mind and body.
>
> This exercise can be practiced once or twice daily, in the morning and evening.

There are various types of *pranayama*, based upon techniques that focus the flow of breath through one nostril or both nostrils. Proper abdominal breathing in these practices is slow and deep, and involves the diaphragmatic muscles. There are three parts of *pranayama*: inhalation (*poorak*), retention (*kumbhak*), and exhalation (*rechak*). These processes are repeated multiple times. As this practice of *pranayama* gradually increases the retention of breath, the *prana*, or life-energy, is enhanced.

Pratyahara, the fifth limb of raja yoga, involves a gradual minimizing of one's needs through control of the mind, in preparation for the various stages of concentration and meditation.

Dharana (concentration), *dhyana* (contemplation or meditation), and *samadhi* (deep contemplation), are the final three limbs of this yoga—aspects of mind control. *Dharana* is accomplished by sitting in a comfortable posture in a quiet place, closing the eyes, and beginning the practice of concentration. This can be done through the internal repetition of a *mantra*, focusing the mind on an inner object such as a picture or geometric form, or gazing externally at the tip of your nose, until you are able to focus. One must try to concentrate by bringing the mind on the desired object. Through the practice of concentration one can progress toward meditation.

The second stage of mind control is *dhyana*, which means meditation or contemplation. In this stage one increases concentration for longer periods of time by constant practice. Meditation is, in fact, a state of continuous concentration and can have an external or internal focus. Meditation is used to still the endless modifications of the mind in order to achieve a state of peace. When the mind is completely focused, there is no sense of time or space. According to the philosophy of yoga, time is nothing but a modification of the mind—time, space, causation, and all other external experiences are creations of the mind.

The ultimate goal of meditation is to concentrate and calm the mind in order to transcend it and rest in an awareness of the inner Self or the spiritual principle in all beings. By turning the mind's concentration inward upon the Self, the experience of concentration expands and deepens. If the various stages of meditation are sincerely and methodically practiced, it can eventually lead to *samadhi*, in which a state of bliss and union are achieved with the Self. Those who achieve this superconscious state all the time are called Self-realized beings, or mystics.

 A Simple Meditation Exercise

Meditation is a simple and natural process that can enhance our ability to deal with the stresses of daily life and help us achieve a heightened sense of well-being and inner peace. As we meditate we learn to calm the restless mind and senses and gain access to a deeper source of well-being, peace, and vitality within ourselves. The simplest and most direct approach to meditation is through observing the breath. When the breath is calm the mind is calm, and when the breath is restless and uneven, the mind is restless. The following instructions demonstrate this principle.

• Find a quiet place where you will be undisturbed for twenty minutes. There should be no distractions or interruptions. This is time for yourself.
• Sit in a comfortable, upright position, and allow your spine to lengthen. You can sit cross-legged on the floor, on a cushion, or in a chair. If you are sitting in a chair, allow your feet to rest flat on the floor. Rest your hands on your knees or your lap.
• Close your eyes and focus on your breath. Observe the rhythm of your breathing—the breath coming in and the breath going out.

- As you focus on your breathing, feel the calming effect on your body. Note that as the breath becomes more balanced and peaceful, the mind and senses become very peaceful.
- If memories, thoughts, and feelings arise, simply observe them and let them pass away naturally.
- If you need help in staying focused on the breath, you can take the assistance of a word or phrase that is spiritually meaningful to you. Silently repeat the word or phrase once on the in-breath and once on the out-breath. This will help you remain focused and become more and more relaxed and aware.

   One effective phrase is the Sanskrit word *So'ham*. *So'ham* is said to be the natural sound that accompanies each cycle of breathing, every day of our lives. Repeat *"So"* on the in-breath, and *"ham"* on the out-breath. Another variation is to simply repeat *"Om"* (aum) on the in-breath and out-breath.
- By focusing your awareness on the natural rhythm of the in-breath and the out-breath, you can begin to experience periods of inner stillness and repose.

Try meditating once a day for twenty minutes. Over time you may want to increase the length up to one hour. If possible meditate in the same place every day, and you will find it easier and easier to meditate. You may want to set up a small room or space specifically for the practice of meditation.

BENEFITS OF YOGA FOR DEPRESSION AND IMPROVED MENTAL HEALTH

The greatest contribution of yoga is in the area of mind control. Quieting the mind by various yogic techniques causes a series of positive outcomes, including increased concentration and improved memory. In addition, mind control leads to positive psychophysiological interactions between the body, mind, and emotions through the neural, endocrine, and immune systems as documented in the medical discipline of psychoneuroimmunology.

The practice of yoga has been shown to decrease the incidence and prevalence of chronic diseases, such as anxiety, depression, cardiovascular disorders, chronic fatigue syndrome, cancer, arthritis, and asthma. In one important study hatha yoga was shown to improve physiological and psychological parameters in healthy women, including a decrease in heart rate and a higher score in life satisfaction.[1] The women demonstrated a decline in excitability, aggressiveness, and psychosomatic complaints. They were better able to cope with stress and displayed an elevation of mood.

Meditation and breathing exercises have been shown to increase physical endurance, fitness, mental well-being, and the quality of life. Regulation of the breath in various *pranayama* exercises have a calming effect on the body and mind and can be helpful to one who is in an agitated and depressed state. *Asanas*, or yoga postures, helpful in alleviating depression, insomnia, and anxiety include the sun salutation (*suryanamaskar*), cobra (*bhujangasana*), lotus (*padmasana*), the "corpse" or resting position (*savasana*), and the headstand (*sirshasana*).

Stress Management.

A regular yoga practitioner conditions the mind so that the body does not react so strongly to stressful stimuli. The controlled mind is better able to discriminate between various psychophysiological phenomena (e.g., stress, anxiety, depression, and phobias), and is therefore less prone to suffer from stress or emotion-related disorders.

Yoga practice has been shown to lead to the reduction of occupational stress as well as societal or community-based stress in numerous studies over the past thirty years.[2] The regular practice of yoga also improves respiratory endurance, muscle strength, and overall physical fitness. The changes in the autonomic nervous system that occur with meditation and yoga enable one to better handle stress.

Cognitive/Psychological Effects.

Yoga practice demonstrates improvement in various psychological parameters including intelligence, memory, and mood.[3] The headstand, for example, is particularly helpful for enhancing memory, in part due to the increased blood flow to the brain.[4] While practicing yogic exercises such as stretching, breathing, and meditation, one tends to feel more relaxed and less stressed.

Effects on Nervous System.

Cortical activities measured by EEG improve with an increase of alpha waves. The practice of yoga and meditation has been shown to increase production of alpha waves in the brain. Meditation has also been shown to bring positive changes in autonomic activity (i.e., pulse rate, breathing, and improvement in intelligence).[5]

Mental Illness and Psychiatric Disorders.

Yoga has been used in various psychiatric disorders including anxiety, depression, bipolar syndrome, and obsessive-compulsive disorders.[6] Meditation helps to reduce anxiety levels, while the practice of yoga has significantly improved mood in patients with post–traumatic stress syndrome.

LOOKING TO THE FUTURE

Ayurveda, like other forms of traditional medicine, is effective and humane because it examines and treats the whole person. For thousands of years it has explored and refined its methods of healing and developed into a safe and reliable science with clinically and scientifically measured results. Its protocols for addressing illness and disease, including mental health and depression, are fairly easy to adapt into our Western lifestyle and by today's standards is economical and cost-effective with minimal side effects. As Ayurveda and yoga become more available to and recognized by Western culture, their methods of bringing health and healing will become more and more integrated into modern medicine. Ayurveda will then take its place as a truly global health tradition.

Qigong, Chinese Medicine, and Depression

✌

Roger C. Hirsh, O.M.D., L.Ac., B.Ac. (UK), Dipl.Ac.

(NCCA)

Thus, without expectation, one will always perceive the subtlety;
Ever with expectation one will always perceive the boundaries.
—*Lao-tzu, Tao Te Ching*

The nature of life demands that we be involved in a process of gathering and expending energy from birth to death. When we expend too much energy or have not acquired enough, imbalance and illness result, including depression. Qigong is an ancient Chinese energy training system based on movement and breath that enhances and refines human energy while replenishing the energies lost in the process of living. It offers a way for individuals to gain mastery over their own destiny. By practicing Qigong one actively chooses to cultivate and collect certain energies from nature and the universe. For centuries Asian peoples have been able to confront the stress and challenges of their everyday lives through the practice of Qigong, and experience the extraordinary fruits of inner peace and well-being.

Qigong is a health care approach and exercise system used to balance the body and promote longevity. In order to live a long and peaceful life, according to the ancient Chinese health classic *Nei Jing Su Wen* (Classic of Internal Medicine, 2500 B.C.), we are urged to reconnect ourselves with our roots, or the *Tao* (*Dao*). This book also suggests that because we have severed these roots, our life span is less than a hundred years. The Chinese people have a 5,000-year history of addressing health issues with preventative medicine that enriches and lengthens life. It is from this fertile heritage that Qigong originates.

According to ancient Chinese medical classics, the universe is principally made up of energy (*Qi*) and the laws that govern it. Qigong (*Qi Kung*) is the art and science of gathering, circulating, and storing the *Qi* that is readily available from nature and the universe. The universe is said to arise from the *Tao*, which means "the way." From a philosophical point of view the *Tao* is considered to be the mysterious unknown at the root of all things, of which nothing can be said. The Chinese believe that it is from the *Tao* that an archetypal paradigm unfolds composed of the concepts of *Yin* (darkness) and *Yang* (brightness), the five phases of transformation (five elements), and a myriad of things that manifest and move through space and time. The *Tao* is expressed by all life through the process of living. We, as thinking or "sentient" beings, experience the *Tao* by interacting with each other, nature, and ultimately spirit.

Qigong is breath and energy work. *Qi* (*Chi*) means energy. *Gong* means training, work, or cultivation. In Qigong we are gathering energy and cultivating our spirit, thereby eliminating adverse reactions to stress that can cause depression and other illnesses. Qigong energy training's techniques involve movements, breathing, and visualizations. These are done while standing, sitting, moving, and even lying down, thus making Qigong available to those people who are bedridden or convalescing from serious illnesses.

In order to understand Qigong, one must first understand *Qi*. It is ever present in nature and it is the foundation of all things. When something is devoid of *Qi*, it is considered to be dead. In the practice of Qigong there is a reciprocity between the body and mind. It is through this relationship that one has the opportunity to experience the subtle energies that permeate the structures of the body such as the blood vessels, nerves, and lymphatic vessels. As one advances in Qigong training, one may begin to experience subtle energies such as the perception of a thought, the sound of a trickling high mountain stream, or the smell of a fragrance on a summer evening. *Qi,* when transformed into speech, can be lightning quick and piercing such as when you are calling out for someone in a crowd.

THE THREE MAIN CATEGORIES OF QIGONG

Qigong is a branch of Traditional Chinese Medicine (TCM) that has ancient religious and shamanic roots. In the Chinese system of Qigong exercises there are over a thousand complete movement systems within three main categories—spiritual, martial arts, and medical Qigong. The various styles of Qigong accommodate the many different kinds of body and psychological types. For example, *Tai Chi Chuan*, a moving Qigong exercise whose lineage traces back to the fifteenth century, traditionally has five main styles and is popular throughout China as the national health exercise. Each style has a different sequence of movements, enabling the individual to communicate with nature in a distinct manner. You may have observed people doing these slow, dancelike movements in a park in the morning.

There are many languages that describe our connection and communication with nature. Scientists, with the languages of mathematics, physics, and chemistry, observe and describe the nature of Qigong in a different way from one who is actually practicing Qigong out on a windy bluff overlooking the ocean. It is the experience of one's own self within nature that makes Qigong what it is, a unique and powerful life-giving experience that takes one beyond the normally understood limits of the body and mind.

Spiritual Qigong (Taoist)

Spiritual Qigong represents the highest level of Qigong, as it addresses the whole person—the spiritual, mental/emotional, and physical aspects of our being. It is from the spiritual Qigong practices that all other categories of this work emanate. These practices help the individual practitioner develop a deep connection with the divine elements of the universe and nature. Spiritual Qigong is rarely taught to Westerners and those who are not Taoist initiates because it is considered to be the more esoterically based. The practical ways of ancient Chinese living combine both the spiritual and scientific perspectives to align and create an understanding of one's own individual genetic heritage.

Martial Arts Qigong

The martial artists in ancient China were the learned scholars, priests, and warriors. Today there are many martial art systems, styles, and schools that still exist throughout Asia. These styles developed from a keen observation of nature, and the way creatures, forces, and elements interact. Martial arts systems and styles were frequently patterned after a battle between great generals or predatory animals, with reenactments around a campfire showing the moves of victory. The practice of Qigong by martial artists is also concerned with the battles that conquer the inner demons and dragons.

The varied martial arts styles of Qigong are specific to the individual systems that they are used to enhance. A system of *Lohan* Qigong may be used by Chinese monks (*lohan*) to give power and dynamic expression to systems such as *Shaolin* temple boxing. Tai Chi also has a specific Qigong system called *Tai Chi Nei Kung* that brings out awesome powers from within the practitioner. These powers allow one to summon at will the kind of energy necessary to perform monumental feats like lifting a car off someone who is trapped underneath it.

Medical Qigong

Most of the Qigong practice in America is in the category of medical Qigong that is similar to classic hatha yoga, with the synchronization of breath, physical posture, and psychological attitude. Medical Qigong involves physical exercises coordinated with breathing practices and sometimes imagery. The purpose of this energy work is to resolve specific organ, meridian, and channel imbalances that may be causing or contributing to an illness. This type of Qigong is excellent for those individuals who are committed to a personal health program. It is especially good for those who are suffering from some form of depression, as it can generate the physical and emotional energy to shift one's state from stagnation to movement and balance.

HOW CHINESE MEDICINE VIEWS DEPRESSION

In Chinese Medicine there is a strong recognition of the role of the emotions in health and illness. When the body and mind move in harmony, positive emotions prevail. Depression, for example, is considered an ancient condition suffered by humankind that is often due to a stagnation of emotional *Qi* within an individual's internal organs. The Chinese medical classic, the *Nei Jing,* mentioned earlier, classifies seven emotions that have a direct effect on the body: foolhardiness, anger, sadness, grief, brooding, fear, and fright. When an emotion has been either excessive or neglected over a long period of time or suddenly erupts with great expression, the internal organs are affected and can cause an imbalance or ill health. Conversely, an internal physiological organ disharmony may result in imbalanced emotional states.

The correspondences between the emotions and all the organs are illustrated in the following chart.

Element	Yin Organ	Yang Organ	Negative Emotions	Positive Emotions
Fire	Heart	Small intestine	Foolhardiness	Joy
Earth	Spleen/pancreas	Stomach	Brooding	Thoughtfulness
Metal	Lungs	Large intestine	Sadness, grief	Inspiration
Water	Kidneys	Bladder	Fear, fright	Courage
Wood	Liver	Gall bladder	Anger	Positive assertion

The organs, in turn, are associated with meridians or channels through which the *Qi* circulates throughout the body. When *Qi* is blocked or deficient within a meridian, or when there is an excess within an organ or meridian, some form of imbalance results. In the same way, an excess or lack of specific emotions can lead to a change in the physical energy of an organ or meridian. In the case of depression there may be a number of interrelated changes within the organs and meridians.

According to Chinese Medicine, each of us expresses and manages our "depression" differently. The stagnated feelings that lead to depression can lodge deep within the organs or just float on the surface. In one person, depression may manifest on the surface with the symptoms of eczema while in another there may be a deep, churning emotional tide that bursts out occasionally in a torrent of anger or uncontrollable fits of tears or laughter. In some cases, the depression may be rooted so deeply that the only way to heal the individual is to employ a multidisciplinary program. This program may incorporate dietary changes, herbal remedies, breathing exercises, a healing system such as acupuncture, along with counseling and when necessary, conventional Western medication. The deepest healing occurs, however, when the individual can support these therapies and manifest the cure from within through his or her own internal medicine factory. The practice of Qigong is an activator of this internal medicine.

Qigong is a self-healing technique that breaks down energy blocks in the body by initiating the relaxation response. This is the physiological mechanism that triggers the body to release endorphins and become relaxed. Endorphins are chemical substances released within the brain when the experience of pleasure is present. This basic type of Qigong work is highly recommended by practitioners of Oriental healing arts to their patients before they embark on more strenuous martial arts and *Qi*-generating exercises, such as *Tai Chi*. Experienced practitioners of Qigong know how to generate the relaxation response in specific muscle groups in order to provide appropriate "nutrition" for the needy organ or meridian. If the *Qi* is flowing along the meridian pathway smoothly, the internal organ connected with that pathway receives the proper nutrition of vital energy and blood.

According to Chinese Medicine, the emotional and mental state is directly affected by the body's organic disharmony or when the *Yin* organs (see chart) are not functioning properly. For instance, if the "kidney" (renal-adrenal) is not functioning properly, depression may result in the form of a lack of self-esteem and courage with perhaps feelings of fear. If the kidney function is not balanced on an energetic level, there may be an underlying stress response, which after many months may deepen into a deep-seated anger. This means that the kidney depression from stress has affected the liver, whose corresponding negative emotion is anger.

Initially, kidney meridian imbalances may not be noticeably significant, as modern living is frequently putting us into a fright-or-flight adrenal response state. In the short term, this response state may be protective so that we are not injured by a careless driver, for example. Minor stresses over several years, however, can greatly affect the internal *Yin* organs by draining energy from their deep reserves and eventually creating disease accompanied by the corresponding forms of depression.

A sign that the kidney organ/meridian may be out of balance can be as subtle as having to get up to urinate in the middle of the night or awakening in the morning with sore feet and back pain. These symptoms can be alleviated with the correct treatment, but if the stress is great enough, the symptoms may persist and worsen. The ear-rubbing exercises "Massaging the Ears" and "Flapping the Ears" on pages 202–204 are beneficial for both physical symptoms and depression stemming from kidney imbalance.

The kidney and bladder organs/meridians interrelate with each other like a husband and wife. If there is an "argument" and a loss of control, then one or both can be challenged. Because the bladder meridian travels over the muscles next to the spine, it affects the whole central nervous system. When a person is depressed, the whole body is affected and needs treatment. Stretching these muscles helps to increase the circulation to the organs themselves, thereby balancing the husband and wife: bladder and kidney.

A great deal of depression among women is due to imbalances in the liver and kidney organs/meridians. These imbalances can lead to stagnation of blood in the pelvic cavity, which can adversely affect the menstrual cycle and result in symptoms of PMS and menopause as well as impairing a woman's ability to achieve an orgasm. Chinese herbal medicines to support the kidney and stimulate the stagnated liver energy can strengthen and balance the system of a woman suffering from these conditions. Over one-quarter of the women in the world for the last two thousand years have been taking Chinese herbal medicines and performing medical types of Qigong exercises for both the prevention and treatment of feminine disorders and imbalances. These exercises, remedies, and practices are visibly prevalent in Asian culture today.

Men may also suffer from depression due to male impotence, or the inability to achieve or maintain an erection and perform sexually. This condition is another symptom or manifestation of a deficient kidney organ/meridian. Increasing the energy or *Qi* in the kidney meridian can be accomplished by tonifying the reproductive system with the proper Qigong exercises and herbs. There is a complex system of postures and positions in Qigong and specific Chinese medicines to remedy this condition; these exercises, however, are rarely taught in the West because of the sensitivity of the American public to sexual issues and the esoteric nature of the subject matter. A few Oriental medical practitioners, however, can prescribe herbal programs that are very helpful.

In my practice I have observed many men who are suffering from depression due to a low sperm count and feelings of inadequacy because they are unable to father a child. This is frequently due to both hereditary and postnatal kidney imbalances. I have also observed these feelings of inadequacy and low self-esteem spilling over into their work life. These men sometimes find it difficult to complete important tasks or achieve their goals, such as meeting their sales quota or finishing a new project proposal. As stress causes fight-or-flight symptomatology, the drain of kidney and adrenal energy is tremendous. This poor and inefficient utilization of creative mental energy depletes the body's ability to deal with deeper fears and depression results.

Depression may also be related to heart disease, with either a deficiency or an excess of *Qi* in the heart meridian. In Chinese Medicine the heart relates to joy, which aligns with the element of Fire and is also responsible for circulation of blood in the vascular system. When someone is depressed, joy is absent from his or her life, and poor circulation may result. The "Shaking the Hands" exercise on pages 204–206, the "Ancient Ho Ho Ho" exercise on pages 206–207, and the "Laughing Buddha" exercise on pages 208–209 all help to stimulate and balance the heart meridian.

Qigong has been hidden to the Western world because of the power of its practices and the lack of scientific equipment sensitive enough to measure and explain the phenomena that occur. It is currently being extensively researched in China, and much of this research focuses on the subtle *Qi* phenomenon. Government constraints, however, keep it away from all but a guarded few in the West.

One study at the Beijing College of Traditional Chinese Medicine quantified the amount of *Qi* emanating from a woman Qigong master who was using the *Qi* from her energy cultivation (Qigong training) to project a force out of her body for healing. The study substantiated that her *Qi* was strong enough in her internal organs to both promote or inhibit the growth of specific bacteria in a test tube.

Principles of Qigong Practice: The Attitude for a Qigong Session

1. When your spirit/mind is relaxed and not focused on immediate results, then your muscles and tendons relax and your Qi will flow.
2. When the mind is strong, the Qi is strong; when the mind is weak, the Qi is weak. Pay attention to what you are doing. If you get distracted, reel your mind back to the practice. Be sincere and committed to the moment and what you are doing.
3. Qigong is a process and a path more than a destination. Be patient. If you have been ill or depressed for a while, although this process can provide immediate and positive affects, it is not a quick fix. It is a day-to-day practice that builds up energy and creates harmony over the long term that is powerful and enduring.
4. Be grateful, but not attached to your results. They may just be sign-posts on the way.
5. Practice in a clean and quiet place. Outdoors is best. Doing the practice, however, is more important than making rules that keep you from taking action. If you are at the office, close the door and open the window. When you are at an advanced level, you should be able to have complete concentration while standing on a busy street corner.
6. Be committed and consistent by practicing daily. Don't be obsessive and overdo it. Attempting to run a marathon when you may not be able to go around the block can be injurious to your health.
7. Wear comfortable and loose clothing that prevents you from getting too hot or cold. If you are at work, loosen your belt so that your waist is not restricted, and remove your shoes if possible.
8. Decrease your food intake. To cultivate Qi it is better to practice on an empty stomach. If you are very hungry, eat a small amount or drink a cup of tea or warm water so that you are not distracted by hunger.

QIGONG EXERCISES FOR DEPRESSION: WARM-UP

The main objective of Qigong exercises is to circulate, cultivate, and store energy; so how does this affect depression? All of the organs in the body are concerned with maintaining a balance, or homeostasis. The process of doing Qigong is a process of moving turbid and toxic energy out of the body while attracting good energy into the body. When this is done, the pathogenic factors can be replaced with positive and vital energy. This clean energy can then shed light into the dark pathways grooved by depression. The following are a series of Qigong exercises for transforming stagnant and depressed energy into vibrant and moving *Qi* that generates and sustains life.

Introduction to Ear Exercises

Rubbing and stimulating the ears is an excellent starting point for the beginning Qigong practitioner. Chinese Medicine has demonstrated the connection between parts of the ear and parts of the body. Massaging the ears has proven to be a direct way of relieving stress and its effects on the different organs and systems in the body. In fact, the ears are considered the "flower" of the kidney, and massaging the ears is recommended for stress and depression stemming from energy blockage or deficiency related to the kidneys. It is recommended to do the ear massage exercises in the morning. Waiting for the water to get hot in the shower or boil on the stove may be just enough time to wake your body up with an ear massage.

Examination of the ear is an important part of the diagnosis in Traditional Chinese Medicine, as the size, shape, color, thickness, position on the head, and significant markings are key indications of health and pathology. Electrical current readings on specific acupoints on the ear can also provide a significant amount of information about the person and his or her state of health. For a depressed patient, an ear examination is an excellent place to begin diagnosis, as the cause of depression can sometimes be quickly recognized, as well as the most effective way to treat it.

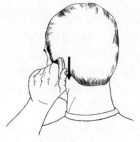

Massaging the Ears

Massaging the Ears

Pull your ears to stimulate and wake up the body and mind. It can be done first thing in the morning or on a study break. The kidney meridian, which reflexes in the ear, also "rules" the brain according to Chinese Medicine and is therefore useful in stimulating your ability to think. This exercise can also be done while sitting or lying down.

> *Pull your ears from top to bottom in a continuous motion (making sure to pull the earlobe) one hundred times to let your whole body know that it is time to wake up. Take your fingers as if you were going to pinch your ears and then pull down from top to bottom of the ears. It is not just rubbing but a kind of pinching and pulling action with the thumbs on the backs and the index fingers on the insides of the ears. When you realize that there are over 200 reflex points on the ear that correspond to the many systems and functions in the body, then you can begin to understand how the whole body can be affected and the benefits that can be gained by doing this simple exercise. When this ear massage is done with the correct intention, it is very relaxing, and when done for five minutes or more can be the equivalent to a full-body massage.*

By doing this exercise, you are not only warming up the body, but you are letting go of fears. If one is extremely depressed and cannot get out of bed, this ear exercise can be done while lying in bed. Several rounds of this may give one just that boost of energy to get out of bed and moving. If only this exercise is done, a lot can be accomplished.

Flapping the Ears

This exercise is a variation of the previous exercise and can be done more actively to stimulate the body. For the greatest benefit, however, it is recommended to do the ear massage and this exercise in sequence.

In addition to activating all of the inner organs, Flapping the Ears most specifically affects the triple warmer (the metabolism meridian) and gall bladder meridians. Energizing the triple warmer (TH) along with its coupled meridian, the gall bladder (GB), can help improve a person's ability to communicate with the world. This pair of meridians is considered the hinge between the inside world and the outside world. In stimulating this coupled meridian pair, the metabolism function in the body is activated. The triple warmer meridian governs the integration between the pelvic, abdominal, and thoracic cavities and will actually warm the body up or cool it down.

Flapping the Ears

Pretend you have huge ears like an elephant. Flap your ears with your palms, back and forth for about a minute or until your ears are feeling warm and tingling with energy. It is normal for the ears to feel a little sore or even hot after doing this exercise because you are not used to stimulating them in this way. After your ears get used to doing this exercise, you can work up to three minutes.

SHAKING THE HANDS

Another way to affect the energy of the whole body is by stimulating the hands. Dr. Tae Wu Yoo, O.M.D., a Korean master acupuncturist, recently discovered an ancient technique of medicine that relates to a very intricate system of hand reflexology. He uses magnets, needles, light, or heat to stimulate different points on the hands for the purpose of healing. It is a very effective and proven technique, and similar in principal to the ear reflexology system in the previous exercises.

There are a number of specific acupoints on the hands, wrists, and forearms that are stimulated by the "Shaking the Hands" exercise that can be useful in healing depression when it is connected to anger or caused by a lack of joy and peace of mind. Stimulating the acupoint called "Palace of Weariness" (*Lao Gong*) located near the center of the palm toward the base of the thumb is beneficial for one who is tired, angry, and unhappy. Another acupoint, sometimes called "Sexual Calm" (*Da Ling*) is located on the center of the wrist crease at the base of the palm of the hand. It helps calm a person who is depressed or frustrated about his or her sexuality. A third acupoint, called "Inner Gate" (*Nei Guan*), located a distance equal to the width of three fingers above the wrist crease, traditionally helps to elevate mood. This acupoint is a gate into your inner self and works on both physical and mental levels. The Chinese steel balls for rotating in your hands work on the same principle of stimulating the hand and forearm points: to calm the mind by first calming the spirit.

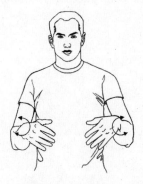

Shaking the Hands

In this exercise you vigorously shake your hands from the wrist in front of your chest for one to five minutes, or a time that is comfortable. When you shake your hands right out in front of your chest and heart region, you are beneficially affecting the body's circulation. You should smile as you perform this exercise, as this helps to balance the spirit (shen) within the heart.

According to Taoist medicine, or Taoist Qigong, this hand-shaking technique is associated with the natural element of Water and its fluid quality. Water corresponds with the ability to penetrate, quench, and soften, as well as to moisten and nourish. It rules the kidney organ/meridian. Because shaking the hands stimulates many acupoints on the front and the back of the hands, it is also invigorating for the entire body. In Chinese acupuncture, the forearm points are used to treat and remedy what we consider to be mental problems in the West, including depression.

THE ANCIENT HO HO HO

This practice is a standing exercise in which you are connecting with your heart energy. Heart energy emanates from the "Palace of Weariness" (*Lao Gong*) acupoint in the center of your palm. By doing this exercise you can connect with your ancestors via the navel, where you were attached to your mother. This simple hand placement, in which you connect with your ancestors, is spiritual Qigong.

The Ancient Ho Ho Ho

Your feet are spaced shoulder-width apart, knees slightly bent. Place your right hand over your navel. Place your other hand on your lower back, palm in, opposite your front hand. Your left hand will be over an acupuncture point between the third and fourth lumbar vertebrae that is the acupoint called "Gate of Life" (Ming-Men). In this placement, one hand connects you with your ancestors (navel), and the other hand with the gate of life in your body.

Now, begin a slow and gentle bounce, up and down, slightly bending at the knees. As you do this, chant "ho ho ho ho ho, ho ho ho ho ho," while exhaling slightly. Do this exercise from one to five minutes or as long as it is comfortable. This exercise will definitely make you smile, and it is good for the type of depression that is heart oriented, stemming from lack of joy. "Ho" is one of the sounds that tonifies the energy of the heart, both physically and spiritually. This exercise is believed to be one hundred times more effective than the same time spent jogging.

BRIGHTENING THE MIND

Once I drove by a bus stop and saw an older Chinese woman doing a particular Qigong exercise involving swinging the arms. I later learned that this exercise is used to "brighten the mind" because it strengthens all the pathways of the meridians that go to the head. It is also very good for the immune system and the lungs.

Brightening the Mind

This simple exercise does not require a lot of physical space. Stand with your feet together and your arms by your sides, palms facing backward. Swing the arms forward to a 45-degree angle and then backward past your legs, again to approximately a 45-degree angle. This is not a slow exercise, but one done vigorously, possibly fifty times a minute. In fact, it should feel as if you are pulling water from the front to the back of you, like in the crawl stroke in swimming. You don't want your hands to touch in the front or the back; you just want them to keep in that same "trough." Do this exercise from three to five minutes a day, or a length of time that is comfortable.

If you cough while doing this particular exercise, don't be alarmed. It means that toxins are being eliminated from the body. The lung meridian is the acupuncture channel that relates to our ability to handle worry and grief. It is the pathway that goes from the front of the shoulder joints along the inside of the arms, and down and out through the thumbs. The idea that the lungs have a relationship with how a person manages worry and grief is found in ancient Chinese medical literature dating back to the *Nei Jing*. Someone who worries a lot or is in a grieving process may have stooped shoulders and therefore can benefit from doing this exercise for ten minutes twice a day.

THE LAUGHING BUDDHA

You may be familiar with Norman Cousins's work with humor and laughter to reverse heart disease. In Qigong our work with laughter is also done to help the heart as well as uplift the spirit. The spontaneity of laughter, in Chinese Qigong, is said not only to open the bodily orifices but also to open the gate to a higher aspect of joy. It is because the heart is related to the emotion of joy that the heart itself vibrates with laughter and accelerates the movement of blood in the vascular system. If you stimulate the heart with laughter, you actually affect every cell in your body, because the blood passes through the heart pump and circulates throughout the whole body.

When you laugh, you take the spirit energy (*Shen*) that is resident in the heart and spread it throughout the body. Laughter can help rid the body of cellular toxicity, which normally occurs through the skin, breath, bowels, and bladder. One way to assist the body in detoxifying is to press a specific acupoint on the side of the thighs while laughing. This turns on an energetic switch that helps the body detoxify.

> *Let your hands naturally fall by your sides. Take your middle fingers and put them along the side of your thighs where the hands naturally fall and press this point. The name of this acupuncture point on the gall bladder meridian is "Wind Market," which means that you can de-stress the nervous system at this point. (See illustration on page 220 from "Raise and Fall on the Heels and Toes" for proper hand placement.) With your fingers on this acupoint on each thigh, start to laugh out loud. "Ha, ha, ha, ha, ha, ha, ha, ha, ha." Laugh until your kidney area hurts on the sides of your back that are protected by the ribs.*

The sides of the legs and body are traversed by the gall bladder meridian, which is psychologically reflected in a person's ability to make decisions. Physically there is a connection with the flow of *Qi* in the reproductive system as the pathway also traverses the pelvis. Because this is where the nervous system's toxins gather, women with PMS will feel considerable pain in this area of the body when massaged. A woman who has depression related to her gynecological and reproductive systems will benefit greatly from this exercise when acupressure massage is applied to this area outside the thigh.

The Laughing Buddha can become a significant form of personal psychotherapy. There are few systems of psychotherapy that you can practice on yourself. If you can laugh for five minutes a day, it will do a lot of good. This exercise makes it easier and easier to laugh and for longer periods of time, thereby multiplying its benefits.

GENERATING ENERGY FOR SELF-HEALING

After doing these Qigong exercises, your hands should be warm. Be sure to take advantage of this newly liberated energy by applying it to an energy-deficient or ailing part of your body. If your elbow hurts, put your hand over your elbow. If you have a knee that is sore, you can hold your knee. You can rub your lower back to stimulate your kidneys. If you have a digestion problem, you can rub your gut. If your thyroid is not functioning properly, you can rub the front of your neck. This is self-healing. If you are interested in cosmetic rejuvenation and want to stay beautiful and young, according to an old Taoist doctors' secret, you can rub your hands on your face. After one hundred days, you will notice a difference, and after a thousand days your friends will say that you look as if you have stopped aging.

 Qigong Exercises for Depression: Warm-Up

> You can begin your Qigong practice with a ten- to twenty-minute daily session, doing some or all of these exercises. The warm-ups, however, can be practiced on their own. If you have a minute here or there, do a few of them. It is important that the exercises be practiced consistently on a daily basis in order to experience the results. Practicing for an hour once a week will not bring the same results.
>
> Once you are comfortable doing these exercises on a daily basis, you can use them as a warm-up for the "Eight Silken Brocades," a set of Qigong exercises.
>
> Massaging the Ears
> Flapping the Ears
> Shaking the Hands
> The Ancient Ho Ho Ho
> Brightening the Mind
> The Laughing Buddha
> Generating Energy for Self-Healing

It must be noted that these exercises and those to follow cannot stand on their own as a cure-all for illness, aging, and imbalance. The effectiveness in addressing any problem is relative to the complex history, lifestyle, habits, and belief systems of an individual. Seeking a proper teacher or guide can be the key to success or failure.

THE EIGHT SILKEN BROCADES

The Eight Silken Brocades is a set of ancient exercises that help stimulate and tonify the biomechanical system of the body. They have been used for many hundreds of years to help relieve stress and maintain youthfulness. These movements provide a subtle yet powerful way of gently stretching and flexing the body in order to open the aerobic channel that stimulates the circulation of blood. Qigong is an "isotonic," or moving isometric, exercise in which the mind provides a kind of static resistance, allowing a balance to occur through a unification of thought and action.

The Eight Silken Brocades, in combination with the warm-up exercises ("Qigong Exercises for Depression: Warm-Up"), takes about twenty to thirty minutes a day. It has been found that even this short amount of exercise is invaluable in the rehabilitation of those who are depressed and looking for simple, self-ennobling ways to balance and strengthen the body. Combating depression is a daily choice for many, in the same way others combat an addiction. Attending group Qigong sessions can help provide the support and momentum needed for a daily practice.

Although the Eight Silken Brocades set of exercises goes back in Chinese history, the proof of its efficacy lies within the practice of the techniques and forms. The Chinese believe that in order to build a foundation for any exercise practice one has to be consistent for at least one hundred days. This is difficult for most Westerners, as discipline seems to have disappeared with the advent of television and modern living. For one who is depressed, the energy needed to even start an exercise program may be almost insurmountable. It is advisable to start with one or a few exercises, like the warm-ups, and build up to these eight exercises. It is also recommended to find a buddy to practice with and eventually a class if one is available. These exercises are simple and can be done anywhere, but preferably outside in fresh air, where there is good *Qi* available.

Warm-Up

Stand with legs slightly wider than shoulder-width apart, and hands on the hips. The tip of the tongue is on the roof of the mouth, not just behind the front teeth but to the upper palate. The chest is relaxed and open, not caved in, shoulders down, and the pelvis is tucked slightly inward. Relax all of the joints from the top of the body to the feet. Stand for sixty seconds, calming your mind with the breath. Inhale and exhale through the nose down to the lower *tantien* (field of elixir), located approximately three finger-widths below the navel. One inhalation and exhalation is considered to be one breath. Do nine breaths, guiding the breath with your mind down to the *tantien*. If the heart is not calm, and you are feeling restless, repeat the breathing until you feel calm.

The Eight Silken Brocades Warm-Up Stance

I. PROP UP THE SKY WITH INTERLACED FINGERS

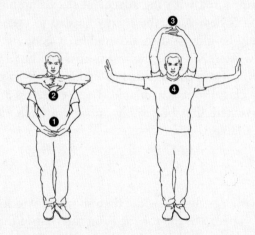

Prop Up the Sky with Interlaced Fingers

Interlace the fingers at the lower tantien *with palms facing upward. Inhaling, rise up on your toes while drawing your hands up the front of the body, turning them outward as they pass the chest and, still on the inhale, raise them all the way above the head facing skyward. Then pause and hold the breath for a moment while still on the toes and stretching, without straining. On an exhale, begin lowering the heels while the hands separate and circle down to the sides, completing one round. Do nine rounds.*

Purpose.

This movement primarily strengthens the muscles, tendons, and bones of the back and spine. It helps to stretch and energize the bladder and small intestine meridians, which are the first line of immunological defense. It also opens the channels and collateral meridians and gives a signal that the set of Eight Silken Brocade movements are going to begin. This brocade is important for anyone who is depressed, as it strengthens the ability to protect oneself against outside negative forces whether they be in thought, word, or action.

2. DRAW THE LONGBOW ON BOTH SIDES

Draw the Longbow on Both Sides

In this brocade exercise, one can assume the attitude of an ancient hunter drawing a bow to shoot an arrow toward dinner or some other worthy objective. From a standing position step to the left into a horse-riding stance, knees slightly bent with the upper body upright yet relaxed, putting equal weight on each leg. Next, cross your arms in front of you with the right hand on the inside, palms facing you. On an inhale, the right hand forms a loose fist as the arm draws back to the right shoulder, as if pulling a bowstring. At the same time the left arm extends out, and the eyes follow the index finger, which points straight up as if aiming an arrow. The chest is gently opened and stretched while pulling back on the bow-string and aiming the arrow.

Exhale slowly while bringing the hands back to center, arms crossed and palms facing you at chest level (left hand on the inside). Stay in the horse-riding stance and strive to be fluid in your motion. Then on an inhale pull the left arm back, forming the hand into a fist, while stretching the right arm out, pointing the index finger upward, thus repeating the same movement to the other side. One bow pull to each side is considered a repetition. Do nine repetitions.

Purpose.

This movement benefits the arms, shoulders, and chest. It opens the ribcage and is good for the circulatory and respiratory systems, as it energizes the heart and the lungs. When the lungs are stimulated and oxygenated, it helps a person deal with grief or loss. Opening the chest also helps to calm the worrisome nature of those with weak lung *Qi*.

This is a very good exercise to aid in the prevention of breast and lung cancer. It is only good as a preventative measure, however, if done regularly with dedication, sincerity, and commitment, and its effectiveness is relative to the personal profile of an individual.

3. RAISE THE SINGLE ARM

Raise the Single Arm

This position begins with feet together and palms at your sides. On an inhale, slowly raise the hands to chest level, crossing the hands with the left hand on the outside. Raise the left hand straight above the head toward the sky while the other hand moves down with the palm facing toward the earth. Hold the inhale, while stretching the top hand up above the head, the fingers pointing to the right, and the palm facing upward. The other arm simultaneously extends downward, and the hand is next to the side of the body, palm facing downward with the fingers pointing to the front. The hands and arms move in a light and fluid motion like those of a ballet dancer. Next, on an exhale, the hands begin to exchange positions and meet at the area halfway between the navel and the bottom of the ribcage, with the right hand on the outside. Then the right hand goes up over the head and the left down the side. Do nine rounds.

Purpose.

This movement benefits the gastrointestinal tract and all of the internal organs by extending and stretching the energy pathways of the arms and hands. If you do not really feel a gentle, even stretch, then you could be stiffening the arms or locking the elbows while pushing up or down. Avoid locking the arms at the elbows. If you have symptoms that accompany depression such as feeling heavy or sluggish, fatigue upon little exertion, indigestion, heartburn, food allergies, or brain fog, repeat this brocade thirty-six to eighty-one times. This is an excellent stretch for the stomach meridian, which runs from the eyes down the front of the body to the toes. It is also good for the metabolism and one's ability to reason.

4. TURN THE HEAD TO LOOK BACK

In this exercise the body is standing facing the front, feet are together with the hands at the sides, and the index finger is pushing inward at the thigh. On the inhalation slowly rotate the head 90 degrees to the left, the eyes following until they look back over the shoulder, dropping the gaze downward, keeping the head straight. Then exhale and slowly rotate the head and gaze back to the center. From the center position repeat the movement to the right side, inhaling and slowly turning the head 90

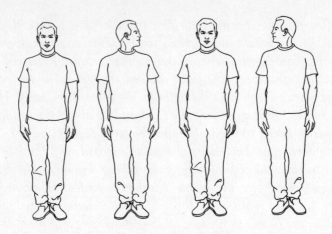

Turn the Head to Look Back

*degrees to the right, the eyes following until they gaze down-
ward over the right shoulder. Exhale as your head rotates back
to the center position. This is considered one repetition. As the
eyes and head rotate in a half circle, the upper torso does not
turn, but faces forward, open and relaxed. Do nine repetitions.*

Purpose.

This movement benefits the eyes and eyesight. It can help a
depressed person see into the heart of a problem. There are many acupoints on the muscles of the neck that relate to consciousness and
understanding. When you stretch the muscles of the neck and stimulate
the cervical bones, it increases blood flow to the brain. By stimulating
the body with this gentle turning action, you are allowing the central
nervous system to adjust and come into balance.

5. CAT GAZING AT THE MOON

*In this position your legs are separated a little wider than
shoulder-width apart, and the knees are bent in the horse-riding stance with hands on your hips. Now bend forward at the
waist, head down, then on an inhale swing and rotate the upper
body to the left side turning the head and looking up at the sky
and to the back, gazing momentarily. Exhale as you rotate and
swing the upper body down to the front again with the waist
bent. Then inhale as you repeat the motion of swinging and*

Cat Gazing at the Moon

rotating the upper body to the other side, looking up and back. This is one continuous, fluid movement. Do nine repetitions.

Purpose.

This exercise benefits the heart and circulation and can be quite strenuous, depending how low you bend at the waist. Do not strain the body. This movement helps a person to cultivate calmness and joy as the heart circulates and pumps blood throughout every cell of the body.

6. Pull the Toes with Both Hands

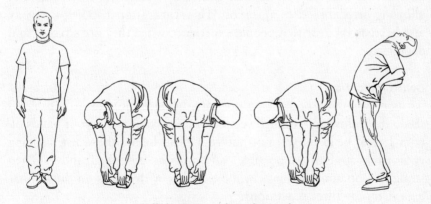

Pull the Toes with Both Hands

Inhale as you bend over at the waist, dropping your head and upper body as far down as you can comfortably go. Bent over, keep your back as straight as possible and your legs straight without bending at the knees and pull up on the toes with your hands. (If you are unable to touch your toes with your legs straight, then place your hands on your knees, shins, or at whatever position is comfortable, while still maintaining a gentle stretch.) The heels are together, and the feet are splayed apart to stimulate the "bubbling wells" that are the acupuncture points at the bottom of the feet.

Holding your toes (or legs) and still on the inhale, turn your head left and look back behind your left side and while still holding your toes (or legs), swing to the right and look behind your right side, as if you are a dog wagging your tail. After each repetition (wagging to the right and left side), on a slow exhale, straighten back up slowly to a standing position and then lean back, bending at the waist, placing the palms of the hands on the lower back, or lumbar area. As you are exhaling and leaning back, imagine your breath going down to the bubbling wells. Do three to nine repetitions.

Purpose.

This exercise strengthens and develops the waist, which is the protector of the internal organs and the lumbar area of the lower back, as well as the hinge for all of the body movements. It relieves strain and benefits the kidneys and adrenal glands by opening the rib cage and allowing better blood energization. This stimulation also helps remedy and balance the fear that people experience when they are stressed and depressed.

Contraindication.

For those with high blood pressure, hypertension, or arteriosclerosis do the following modified version of this exercise. Put your hands on your knees, bend but do not put your head below the waist, keeping your back straight as possible, and wag as described above. Then straighten up and lean back while exhaling with hands on the lumbar area. Do only three repetitions.

7. PUNCH WITH ANGRY EYES

Punch with Angry Eyes

Begin this exercise by inhaling and squatting down in the horse stance. With thumbs inside, form fists facing upward at the waist level, exhale and punch out the left arm at chest level, rotating the wrist so that the fist is facing downward at completion. Inhale as you pull the left arm back to the waist. Now exhale and punch out the right arm at chest level, rotating the wrist so that the fist is facing downward at completion. Again inhale as you pull the right arm back to the waist. Do not lock the arms at the elbows or hyperextend them. The eyes should focus with the fierce energy of punching. Your head faces center front and remains stationary while your eyes move and follow each punch to the right or left side. At the last expression of the punching movement, squeeze the fist of the extended arm. Do nine repetitions.

Purpose.

This practice benefits the cerebral cortex and autonomic nervous system, promotes blood circulation, and enhances muscle strength and stamina. It also helps to clear and release anger and unwanted aggressiveness that often underlies depression.

8. RISE AND FALL ON THE HEELS AND TOES

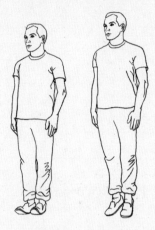

Rise and Fall on the Heels and Toes

In this exercise, you are in a standing position with the feet together. While inhaling, rise up on your toes, lifting both heels from the floor, and then while exhaling, rock back on the heels, lifting the toes. Do nine repetitions. Concentrate your energy on the navel. Relax while you stand and let the energy settle.

The Eight Silken Brocades

The pace of doing the exercises should be natural. If you are unable to do nine repetitions of an exercise, work up gradually, or you may want to do more. The main idea is to do it consistently on a daily basis, as this will produce the best results.

Eight Silken Brocades Warm-Up

1. Prop Up the Sky with Interlaced Fingers
2. Draw the Longbow on Both Sides
3. Raise the Single Arm
4. Turn the Head to Look Back
5. Cat Gazing at the Moon
6. Pull the Toes with Both Hands
7. Punch with Angry Eyes
8. Rise and Fall on the Heels and Toes

Purpose.

This practice helps to release, disperse, and recirculate all the blood and *Qi* after performing the other Qigong exercises in the Eight Silken Brocades. It is important to let the body settle after completing this series and before launching into a new activity.

WHY PRACTICE QIGONG?

During the last century in the United States, conventional approaches to treating depression have been primarily through drugs and psychotherapy. In my clinical practice, I have come to understand that to treat mental or mood disorders, not only must one's mind/brain chemistry be affected but also one's internal physiology through movement and exercise.

The Spiritual Dimension of Depression

Carlos Warter, M.D., Ph.D.

Speak little,
Learn the words of eternity.
Go beyond your tangled thoughts
and find the splendor of Paradise.
Go beyond your little world
and find the grandeur of God's world.
There's only one thing stopping us
from having heaven on earth—
"that we can't believe it can be."[1]
—Jalal Al-Din Rumi

As humans we make a fundamental choice, whether consciously or unconsciously, about how to live our lives. We live either from the grandeur of our spirit or the limited perspective of our personal story. When we live from our smaller story, even the best of us when faced with adversity are tainted with the conditions and conditionings that create patterns that can send us spiraling down the abyss of pain and depression.

There is yet another option of living our life. In this one we have our feet firmly planted on earth and our hearts rooted in heaven, moving through our world for the sake of service and with the clear intention of making a contribution that emanates from the big story of who we truly are as spiritual human beings.

This approach to living has been a basic principle of many spiritual traditions throughout the ages as well as by some modern scientists. In his classic book, *The Perennial Philosophy,* Aldous Huxley describes the core tenet running through all major spiritual traditions—the divinity of man or the identity of God and the individual soul—as captured in the Sanskrit phrase *Tat tvam asi,* or "Thou art That." According to the perennial philosophy, we have forgotten our divine heritage, and the larger purpose of our lives is to "remember" who we truly are. From the scientific perspective, Nobel Prize–winning neuroscientist Dr. Roger Sperry reports finding distinctions both in the brain and in the lives of those who hold themselves to be cosmic individuals versus people with identities bound primarily to sociological and psychological factors. This perspective is reflected in the words of the great scientist Albert Einstein:

> *A human being is part of the whole, called by us the "Universe," a part limited in time and space. He experiences himself, his thoughts and feelings, as something separated from the rest—a kind of optical delusion of his consciousness. This delusion is a kind of prison for us, restricting us to our personal desires and to affection for a few persons nearest us. Our task must be to free ourselves from this prison by widening our circles of compassion to embrace all living creatures and the whole of nature in its beauty.*

For over twenty-five years I have worked with people as a psychiatrist and physician board-certified in Family Practice. During this time, I have treated hundreds of people reporting symptoms of depression with various treatment modalities, both conventional and alternative. I have found, however, that while every treatment modality can work to some extent, to be truly effective one must not only look into the physical, biochemical, mental, and emotional causes but also cross into the realm of the spiritual to create a comprehensive approach to healing. In the majority of depression cases that I have treated, the essential problem has been that the individual's identity is firmly established in the smaller story of the personality, and the person's larger, divine identity has been "forgotten." The transmutation that must occur in order for healing to take place is to move from the small, contracted story where depression brews to the awareness of a larger dimension of one's being, the large or big story of human life. In addition to all known physiological, psychological, medical, and natural approaches to treatment, this elevation in awareness entails a fundamental shift in the very notion of who one is and how to operate on many levels simultaneously while maintaining the necessary attitude to live a healthy and fruitful existence.

There is a wonderful story that illustrates how people's perception of the context within which they live affects the way they perceive their day-to-day existence, and whether they live in the large or the small story.

One day in the Middle Ages three masons were busily at work, laying bricks. A young man was walking by and noticed that although all three men were working and doing the same thing, only one of them looked happy! The young man approached one of the men that looked unhappy and asked him what he was building, and the man answered gruffly without even raising one eyebrow from his work, "I'm laying bricks." He then walked over to the second man, who looked a little happier, and asked him the same question. The second man replied, "I'm building a wall." Finally, he walked over to the third man, who was doing his work with an ecstatic expression, and asked the same question. The third man replied enthusiastically and with obvious pride, "I'm building a cathedral."

THE BIG STORY VS. THE SMALL STORY

The truly impossible dream is the kind of conventional happiness that most of us seek. We imagine being in a state of physical and material perfection, safe from illness, death, or any other kind of pain. We desire a solid, unmoving place—just the opposite of what we are and our essence, which is the kernel of awareness and substance of our sense of constancy. It is the inner witness that provides our awareness of this continuity.

Instead of living from our essential self, we try to create that kind of fixed, stable, and unmoving place—a reference point—by telling little stories to ourselves about what is happening in a way that suits our limited, preconceived notion of reality. No matter how profound and deep an experience we have, we try to squeeze it down and make it fit into our world, our comfort zone or ego bubble. Then we try to hold on to it firmly, forgetting that it is physically or psychologically impossible to do so when the fundamental nature of the universe is constant change. As we spend our lives trying to establish such an unmoving place, our hearts become closed, and we become less able to experience the power of love, wonder, and spontaneity in life.

The conflict between our desire for "fixed" security and happiness, coupled with the basic truth of impermanence and evolution, produces great friction and stress in our lives. In turn, friction and stress produce all kinds of ill health—emotional, spiritual, or physical. The choices become clear: learn to embrace the truth of uncertainty, impermanence, and change, or become more and more contracted, crystallized, and depressed, vainly seeking control and a sense of security that does not exist. Essentially, I believe that this basic contradiction about the true and false nature of reality is the source of much of the depression we experience today. As long as we view ourselves and our lives in this small, contracted way, we will never be truly happy or at peace with ourselves.

THE SEED OF SPIRIT WITHIN

We live in a time of great spiritual hunger, but within each of us is the means of ending this famine. People around the world are beginning to sense the presence of a seed inside them. This seed has long been ignored by psychology, sociology, and the medical profession. Without guidance from these fields, we have been forced to search on our own to discover the proper care of this seed: how to water it, fertilize it, and make sure it receives enough light. Some have looked to ancient wisdom, some to religious traditions, and others to modern science for recognition and nurturing of this seed. Regardless of the path taken, we all are looking for the same thing: the maturing of the seed into the fruit of the spirit and soul that will feed all of mankind.

In our present time, most human experience does not integrate the sacred and the secular. We tend to separate the two, giving each a place that is completely unconnected to the other. As our world shrinks and speeds by at an ever-quickening pace, we seem to have placed all things having to do with the contemplative nature of the soul far down on our list of priorities. We have viewed altered states of consciousness and states in which we perceive an existence beyond our own as signs of illness or psychosis. We have viewed ancient mystical traditions that talk of living a life of spiritual pursuits in combination with service to our fellow man as superstition. Doctors who utilize spiritual psychology as a means of radical self-transformation and prayer as a means of healing the body have been viewed with suspicion and criticized by the medical profession. From an historical perspective, this separation is an unusual development because throughout history human cultures have joined the mind, body, and spirit in their approach to all aspects of living.

The emphasis in modern Western culture on the importance of the separate individual, the exhaustive analysis of the individual's psychological makeup, and the antiquated view of science as adversarial to spirituality, all makes for a fertile breeding ground for depression. It is therefore understandable why the majority of Westerners report periods of depression in their lifetimes, and that major depressive episodes are the most common problem facing psychiatry.

But all of this is beginning to change. A new spiritual consciousness is emerging that connects all of us, and we see it manifesting in many ways. People are reevaluating what they want in life and are finding that their families are more important than their careers and making more money. There is a movement in progress in this country that involves people acting with kindness toward others for no other reason than the connection that exists between all people. The *New York Times* Science section (June 30, 1998) heralds "Science and Religion: Bridging the Great Divide." Best-seller lists are full of books on the human soul, angels, near-death experiences, and the importance of virtues. We are realizing that the cultures of the world have similar traditions, and the world's religions developed from these shared traditions.

Current science is also a part of this change. The development of quantum theory in the past twenty-five years has led physicists to view the world and the universe as an organic whole, not a fragmented reality. It is the realization of these numerous connections that is bringing mankind into a time of spiritual awakening.

ANCIENT AND MODERN VIEWS ON THE SOUL, MIND, AND MENTAL ILLNESS

Many sacred traditions, cultures, and even various historical periods model for us different viewpoints on mind, soul, and the nature of mental illness and depression. Plato, the ancient Greek philosopher, discussed his philosophy for health and balance:

There is no proportion or disproportion more predictive of health and disease, and virtue and vice, than that between soul and body . . . the due proportion of mind and body is the fairest and loveliest of all sights to him who has the seeing eye. . . . We should not move the body without the soul or the soul without the body.[2]

The concepts of mind and soul were almost interchangeable in Plato's world, which raises an interesting point for our modern times. When we speak of "mental illness," are we referring to a disease of the mind as defined in the West as intellect or disease of the mind as defined in the perennial philosophy as lack of soul awareness?

The desire for a deep spiritual awareness as well as the pain of its absence, is described in many religious traditions and historical periods. St. John of the Cross, a sixteenth-century Spanish mystic, described "the dark night of the soul," or the deep depression often experienced by those on the spiritual path as a result of their intense yearning for union with God.[3] In Tibetan Buddhism the basic cause of mental illness and depression is thought to be rooted in leading a life that runs counter to the deepest spiritual inclinations, insights, and inherent disposition, especially if they are resisted, denied, and repressed.[4] In this tradition a combination of somatic medicines, herbal mixtures, and spiritual practices are prescribed to combat mental illness, as well as the practice of *dharma*, the Sanskrit term for right livelihood, and meditation to deepen understanding, strengthen character, and steady the mind.

There is scientific evidence that depression may be partly a spiritual phenomenon. Several interesting studies have been performed showing that traditional spiritual remedies such as prayer are beneficial for depression. In one experimental study on the effects of distant intercessory prayer on self-esteem, anxiety, and depression, some people were prayed for and some were not, and no one was informed which was the case.[5] The study showed that the mental state of those who were prayed for was significantly improved compared to those individuals who were not prayed for. This suggests that there may be some spiritual basis for depression and negative mental states may be positively affected by prayer or spiritual intention.

BARNACLES OF PERSONALITY

How have we forgotten our soul or essence? Why do we habitually resist who we are? Why are so many people becoming depressed? Is depression connected to forgetting who we truly are?

When a baby is conceived, the light and wisdom of universal energy develops into a human being. Over a span of nine months two cells multiply into a trillion, and the result is the marvelous, intricate mechanism that is the human body. Our nature at birth is the nature of essence— open, receptive, and radiant—pure divine love. Our basic impulse as newborns is to love and be loved. Within each of us is the seed or essence of universal light and at this stage, energy is fully expressed through our being. As we look around for reflections of this unconditional love, most of us, however, find something else. The world into which we are born has almost universally forgotten the essential connection. It is as if we, as humans, have forgotten the meaning of humanity.

If essential connection is the universal currency, being born is like coming into the world with lots of money but no place to spend it. We find ourselves looking into the eyes of mothers and fathers or caregivers who have long ago forgotten who they truly are. They have lost touch with their own connection to essence. Without the ability to see themselves in this deeper light, it is impossible for them to see their offspring in this light.

As a result of looking into the faces of those who have forgotten their essence, we as infants begin to believe that who we are is not acceptable. We notice that we are loved only if we behave in a particular way—for example, when we are quiet, when we do what our parents tell us, when we are amusing, or when we don't exercise our natural predilection for exploration and curiosity. Based on the feedback we are given, we decide that we are not valued as ourselves, not worthy of unconditional love.

Because giving and receiving love is our primary motivation, we as children soon set out to discover ways by which we can become "worthy" of love. Even as very young children, we learn to assess each situation and then make decisions about who we need to become in order to find acceptance and love as well as a sense of belonging. Our basic motivation is to be who we need to be in order to get the love we need, and this becomes a habitual pattern. The currency of conditional love is: "You be who I want, and I will love you."

These beliefs, assumptions, and decisions about who we need to be begin to form around our true identity like barnacles on a ship's hull. As our essence becomes obscured and we forget who we are, we develop "personality." As we grow and develop further, we make more and more decisions and form more and more beliefs based upon what happens to us as we live our lives. You fall in love; you get hurt. You'll never fall in love so hard again. You trust a friend; your friend betrays you. You don't trust people so easily after that. Or maybe no one betrays you, and you trust everyone. You become gullible, and people take advantage of you. Whatever happens to us, the layers around our essential being become thicker and more impermeable. Our hearts begin to close. We forget our conscious connection with the natural flow of divine love through our lives. We forget the inner peace, wisdom, and wholeness at our core. We learn to look outside for these things as we become more and more identified with the crusty layers of personality around our essence, based upon who we thought we needed to be in order to be loved. All too soon, we regard these layers or barnacles of personality or self-image as who we really are.

THE PATH OF THE HEAD

Our bodies magically arise from "nowhere" before birth and after death dissolve into the elements. Still, even in the face of this great mystery most of us develop the attitude that our body is "ours" and that we are our body.

We also begin to identify with our thoughts and "story lines," regarding them so strongly that we spend much of our lives being unaware of what is outside and around us. Living in our heads allows us to have any number of fantastic experiences while we shut out the one truly important experience: the present moment. The same thing happens with our emotions, which are thoughts amplified. We solidify them into something monumental and important, such as "I love you" or "I hate you," and we take the energy of the emotion to be ourselves. We are willing to invest heavily in these emotions. How many wars have been fought on the battleground of "I love" and "I hate"?

Stuck in the engineering of our own self-image, we regard even our soul as solid—something we "have" that we could therefore lose. Since our soul or essence is what we are, how can we lose who we are? But because we forget the infinite energy that we embody and instead identify with what is finite, we live in fear of loss. This is not a sin, but an illusion that comes simply from having forgotten who we are.

Our self-image is woven from the threads of limitations and restrictions. And because every aspect of our small world is finite, it is all subject to change. Nevertheless, we draw these boundaries tightly around ourselves in a fortress that we learn to call "me." Having invested so much energy in drawing our boundaries and resisting the natural urge of the heart to stay open, we now attempt to control our world. We let in only what will reinforce our fortress. We try to keep out anything that would rock the boat and cause us to question what we have so carefully built. It is not the path of the heart that comes into play here, but the path of the head.

In an effort to control our world we conceptualize, judge, label, and thus essentially deny it. It takes a great deal of mental energy to shrink our world into a manageable, dependable size. We even do this in the name of knowledge by acquiring a few tools and bits of data, and then we fall asleep and automatically repeat the same thing over and over again. If it works, why change it? Why change our hermetically sealed environment, which we've equipped with our favorite food, music, friends, and temperature controls? Our ego bubble becomes stronger and stronger as it tries to protect what we've acquired. It expends tremendous energy maintaining itself, not letting in anything new. And because this process denies the reality of change, it also denies us the opportunity to truly contact our experience.

There's a German expression that says, "Wash me, but don't get me wet." When we encounter something that might touch us, change our belief, or shift our perception a little, we normally develop a stress reaction, shut down our hearts and minds, and automatically begin to perform actions that remove us from the "threat" and bring us back to safe and familiar ground. This includes overeating, working out, watching TV, gossiping, becoming angry or depressed. Any means of returning to the superfamiliar does the trick.

We retreat into these habitual patterns because they seem solid and comforting. We might even regard them as our power. Because we see this power as coming from our own limited resources, however, and not from something greater, we believe we have to work very hard to maintain it, as we fear that this inner power might run out. We then try to undertake many activities at once to enlarge this power and attempt to dance in many relationships at the same time. In fact, we become so busy at this that we hardly breathe—and we do not take the opportunity to really focus our life-energy on our daily activities. This leads to even more stress.

When we identify with our small, habitual patterns instead of with the greater being that we are, our perception is restricted and true relationship—from which health, peace, and healing energy spring—cannot occur. We wind ourselves up tighter. This tension crystallizes into mental, physical, and spiritual "identities"—closed systems of habitual energy patterns that cause us more pain.

"Fixing" ourselves in this matrix and projecting it onto others and the world around us leads to mental, physical, and spiritual disease—individual and collective. Death, decay, degradation, dominance, and control come from resisting our own expansive nature. The stress created by the resistance acts to harden our consciousness. On the physical level the patterns of rigidity can manifest as arthritis and atherosclerosis. On the emotional and spiritual level, the rigidity can manifest as depression.

NORMALITY OR ARRESTED DEVELOPMENT?

Culturally, there is little incentive to practice living from our essential identity. Indeed, there is heavy pressure to be "someone," to achieve something, to have and do it all in a world bombarded with heart-numbing stimuli. No wonder we forget who we are and are unable to fully live in the present moment.

When we make an intellectual judgment about something that enters our field, we stay with that judgment or definition. This is the definition of "normality." My definition of this sort of normality is "arrested development," and we are in it together. Our collective fog becomes the distorted lens through which we see ourselves, our world, and each other. There is a conspiracy of ignorance that is perpetrated throughout humanity to fall asleep, stay asleep, and remain ignorant of innate human dignity, true wealth, and true healing medicine.

Luckily, it works the other way around, too. Any effort that any one of us makes to wake up affects everyone else. Therefore, as it is said in the Diamond Sutra of Theravada Buddhism, "What use is my own enlightenment if all others are asleep . . . and it is thanks to my own enlightenment that I dedicate myself to serve the enlightenment of all other sentient beings." Healing ourselves creates a field and context that facilitates the healing of others.

While we aspire to the larger picture, we cannot avoid the materialism of the small world and life's day-to-day activities. Someone has to make the money, take care of the children, put a roof over their heads, plant the crops, and cook the food. All these activities require careful tending of the "outer." But the small story becomes problematic when we become stuck in it and believe that that's all there is, losing touch with our essential nature. When this happens, we reduce our understanding to the mere survival of our narrow views about reality. This does not allow for the full unfoldment of our psyche and leads, instead, to a compression or "depression" of our own life-energy.

INTEGRATING THE BIG AND SMALL

Both roles—the person of the world and the man or woman of spirit—must come together. When we begin to see ourselves as an eternal life force—a very mysterious one—that is for now operating in a human body, we are able to surrender and experience miracles. Miracles are waiting for us to look up from our identification with our small story, from our belief that our imaginary bubble of survival is all that there is.

A few years ago I met His Holiness the Dalai Lama, the spiritual and political leader of Tibet, when we were both speaking at the Congress of Holistic Medicine in Bangalore, India. The day after the ceremony, I had been meditating in my hotel room and suddenly felt an urge to put on my jogging shoes and get some fresh air. Instead of being stuck in my small story that said this was "meditation time," I followed my inner guidance. As I left the hotel, I met His Holiness! We went for a long walk together, and I felt a very strong connection to him. After our walk he invited me to visit him in Dharamsala. This small yet miraculous encounter for me was only possible because I acted spontaneously from the heart and was willing to surrender to an expanded idea of what was possible in the universe.

FORGETTING OUR ESSENCE—TAKING ON LIMITING IDENTITIES

In the process of development, our essence tends to get overshadowed by false identification. That is necessary for the purpose of learning techniques to operate in this third-dimensional world. For example, it is good for a baby to be physically conscious when beginning to walk.

It is good for a teenager who starts to use discernment to be emotionally aware and selective in choosing friends and environments. It is helpful for a person who is designing a career, a life, or a service to be intellectually conscious. When we believe, however, that we are just our bodies, emotions, and minds, then we are clearly on the third-dimensional road to the three D's: death, decay, and depression.

As beings of embodied essence, we constantly move in and out of temporal identities, taking on different ones at different times in our lives—even at different times of the day. This is necessary action to survive as social beings in a social world. It is natural and healthy to invest ourselves in a role, subpersonality, reactive "animal" self, or *naf*, as the Sufis say, so long as we do it with a sense of surrender and detachment. When we have big-story vision, we can move into the appropriate role when necessary and leave it when we need to do something else or when it's no longer useful. But we do not want the roles or *nafs* to acquire a life of their own.

When you wake up in the morning, you may be in the *naf* role of spouse or lover (or zombie, if you are not a morning person). Then someone calls from work and you switch to your professional *naf*. Then your mother calls with some advice and you switch into your adult child *naf*. Then the kids are not dressed for school, so you switch to your parent *naf*. You've already gone through four *nafs* even before you've had your shower or your morning drink. Through the course of the day you might also be a carpool driver, a teacher, a secretary, a soccer player, and so on. These roles are our outer identity. We identify with our appearance, with what we do in order to make money, who our family is, whom we are married to, where we live, and our favorite athletic team. "I'm a beautiful woman." "I'm a doctor." "I'm a mother." "I'm an African-American." "I'm a Dodgers fan." "I'm a spiritual person." Each of these roles is just a small expression of the essential self that is intrinsically complete and not altered by external circumstances.

When we identify with any of these roles our self-image and self-esteem become dependent on them. We begin to believe that they are "solid" and constitute our permanent self. However, if we allow ourselves to move unencumbered through space as the energy beings that we are, we become as flexible as bamboo in the wind, no longer holding ourselves frozen in defense against any change that might arise.

Psychological identities or inner identities can be as powerful as expressions anchored in profession, appearance, or family. For example, a disheveled, anxious-looking woman came into my clinic when I was living in Colorado years ago. She had been referred to me by another doctor.

"How can I help you?" I asked.

With hardly a pause the woman breathlessly replied, "I'm a paranoid-schizophrenic alcoholic."

I was taken aback. As I looked at her in amazement, I responded, "But aren't you still a human being?"

"Still?" She pondered for a moment. Then, "You're right. I guess I'd forgotten that."

Labels like "paranoid-schizophrenic," "addict," or even "upwardly mobile" are useful in defining a complex set of motivations and behaviors. Sometimes, however, we identity ourselves or others so strongly with the label that we do not allow for change or growth. For example, although the woman who came into my office had abstained from alcohol for over three years, she was still calling herself an alcoholic. Although such identification is encouraged by Alcoholics Anonymous, I prefer to call it "expressing the *naf* of drinking alcohol." In this way, we do not tie our entire identity to a narrow diagnosis. Was it possible that this woman could start drinking again? Of course. But the identification with her past life and her future potential to abuse alcohol was obscuring her present life, where she was an ordinary human being expressing her essence.

THE SUBPERSONALITY OF VICTIM

The "victim" subpersonality is an ultracharged, false identification that is often accompanied by anger and powerlessness combined with a healthy dose of "What if": "What if I hadn't walked down that street?" "What if I hadn't pushed so hard?" "What if I hadn't been going so fast?" All of these statements arise from our belief that we have control over everything that happens to us. Oddly enough, when something good comes to us unexpectedly, we are just as likely to attribute it to ineffable factors such as synchronicity and luck. What it all comes down to is that we often have no control, and there are also times when we have no choice.

For many people, this realization leads to a feeling of victimhood and ultimately depression, caused by a lack of taking charge and responsibility for our own lives. If we turn control of our life over to an outside authority, we automatically feel compressed and at the mercy of the situation. Depression in this case stems from giving away our power to someone or something else at the cost of suppressing the outward expression of our own energy.

However, how we deal with what life dishes out is up to us. Whether our situation is heaven or hell depends on our perception. If we keep our contracted awareness focused on what happened, our world will get pretty small. If we are able to find a way to accept what happens to us, process it, and move on, we are less likely to dwell in the past and identify with the victim. Forgiving ourselves and others can be an important part of the inner work involved here.

One example of true victimization is the people who survived the Holocaust, with the exception of some people like Victor Frankl, Elie Wiesel, and others who kept their inner core intact. These unique survivors, rather than withering inside, used their Holocaust experiences to nourish their inner strength and then passed it along to others in service or teaching.

A paraplegic woman in her midthirties named Carol came to me recently for help with depression and marital discord. Two years earlier she had been left paralyzed by a car accident. The fears, worries, and discontent that she brought up in our sessions were affecting her marriage, which had been healthy before the accident. Although her feelings sounded reasonable, it seemed to me that everything she was saying led back to a "victim" identity.

"If you will allow it to happen," I told her, "something in this experience is leading you toward greater awareness of your essential self. First, can you forgive yourself for being in that car accident? There was nothing you could have done to prevent it. It was a rainy night, visibility was bad, and you did all you could to avoid the accident."

Carol's anger at herself gradually dissipated over the next several sessions. At the same time, her contempt for the driver who had crashed into her car grew and grew. "How can I ever forgive something like that?" she demanded. The way she tried to shift her body in her wheelchair was a reminder of the heaviness, inertia, and helplessness that she seemed to feel.

"Your future happiness and health depends on your ability to forgive him," I said. I explained how her hatred for the driver of the other car was a stressful inner energy that, if unreleased, would slowly contribute to the deterioration of her body.

I had recently realized that I, as a Jewish person, had let myself remain an indirect victim of the Holocaust by not forgiving Adolf Hitler for his crimes against the Jewish people. As a result, I had often been defensive when issues about religion and ethnic identity came up.

I used my recent insight as an illustration for Carol.

"How can you forgive someone as evil as Hitler?" she asked. "After all he did?"

I leaned back and smiled. "Forgiving Hitler doesn't mean that I think what he did was all right," I told her. "I can recognize that he was following his own misguided, and in my view evil, path, which led to incalculable suffering for millions of people. However, he is dead now, and forgiving him means that it's high time I release the negative energy I have been harboring. That energy is not hurting him or avenging my relations whom he killed. On the contrary, that energy is hurting only me—destroying me, in fact."

Awareness of her "victim" identity along with genuine feelings of forgiveness opened up my patient's life. Now she is combining trips to her neurologist with Qigong and acupuncture treatments. She is much more relaxed and accepting of her physical condition. Releasing the solidly held view of herself as "victim" has also helped her family and friends, as she realized they had been supporting, reinforcing, and enabling her victim identity.

Forgiveness also gave Carol a greater sense of power and energy, which helped lift the burden of depression she was carrying from the accident. Even though she was still in pain, she saw that by holding a grudge, she lost even more energy to the circumstance. Becoming fully alert and forgiving the other driver allowed her to release her burden and become free from the circumstance.

The Healing Pyramid

I have developed a model called "The Healing Pyramid" that I have found to be a powerful healing vehicle for my patients dealing with depression. The Healing Pyramid integrates the full range of healing modalities with the power of our open hearts and heaven—divine love. As we ascend this imaginary pyramid, we are led to spiritual health and a fully integrated state of well-being. The Healing Pyramid incoporates the force of heaven at the apex, earth at the base, and the path of the heart in the middle.

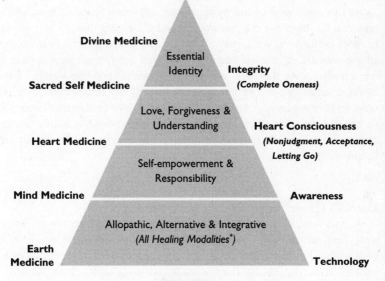

GOD AS LOVE

Divine Medicine

Essential Identity

Integrity
(Complete Oneness)

Sacred Self Medicine

Love, Forgiveness & Understanding

Heart Consciousness
(Nonjudgment, Acceptance, Letting Go)

Heart Medicine

Self-empowerment & Responsibility

Mind Medicine

Awareness

Allopathic, Alternative & Integrative
(All Healing Modalities*)

Earth Medicine

Technology

GRAVITY

*The term ALL HEALING MODALITIES includes Acupuncture, Allopathic Medicine, Applied Kinesiology, Aromatherapy, Ayurvedic Medicine, Biofeedback Training, Biological Dentistry, Bodywork, Cell Therapy, Chelation Therapy, Chiropractic, Colon Therapy, Craniosacral Therapy, Detoxification Therapy, Diet, Energy Medicine, Environmental Medicine, Enzyme Therapy, Fasting, Flower Remedies, Guided Imagery, Herbal Medicine, Homeopathy, Hydrotherapy, Hyperthermia, Hypnotherapy, Juice Therapy, Light Therapy, Magnetic Field Therapy, Meditation, Mind/Body Medicine, Naturopathic Medicine, Neural Therapy, Neuro-Linguistic Programming, Nutritional Supplements, Orthomolecular Medicine, Osteopathy, Oxygen Therapy, Pharmacology, Qigong, Reconstructive Therapy, Sound Therapy, Surgery, Traditional Chinese Medicine, Yoga.

Level I (Earth Level)

Level I is the "well" containing every technique and healing methodology that we dip into when we need help. At this level we are actively involved in doing things to improve our health. In the case of depression or mental illness, we may consult with practitioners in a wide variety of traditions, ranging from allopathic medicine, psychology, and psychiatry to homeopathy and Chinese Medicine, including diet, exercise, botanical medicine, and a myriad of other approaches. At this ground level, the specific approach within the healing modality and the responsibility for healing reside primarily with the physician or practitioner.

Level II (Heart Level 1)

At this next level of the pyramid, our approach is interactive, and we take responsibility for our healing. Instead of heading directly to our usual doctors or healers, we survey all the healing traditions and practitioners, all the modalities, and choose the ones that seem most appropriate for our condition. At this level we use our intuition and knowledge of ourselves. In opening our awareness to this level of self-responsibility, we seek ways to fully engage our innate healing energy. We realize that healing has to come from within, and the practitioner we choose will only facilitate that process. Even the most skilled healer cannot help us if we do not want to get well.

Level III (Heart Level 2)

At this level we approach our condition with understanding, compassion, forgiveness, and love. We recognize that in some way we are responsible for our depression, although we may or may not have had control over the cause. For example, we may suffer from hereditary manic-depression. Regardless of the cause, at this level we learn to let go of any guilt, shame, or blame that we feel because of the condition and learn to accept and tolerate the cause. This acceptance transforms any negativity into forgiveness and compassion toward ourselves. In the silence of the heart that follows, gentleness arises, as well as self-acceptance and self-love.

At this stage we have the power to heal ourselves. We choose to work with healers who are in touch with their own inherent healing energy and will help ignite ours. Tools for healing our depression at this level include all those available at the previous levels as well as strong doses of loving kindness, compassion, acceptance, and forgiveness.

Level IV (Heaven Level)

Directing loving kindness toward ourselves is the route to mastery in healing—the top of the pyramid. Here the self merges with the divine, and here love of self becomes love of soul. When we reach the top of the imaginary pyramid and are surrendered to self-love, we reach a frequency of coherence for body, mind, and spirit—the frequency of essential identity.

At this level we feel a certainty, a peace, a love that surpasses everything. Here it is obvious that we are on a journey toward the divine. We are at one with ourselves, with others, with our surroundings—indeed, with life itself. This state is the raw source of all healing. We wake up each morning fully grateful for life, the restoration of consciousness, and for everything else in the day. We wake up well. Gratitude shifts to a "biology of hope," in the words of Norman Cousins, thus relieving the hopelessness that the state of depression causes.

An Integrated Approach to Healing Depression

This Healing Pyramid model can provide an integrated approach to the healing of depression.

At Level I, or Earth Level, all treatments, remedies, and techniques can be utilized without conscious awareness of the actual shifts in mood and state of being. At Level II, however, the individual seeks to understand the deeper level of causality for the situation beyond the physical dimension. How does someone get into a traumatic self-inflicted circumstance that leads to a depressive mode in his or her life? For example, in early childhood, children's experience of love is often not a positive experience. They begin to learn, through parental reinforcement, that in order to get love they must act out certain negative patterns. Over time these patterns can develop into responses that lead to melancholy and depression.

I have developed a process called the Psychospiritual Integration Process (PIP)[6] that allows people to identify the negative patterns that they have internalized from their parents and society and transform them into positive alternatives. This process brings a person to Level III of the pyramid, where love, understanding, and forgiveness are directed toward both the self and circumstances. Preliminary findings from a study I am conducting on this process using the MMPI-II (Minnesota Multiphasic Personality Inventory), shows a significant reduction on the depressive scale for participants who complete the process.

As one moves through the pyramid, each level produces a different state that is embraced and then de-identified with in order to continue to move toward higher levels of healing and consciousness. These levels are:

1. Awareness
2. Responsibility
3. Understanding and No Condemnation
4. Compassion
5. Love
6. Inner Silence
7. Source

By surrendering to the inner understanding of the power of love and the force of grace and by balancing this understanding through meditation and contemplation, one comes in direct contact with one's essential self and the divine.

At the top of the pyramid, Level IV, the person is able to connect with their essential self, allowing them to have a transcendent experience of who they really are. This experience provides a sense of unshattering, unbreakable identity that is fully immersed in positive love and connection to the divine. All healing modalities are available at this level, empowered with not only self-responsibility but divine love. Here we also have the added aspects of community, selflessness, clear vision, and direct relationship with the divine.

THE SEAT OF CONSCIOUSNESS: LOWER MIND OR HIGHER HEART?

If we consider the terminal of the computer—the brain—to be the seat of consciousness, we flatten our holographic awareness into a small screen in our heads and project this imaginary screen into the world around us. In effect, we are flattening our perception. But if we acknowledge the heart as the seat of consciousness, our experience is totally different. We see that in truth, we are a door. Through the awareness of the heart, our consciousness is an open door or portal. The heart is not just something that receives images through our brains or projects images on the small screen of the third-dimensional or "objective" reality.

Ironically, regarding the brain as the seat of consciousness only leads to clouding the clear, diamondlike quality that the brain has when receiving the heart's intelligence. The brain is the transducer for the heart's wisdom. Unclouded by our core beliefs, the brain works in tandem with the heart, guiding us directly and straightforwardly on our path as a soul in a human body. Allowing the brain to do its job efficiently is a matter of unlearning the core beliefs of the head, while at the same time tuning in to the energy of the heart.

When we identify with the path of the heart, the brain enables us to see ourselves and others clearly, speak with meaning, and act from the higher frequencies of the heart, which we call core values.

The different wisdom traditions and religions have reinforced those core values through their moral codes and prayers, rituals, and practices. The Bible tells us, "Love thy neighbor as thyself." Tibetan Buddhists say, "Be grateful to everyone." The Sufi sage Hadrat 'Ali said, "Faith is experienced by the heart, avowal by the tongue, and action by the limbs." These traditions know that the higher frequencies of the heart are the doorways to universal or cosmic intelligence.

By awakening the energy of our hearts, we give ourselves the power to release judgments, communicate honestly, enjoy inner self-esteem and security, and uncover the frequency of compassion. We can surrender to the higher intelligence and power that enters through the heart.

The coherent frequencies of the heart also have healing power. It has been shown that by tuning in to the higher frequencies (shifting from anger to forgiveness, for example), we can lower our blood pressure and increase T-cell counts. These systematic and immunological changes take place when stress and tension subside. Thus tuning in to the holographic awareness of the heart can be a way to change the frequency patterns that cause illnesses such as depression. When these higher frequencies of the heart are activated, we can then forgive ourselves and others, magnetize our appreciation and caring, and even see death and dying as a frontier in which to learn and move toward higher consciousness.

Heart values are fluid and flow freely in and out through the heart's open doorway. They make a bridge between what we so often see as our "separate self" and the vast ocean of the interdimensional and interconnected world around us. They are the vehicles by which we express the essential fluidity of our being; they are the means by which we receive the divine energy we embody. These values connect us with one another. Opening to these core values, we no longer feel or see ourselves as separate. At the same time, we can see others as ourselves.

When we identify with lower frequencies such as depression, anger, fear, apathy, boredom, anxiety, irritation, frustration, exhaustion, low self-esteem, disappointment, tension, discouragement, and stress reactions, we are barricading the entrance to these higher human values. Solidifying the lower frequencies blocks the love, forgiveness, and compassion that inhabit our hearts. It keeps us from embracing the human realm, which is also the realm of the divine.

These solidified negative emotions can also lock into our bodies with an explosive force that, if left unchecked, will create disease. They are like sticks of dynamite that sooner or later will implode and cause heart disease, kidney failure, cancer, severe depression, or a fatal accident. Unfortunately, because we hold on to negative emotions, some of us die with a lifetime of unexpressed love still locked up in our hearts.

One interesting phenomenon, readily experienced on the path of the heart, is that it takes much more energy to harbor negative emotions than it does to let them go. But first it is important to acknowledge and feel these emotions and after doing that, it takes much more energy to retain negative feelings—clinging, grasping, defending, clutching at, holding a grudge—than it does to flow with the gentle path of the heart. In fact, this holding on to negative feelings leads to depression. Touching and feeling our hearts takes us beyond these negative emotions into higher frequencies of forgiveness and love. We do not have to create these higher frequencies; they are already there.

Inner work entails unlearning our attachments to the lower frequencies. We will always experience the lower frequencies, but we can learn to work with them in creative ways. We could consider inner work as simply "attention to essence." The more we attend to essence, the less likely we are to let temporary identifications crystallize in our psyche and body. The inner work unblocks the door and allows our true heart power to flow naturally. It also clears the heart so it can actively receive the divine energy that flows around us and through us.

Unlearning attachments to lower frequencies leads us away from depression. In the Psychospiritual Integration Process (PIP), participants learn and use a process I call "recycling." In simple terms, recycling involves the deep recognition of an attachment that we have to a particular negative frequency or pattern and transmuting it into a positive alternative. With daily recycling, a person releases his or her attachment to the negative or lower frequency and creates an attachment to a positive pattern or higher frequency. Because it is often the attachment to the lower frequencies that causes depression, as the person recycles, his or her depression is alleviated.

EMOTIONS AS FREQUENCIES OF THE HEART

Some of us repress our emotions, some of us act them out, and some of us try to suppress others' emotions. None of these approaches works. On the path of the heart, we learn to see our own emotions clearly and manage them. We find out that any emotion presents an opportunity to connect with our essence.

We quickly learn that when we align our emotions with the wisdom of the heart, we also have fun. The more we listen to the heart, the more we hear it. I find it useful to think of emotions as frequencies we can tune in to. We can visualize higher and lower heart frequencies as well as higher and lower bands of emotions. It is as if the universe were filled with radio stations or television channels with their own patterns—their own sonics, their own style and design. Each station is tuned to a band or to many bands at different times. Although some frequencies affect us subconsciously and we cannot do much about them, we have a choice of how to respond to those we are aware of.

For example, the thought "I forgive myself" is powerful because it cuts through our story lines and resonates with a higher frequency of emotions than the thought "I am bad because I have made myself sick by eating the wrong foods." Saying with commitment and devotion "I forgive myself" transcends the static state of the lower frequencies of emotion. It does not try to obliterate or argue with them. It rises above them. If we tell ourselves with conviction "I forgive myself" and feel it deeply in our heart, then the other story lines like "I'm a lousy person because I did this-and-this-and-this" or "I can never do anything right" simply crumble and die in the blazing light of the truth.

The energy of "I forgive myself" in what I have learned, what I have been taught, for my culture and the culture of my parents, my religion, and the religions of my ancestors, stands to acknowledge and thank a higher power for giving the gift of life. As an affirmation of truth, a shift takes place in our understanding. It engages a transformative energy—the energy of forgiveness.

In Hinduism, our *sanskaras* ("impressions on the soul"), or what we are calling set false identities, are erased or healed through attunement with the frequency of love and forgiveness. Hindus believe that *sanskaras* impact the life force of the heart; they represent a cycle that we are forced to repeat until they have been removed from their hardened position around the heart. Forgiveness removes them. As we forgive ourselves and release these false identities, our hearts become lighter. We can more easily tune in to the higher heart frequencies and experience life in a more positive way.

Forgiveness releases resentment, hurt, pain, and stressful emotions, thereby erasing negative associations from the holographic field of the heart. Nonforgiveness can lead to self-loathing or hate that damages the heart emotionally, contracts it electrically, and pollutes it spiritually, sending the person down a progressive path toward illness and depression.

In tuning in to positive frequencies, we move back into the flow of our lives. We create a new standard—one that is based on our own inner truth rather than an externally imposed and arbitrary "truth." Empowered by our own deepening awareness, we are no longer dependent on others for validation and approval. We free both ourselves and others to be who we are. We begin to see ourselves as essence and see the essence within others, regardless of outer appearances.

The Higher Heart Frequencies

Heart frequencies are feelings, and feelings are what make life worthwhile. Higher heart vibrations reflect the higher aspects of human nature—serenity, laughter, love, compassion, forgiveness, tolerance,

---

 Exercise: Self-Forgiveness Meditation

The following is a meditation used by knights during the Crusades before battle in order to cleanse themselves of all past sins. These knights knew that they would quite likely die in battle, thousands of miles from home. Purifying themselves before the fight served a double purpose: to perform well in battle and to supply the confidence that, should they be killed on the battlefield, they would go to God with a pure heart.

To do this meditation, lie on the floor facedown with your toes crossed. Intertwine your fingers, with your knuckles placed across your third eye, which is in the center of your forehead.

In this position of surrender and supplication, repeat the prayer, "Forgive my sins, thou the most merciful." Say this prayer over and over as you review your life. Mentally picture all of the errors, sins and transgressions that you would like to have forgiven. Do this exercise until you feel a surge of pure, clean, fresh energy arising in your heart.

gratitude, appreciation, kindness. These frequencies are in sync with core values and are accessed from the core or the heart. The primary feeling is simply unconditional love.

The higher heart bands are a guide into the field of essence. They are the highways of divine energy. Accessing these higher bands regenerates the immune system. They're in charge of the fountain of youth. Our "ageless body" resides in the higher frequencies.

The way to tune in to these higher frequencies is to connect with our hearts at the deepest level. One of the basic ways to do this is by repeating certain phrases to ourselves such as "I am present in the moment," "Stay in the heart," and "Open the heart." If we feel ourselves closing down, turning off, or erecting a defensive wall, we can consciously remind ourselves with these statements from the heart. If we feel afraid, depressed, irritable, or if things are not going our way, we can return to the source of "flow" by silently repeating words like these.

Another method for tuning in to the higher frequencies is through deep, conscious breathing. Focused attention on the inner rhythm and tempo of breath helps to balance the brain waves, allowing one to go beyond the actual exercise and enter into a realm of beingness that transcends the scattered thinking that is usually present in nonharmonious living.

One way to consciously breathe is to imagine that we are breathing in the luminous golden light of the higher frequencies while dissolving into that flowing, nectarlike energy of love. This love serves as the ultimate healer because it keeps our hearts and heads in balance.

The Middle Heart Frequencies

The middle emotions on our frequency band are sentimentality, expectations, attachments, desires, sympathy, and pity. These are some-

 Exercise: Opening the Heart

Opening the heart can be easy; it is an act of surrender and will. Will lies below the heart in the solar plexus. Start by relaxing your solar plexus by taking a few deep breaths into your belly. Then relax your belly. Concentrate the will that is there to say, "I am going to open my heart, now." Stay in your heart and listen to each beat. Soon you may feel a tunnel. Follow that tunnel and see where it leads.

what neutral in affect, depending on how we use them, thus making these emotions difficult and challenging fodder for inner work. With awareness, they can be used as a road in to the higher frequencies. Without awareness, they can draw us into a web of negative emotions.

For example, when love turns to attachment, or compassion gets colored by sympathy, the heart-energy condenses into sadness or pain, and we become "heavy-hearted." This brings up feelings of disappointment and the need to replay our sad old movie, each time reinforcing the hurt feelings. But in truth, a broken heart is a head-on collision between the middle heart and higher heart frequencies. Here, the love that we experienced drifted to the middle heart frequency, where it became expectation and attachment. If we have the inner awareness to see what happened, our disappointment can become a path to liberation. We can rejoice in our ability to love, in our longing to love, in love itself. We can release our pain and move on. If we have been victims of traumatic abuse and are suffering from depression, hostility, or melancholy, we might need to access some other higher-frequency feelings to help us move along the path of the heart, such as forgiveness. Forgiving ourselves first and then others paves the way to releasing self-pity.

Real love is caring and forgiving and transcends even the limitations we make up in the name of love. If we can find a way to transform attachment into unconditional love or pity into compassion, our heart-energy is enlightened and we feel "light-hearted." We can also align ourselves with wholesome desires such as ardently wishing that we reside in the resonance of the heart, thereby tuning in to the higher frequencies.

The Lower Heart Frequencies

The negative emotions are anger, fear, depression, apathy, boredom, anxiety, irritations, frustration, exhaustion, low self-esteem, unfulfillment, tension, discouragement, and stress reactions. When we solidify these, we cut off our connection with the world of essence. Just because these emotions vibrate at lower frequencies, however, does not mean that we should turn away from them when they arise. In fact, we must allow ourselves to feel their energy fully before we can productively work to transform them into positive energy.

When we identify with negative emotions such as depression, they increase our sense of separateness. When we allow ourselves to experience them fully, however, by moving toward them, they can be extremely useful on this healing path of the heart. Connecting with and feeling our negative emotions can lead to compassion and loving kindness for ourselves. Working creatively in this way can bring us back to higher-frequency feelings. Knowing them ultimately leads to knowing ourselves, helping us to lift the veil of depression.

Exercise: Embracing Negative Emotions to Release Them

Making friends with negative emotions is a powerful practice. Most of us have never been encouraged to do this. Like a moving iceberg or a fire racing through a forest, negative emotions can seem overwhelming, scary, and dangerous. Our habitual response to a strong emotion may be to try to deny it or to get rid of it in the quickest possible way. Yet if we learn to accept our emotions, even make friends with them, we can use their energy in positive ways.

Embracing negative emotions is a technique that is practiced over the long term. There are countless opportunities to practice it even in a single day. First, it helps to cultivate feelings of generosity toward yourself that can give you the space to experience your feelings directly. Most of us have never learned to do this, because we judge our feelings as "bad" and inherently want to avoid them. Patience is another helpful tool that comes in handy when encountering our desire to be rid of our undesirable feelings as quickly as possible.

Next time you feel a particularly keen emotion that you'd rather avoid—let's say anger—notice what you do with it. Do you get rid of it as quickly as possible by acting it out, yelling at whoever or whatever made you feel angry? Or do you try to drive it away by repressing it? Some people repress their anger by literally swallowing it. They take a drink, eat a cookie, or smoke a cigarette, for instance. In all of these cases—acting out and repressing—we're denying the opportunity to genuinely connect with ourselves and in the process may be creating harm for ourselves or others.

Do you allow yourself to feel what you're feeling? It's hard. Vipassana meditation, a form of Buddhist meditation known for its focus on "mindfulness," is a particularly good method for watching emotions rise, noticing them, and letting them go. It helps to observe within the concentrated context of meditation practice that no matter how strong the emotion, it is not permanent, and it doesn't have to be particularly threatening, either. Meditation practice strengthens the possibility of being aware of our emotions when we are relating with others. Emotions are powerful surges of energy, almost guaranteed to spirit us away if we haven't cultivated mindfulness of the light that lies beneath them.

Once you've become aware of your feelings, you can begin to notice which ones are acceptable to you and which ones aren't. For men, feelings of sadness are often judged as weak or unacceptable (did you ever hear the phrase, "Boys don't cry"?), whereas for women, the most unacceptable emotion may be anger. And in our society, feelings of depression are viewed as mysterious, frightening, and unacceptable. What is your attitude toward your feelings?

Now when you feel a surge of strong emotion, you can begin to accept it by taking a gentle and friendly approach to it. Instead of trying to banish it from your kingdom, engender curiosity about it. Cultivate the habit of asking yourself questions about it. "Where is this sadness coming from?" "Why am I suddenly so irritable?" Try to be open to your emotion without judgment.

Judgment is usually the first step we take away from our emotion, and it only serves to give the emotion a double-negative edge. An open, accepting, and curious attitude about what you're feeling moves you into direct contact with your negativity.

Once you've become aware and accepting of your emotions, you can ask another question. "What is this emotion saying to me?" "What can I learn from it?" You may notice that underlying a lion's share of negative emotions is the fact that you want something that you can't have, or you've got something that you don't want. Negative emotions usually have something to tell us, and often in a most sharp and accurate way if we don't let hostility obscure their passageway.

An important practice here is to see emotions as neither good nor bad. When you feel yourself judging your emotional state, mentally take out a golden sword and slay the judge on the spot. Let yourself feel the hot energy of anger and imagine it as a flame cleansing you of impurity. When you feel sad, don't try to brush it under a rug. Feel your sadness and imagine the tears are washing away everything that conceals your inner light. When irritation or frustration seems to be making you anxious or "speedy," harness its wind and imagine it blowing away any clouds that darken your path.

Unless we feel compassion for our pain, we will not know how to extend loving kindness toward ourselves. And unless we know ourselves fully and are able to feel compassion and loving kindness toward our own being, we can never fully extend ourselves toward or understand others. Being there for others in relationship and service is the next step on the healing path of the heart. In the big story, all emotions are part of the human experience. We do not have to beat ourselves up for experiencing a negative emotion that so often takes the form of reinforcing our negative story line or retreating into addictive behavior. Negative circumstances offer a great opportunity to see ourselves as a healing instrument. Even when we are in pain, we can use whatever we encounter to rise into a higher consciousness, heal ourselves, and emanate this energy into the world.

SHIFTING NEGATIVE EMOTIONS INTO POSITIVE ONES

If you are suffering from depression, a way to help drop your attachment to negative feelings or situations and expand into the higher frequencies is to attach yourself to something more positive. Our entire energy system is more efficient when we learn how to "time out" negative mental imagery and surrender to heaven and earth. Surrendering to heaven and earth means that we accept both the high states we have as well as the daily, ordinary states. Once we let go of a false identification that is negative, we can then actively embrace a positive image.

Years ago I was having dinner with Norman Cousins in Los Angeles. We talked a lot about his famous recovery from ankylosing spondylitis (a disintegration of the connective tissue in and around the spinal column), as recounted in his book *Anatomy of an Illness*. We talked about how the diagnosis of his illness had first sent him into a state of depression. Then he told me in detail how he started to laugh at his diagnosis of terminal disease, giving rise to an exhilaration attack that shifted the focus of his whole life and set him on a course of action. As he was healing, he actively cultivated the higher heart frequency of humor and bliss that successfully turned any negative emotions of depression, anxiety, or melancholy into a positive alternative. His therapy included, for example, watching Marx Brothers movies and anything else that would make him laugh.

What he experienced not only healed him; he also ended up being the only nonmedical doctor on the faculty at the UCLA center for research into psychoneuroimmunology. His healing approach, as detailed in the many books that followed, continues to have a positive influence on individuals and research worldwide on fourth-dimensional (transpersonal) healing.

Norman Cousins's experience is a perfect example of the interdimensional quality of the healing experience. In terms of the healing pyramid, he took responsibility for the method he chose and empowered his treatment with love, compassion, and forgiveness. Through the practice of humor and positive, light-hearted imagery and thoughts, he was able to transcend his "small" story, heal his "incurable" illness, and live his life focused on the "larger" story. His legacy of books and research following his recovery are his great contribution to the world.

OFFERING UP OUR NEGATIVE EMOTIONS

Working with our own pain and negativity allows us to develop skills for dealing with problems from a higher perspective. We can move bravely toward and through our negative emotions. There is no way we can know courage without knowing fear, no way to know confidence without knowing doubt, no way to know peace without knowing turmoil.

We can also take these lower-frequency feelings and dedicate them to a higher purpose. We can offer them up to ourselves, others, or God. For instance, you can say, "I will experience this fully for the highest good of myself and others."

To offer them to ourselves, we can simply allow these emotions to exist, since they are a natural part of our emotional terrain, enabling us to transform them into positive action. We can wear them as an ornament or utilize them in service to others.

For example, the Dalai Lama does not hate the Chinese Communists who overran his country in 1959, killing monks and laypeople, destroying monasteries, and driving hundreds of thousands of Tibetans into India as refugees. He is very angry with them, but is not holding on to anger and turning it in on himself. Instead, he uses the anger to call attention to the plight of Tibet in his travels throughout the world. The Dalai Lama thus engages his feeling in an active way to help others.

SURRENDERING TO A HIGHER POWER

In recent years the idea of surrendering to a higher source or power has become especially popular in addiction and recovery circles. Many people in a variety of organizations will attest to the strength of this technique.

In a sense we are all addicted to an idea of ourselves, and this is where surrender comes in handy. It is the false idea of who we are that keeps us from realizing our true identity as souls and great beings. By clinging to the sense of what is safe and permanent, which is our idea of ourselves, we think we can avoid traveling into unknown territory (the land of the present moment) where we can experience our true selves or essence.

In the following exercise you're going to practice surrendering to the immediate and available higher sources of heaven and earth that are imminently accessible to each of us in the present moment.

Exercise: Surrendering to a Higher Power

This is a visualization and relaxation exercise to help us give up control. Through it we may discover that it is not necessary to hold on to ourselves all the time. We can trust the power of earth, which is gravity, and the power of heaven, which is love, to support us.

Lie down in a quiet, comfortable place where you will not be interrupted. Take a few deep breaths. Start by relaxing your head. Repeat to yourself while you relax your head: The earth will support my head. I am letting go of my head. My head is completely relaxed. I surrender my head to a higher source (power). When your head feels totally relaxed, move down to your neck. If there's tension in your neck, acknowledge that it's there and then begin to relax. "I don't have to hold on to my neck. The earth will support my neck. I let it go. I totally surrender my neck."

Repeat this exercise with your trunk and limbs. You can do it as slowly or quickly—joint by joint—as you wish. But be sure to relax into the earth as much as possible. After you've repeated this exercise with your trunk and limbs, move on to your inner organs. Feel any accumulated tension in your heart, lungs, liver, kidneys, and reproductive organs, let it go, and surrender.

When you have surrendered your entire body to the earth, surrender your mind and heart to heaven. Visualize a golden globe of light in the sky in front of you and above you. This is the higher power of heaven. Visualize the golden globe growing bigger and bigger, until it envelops your body. Relax into the light of the higher power.

Now surrender to the light of heaven. Surrender your thoughts, your feelings, your insecurities, and your joy. Tell yourself, "I surrender to heaven. I can trust the power of heaven. In this moment I release my anxiety about the future. I release my guilt about the past. Whatever I think, whatever I feel, whatever I think I am, I surrender it to heaven," and so on. You can make this surrender as personal as you like. If you feel hurt, angry, disappointed, depressed, or if you're carrying a grudge, surrender it to heaven. If you're grief-stricken, you can surrender your grief. If you're full of joy, you can offer your joy.

Whatever you surrender, now feel yourself melting into the light of the higher source of heaven. Then bask a while in the brilliant light and beauty of heaven, earth, and the present moment.

Surrendering to a higher power means integrating oneself with the flow of living, recognizing with gratitude the continuum of life, and living rather than worshipping the false ideas of our separateness. Surrendering is not submission. It is exaltation to the supreme physiology of being.

REGAINING OUR SPIRITUAL HERITAGE

As a psychiatrist, I remind patients who are in emotional pain and depressed that pain can be a compassionate aspect of our mission as human beings. As essential beings, perhaps we place ourselves in painful circumstances for the very reason that in order to resonate with the morphic field of others who are feeling similar pain, we must first experience it ourselves. Whether or not our pain has some karmic or missionary aspect, we can definitely use it to make a heart connection with others.

We live in a constantly shifting world in which we have sacrificed, for several hundred years, the development of spiritual understanding to master physics and materiality. In this time, and at the turn of the century, we are integrating the coming together of the mystical and the scientific through the unified field of awareness. For the first time, we are able to reclaim our spiritual heritage for our personal selves. We are also now able to apply the sacred aspect of spirituality to the way we approach health and wholeness, not to the exclusion of the great discoveries of science and technology, but to the enthronement of essence as the clear and central pivot to our understanding of life.

e l e v e n

Where Do I Go from Here?

The greatest discovery of any generation is that human beings can alter their lives by altering the attitudes of their minds.
—Albert Schweitzer

In developing your own program for healing depression, you will want to establish some criteria. You may want to assess the safety of the treatment, its reported efficacy, the speed with which the therapy works, its cost, and availability in your area. Considering these aspects will give you a clearer picture of the therapies in which you can place the most confidence.

If you are interested in investigating the innovative laboratory tests that address many of the potential health factors underlying depression, Appendix E, "Diagnostic Laboratories," offers detailed information about many of the best laboratories that perform these tests.

FINDING THE APPROPRIATE HEALTH PROFESSIONAL

After you have selected the approach(es) for healing depression, you will want to take the steps to finding the right health professional with whom to partner in your journey to health. In selecting a health professional there are a number of points to consider.

Referrals

Check with friends, relatives, and associates who have had positive experiences in the treatment of depression or related conditions. The referral of a trusted individual can be worth its weight in gold and time.

Professional associations are another good source of referrals for a specific therapy or modality. Appendix B: "Resources for Alternative and Complementary Health Care," offers an extensive list of professional associations and organizations that can help you find practitioners of a specific modality in your area.

The compounding pharmacies in Appendix F, which provide compounded natural hormones according to a doctor's prescription, as well as the diagnostic laboratories in Appendix E, can also be a source of referral to health professionals who use natural hormones and utilize the respective laboratory tests.

If you have Internet access, you can utilize HealthWorld Online's Professional Referral Network (www.healthreferral.com). This is the most comprehensive on-line resource for referrals to alternative/complementary and integrative health care professionals, with searchable membership databases for over twenty professional associations. Each practitioner database is searchable by last name, zip code, area code, city, state and country. Some of the practitioners in the databases have home pages that provide additional information that can be invaluable in making a decision, including the practitioner's philosophy, training, practice, insurance coverage, and office hours.

Educate Yourself

Educate yourself about any therapy or modality you would like to pursue. Check "Resources for Alternative and Complementary Health Care" in Appendix B, "Recommended Reading" in Appendix C, and the "Internet Resources on Depression and Alternative/Complementary Medicine" in Appendix D. Your research will yield further information and solutions, allowing you to interact in a more intelligent and fruitful manner with a health professional.

Screening Health Professionals

Develop a list of criteria to help you screen health professionals to determine which ones are a good fit for you. You can screen the candidates by asking questions of their office staff. How long have they practiced? What certifications do they have? What complementary therapies do they include in their practice, and where did they receive their training? What success have they experienced in treating depression? What is their attitude toward integrating alternative/complementary and mainstream practices? Are they part of a multidisciplinary integrative medicine clinic? Do they accept insurance? Which therapies are covered? What are the office hours?

Interviewing Health Professionals

In interviewing a health professional you should ask the questions that will elicit the information you need to make a decision. You also need to assess if you are comfortable with his or her personality and medical "bedside manner." In the interview you will want to:

- Describe to the health professional what you know about your depression and related symptoms as well as any hunches regarding the possible underlying causes.

- Share what you have learned from this book and other resources about your favored treatment options.

- Listen. You may want to bring a notepad or tape recorder to record the health professional's observations, diagnosis, and recommendations.

- Be firm. Do not be afraid to respond to his or her recommendations if you do not understand or if you disagree.

- Ask yourself: "Is this a health professional with whom I have a good communication and rapport and someone I can work with as a partner in reestablishing my health?"

- Is the health professional knowledgeable about the characteristics and efficacy of a wide variety of treatments? Such a professional will be able to more closely match the appropriate treatment to your situation and will be more open to developing a comprehensive treatment program. Often health care practitioners specialize in one or two treatment approaches and may attempt to fit the patient into their area of expertise.

- Remember, not every health professional is the right one for you.

Last Words

In this book we have endeavored to provide you, the reader, with a map and compass to help you navigate through the wilderness of depression. We have also provided you with many signposts and tools along the way to enable you to emerge healthy and whole from this journey into the light. The choices are yours.

> *You already have the precious mixture that can make you well. Use it.*
>
> —*Jalal Al-Din Rumi*

Quick Reference
to Natural Therapies in
Natural Healing for Depression

- **Amino Acid Therapy:** Utilization of the neurotransmitter precursors (amino acids that form the neurotransmitters or brain chemicals that affect mood) such as tryptophan, tyrosine, and choline.

- **Aromatherapy:** Essential oils of such plants as bergamot, jasmine, lavender, lemon, sandalwood, and ylang-ylang have long been used in cultures throughout the world for their mood-elevating effects.

- **Ayurveda:** The traditional system of medicine in India, the practice of Ayurveda extends to 3500 B.C. *Ayurveda* means "Science of Life," and has a long history of working with rejuvenation, longevity, and mental health through diet, lifestyle, herbs, massage, yoga, and meditation.

- **Bach Flower Remedies:** The thirty-eight flower remedies were discovered by Dr. Edward Bach beginning in the 1920s in England. These official homeopathic medicines are made from flowers. They are traditionally used to balance various mental/emotional conditions, and can be self-prescribed according to one's emotional state in mild depression.

- **Biochemic Tissue Salts:** The twelve biochemic tissue salts are some of the many mineral medicines listed in the homeopathic pharmacopeia for treatment of mental depression, insomnia, and neurasthenic conditions.

- **Biofeedback:** A modern form of psychophysiological self-regulation that can be learned with the assistance of electronic biofeedback devices.

- **Chinese Medicine:** Practiced for over 5,000 years, Chinese medicine includes the use of herbs, acupuncture, dietary therapy, massage, lifestyle, and physical exercises called Qigong. Chinese medicine is based on balancing the flow of *Qi*, or energy, through the body's organ/meridian system.

- **EMDR (Eye Movement Desensitization Reprocessing):** A new psychotherapeutic technique, EMDR involves the evoking of rapid eye movement in the patient to help him or her get in touch with and reprocess old traumatic feelings and events.

- **Exercise:** Physical exercise is a great benefit in preventing depression and is often part of a holistic treatment program for depression.

- **Guided Imagery:** A mind/body technique for helping people refocus their attention on their inner wisdom, the part of the nervous system that has answers and solutions to many of our problems.

- **Herbal Medicine:** The therapeutic use of herbs to alter physiology and mental/emotional states. This book addresses both Western and Chinese herbs used in the treatment of depression, and includes St. John's wort, currently the most highly researched and publicized herb for treating depression.

- **Homeopathy:** Homeopathic remedies are designed to stimulate the body's own natural powers of recovery to aid in overcoming the disease rather than simply suppressing symptoms. Homeopathy aims to treat the patient rather than the disease and is effective in treating mental/emotional disorders.

- **Integrative Psychiatry:** An emerging field of psychiatry that integrates the most effective alternative and complementary therapies in the field of mental and emotional health with conventional psychiatric practice.

- **Light Therapy:** Use of full-spectrum light or special bright lights for those suffering from depression or seasonal affective disorder can lead to a 50 percent decrease in symptoms by raising serotonin levels.

- **Massage and Bodywork:** Chronic stress and emotions can be somatized or held in the tissues of our bodies. Massage and bodywork can help release the stress, tension, and repressed emotions.

- **Mind/Body Medicine:** The use of stress-reduction techniques, guided imagery, biofeedback, meditation, and other modalities to achieve higher levels of mind/body integration, greater capacities for self-regulation, and inner peace in order to better control anxiety and mood swings.

- **NAET (Nambudripad's Allergy Elimination Technique):** A technique to desensitize individuals from a substance to which they are allergic, involving muscle testing and acupressure.

- **Natural Hormone Therapy:** The use of natural hormones such as progesterone to address female hormonal imbalances and mood swings during PMS and menopause.

- **Naturopathic Medicine:** A natural approach to medicine that considers all of the factors needed to help move a person toward health. This medicine looks to understand the underlying causes of illness and then addresses these causes with natural therapies such as diet, lifestyle, herbs, homeopathy, nutritional supplements, hydrotherapy, acupuncture, and massage.

- **Nutritional Medicine:** This approach involves the use of diet and nutritional supplements to correct nutritional deficiencies as well as the use of high dosages of nutrients (Orthomolecular Medicine) to push biochemical reactions in the desired direction.

- **Psychospiritual Integration Process (PIP):** A powerful process that allows one to identify the negative patterns that have been internalized from parents and society, and transform them into positive alternatives.

- **Qigong:** The Chinese art and science of gathering, circulating, and storing body/mind energy (*Qi*) through breath and energy work. These are techniques that involve movements and visualizations while standing, sitting, and moving.

- **Spiritual Psychology:** An emerging field that explores the spiritual dimension of health and psychology, utilizing psychospiritual disciplines such as visualization, relaxation, meditation, breathwork, and self-inquiry.

- **Voice Dialogue:** A powerful form of Jungian psychotherapy that involves talking with the different subpersonalities of an individual to create a greater sense of awareness and integration in the personality.

- **Yoga:** A spiritual discipline practiced in India for many thousands of years, yoga employs diet, lifestyle, postures, breathing practices, and meditation to promote optimal health and spiritual development. Yoga is particularly effective in promoting mental clarity and balance.

A p p e n d i x B

Resources for Alternative and Complementary Health Care

ACUPUNCTURE AND CHINESE MEDICINE

American Association of Oriental Medicine
4101 Lake Boone Trail, Suite 201
Raleigh, NC 27607
(919) 787-5181
E-Mail: aaom1@aol.com
Web Site: http://www.aaom.org

Provides referrals to acupuncturists in your area.

American College of Traditional Chinese Medicine
455 Arkansas Street
San Francisco, CA 94107
(415) 282-7600
E-Mail: lhuang@actcm.org
Web Site: http://www.actcom.org

Offers information and referrals to licensed acupuncturists and Oriental Medical Doctors (O.M.D.'s).

American Foundation of Traditional Chinese Medicine
505 Beach Street
San Francisco, CA 94133
(415) 776-0502
E-Mail: aftcm@earthlink.net

Write to request information on Chinese Medicine or referrals to acupuncturists or O.M.D.'s in your area and large cities near your area. The foundation is nonprofit, and donations are requested to help defray costs.

National Acupuncture and Oriental Medicine Alliance
14637 Starr Road SE
Olalla, WA 98359
(206) 851-6896
(206) 851-6883 FAX
Web Site: http://www.healthy.net/naoma

The National Alliance is the national professional membership association founded in 1993 to represent the diversity of practitioners of acupuncture and Oriental Medicine in the United States. Professional referrals available at the NAOMA web site.

Internet Resources:
http://www.acupuncture.com

AROMATHERAPY

American Alliance of Aromatherapy
P.O. Box 7309
Depoe Bay, OR 97341
(800) 809-9850
(800) 809-9808 FAX
Web Site: http://www.healthy.net/aaoa

A nonprofit organization and resource center that allows aromatherapy practitioners, educators, manufacturers, retailers, and consumers to share valuable knowledge, encourage education, and promote ethical and equitable business practices. Offers subscriptions to The International Journal of Aromatherapy *and the* American Alliance of Aromatherapy News Quarterly.

Internet Resources
http://www.healthy.net/aromatherapy

AYURVEDIC MEDICINE

Ayurvedic Institute
11311 Menual NE, Suite A
Albuquerque, NM 87112
(505) 291-9698
Web Site: http://www.ayurveda.com

Founded by Dr. Vasant Lad, the institute trains general public and health professionals in all aspects of Ayurveda. Correspondence course, newsletter, and mail order sale of Ayurvedic remedies.

The College of Maharishi Ayur-Veda Health Center
P.O. Box 282
Fairfield, IA 52556
(515) 472-8477
(800) 248-9050 (For referrals)
E-Mail: theraj@lisco.net
Web Site: http://www.theraj.com

Provides information on Ayurvedic medicine to the general public and offers referrals to health centers that offer Ayurvedic methods for the prevention and treatment of a wide range of health conditions.

Internet Resources
http://www.ayurvedic.com

BIOFEEDBACK

Association for Applied Psychophysiology and Biofeedback
10200 West 44th Avenue
Wheat Ridge, CO 80033
(303) 422-8436
E-Mail: aapb@resourcecenter.com
Web Site: http://www.aapb.org

Send a self-addressed, stamped envelope to receive information, a list of publications, and contacts in your state for obtaining referrals.

BODYWORK, MASSAGE, AND ACUPRESSURE

Acupressure Institute
1533 Shattuck Avenue
Berkeley, CA 94709
(800) 442-2232 (Outside California)
(510) 845-1059 (Inside California)
E-Mail: info@acupressure.com
Web Site: http://www.acupressure.com

Provides trainings in acupressure and Oriental bodywork as well as books, audiotapes, CDs, and videos on acupressure.

American Massage Therapy Association
820 Davis Street, Suite 100
Evanston, IL 60201-4444
(847) 864-0123
(847) 864-1178 FAX
Web Site: http://www.amtamassage.org

Offers referrals of certified massage therapists throughout the United States. Call the main office for the number of AMTA chapter in your state, and your state chapter will provide referrals in your area based on zip code.

American Oriental Bodywork Therapy Association
AOBTA National Headquarters
Glendale Executive Campus, Suite 510
1000 White Horse Road
Voorhees, NJ 08043
(609) 782-1616
(609) 782-1653 FAX
E-Mail: ShinnAOBTA@aol.com
Web Site: http://www.healthy.net/aobta
For information, practitioner directory, and referrals.

American Polarity Therapy Association
2888 Bluff Street, Suite 149
Boulder, CO 80301
(303) 545-2080
(303) 545-2161 FAX
E-Mail: satvahq@aol.com
Web Site: http://www.polaritytherapy.org
Provides referrals to practitioners and information about trainings.

Associated Bodywork and Massage Professionals
28677 Buffalo Park Road
Evergreen, CO 80439-7347
(800) 458-ABMP (2267)
E-Mail: expectmore@abmp.com
Web Site: http://www.abmp.com

ABMP is a professional membership association that provides practitioners with services and information. ABMP is devoted to promoting ethical practices, protecting the rights of practitioners, and educating the public as to the benefits of massage, bodywork, and somatic therapies. On-line referrals to massage and bodywork professionals available on Web site.

Feldenkrais Guild
524 Ellsworth Street SW
P.O. Box 489
Albany, OR 97321-0143
(800) 775-2118

(541) 926-0981
(541) 926-0572 FAX
E-Mail: website@feldenkrais.com
Web Site: http://www.feldenkrais.com

Provides information on the Feldenkrais Method.

Hakomi Institute
P.O. Box 1873
Boulder, CO 80306
(888) 421-6699
E-Mail: institute@hakomi.com
Web Site: http://www.hakomi.com

The Hakomi Method of body-centered therapy is the integrated use of mindfulness, the body, and nonviolence in psychotherapy that originated in the mid-1970s by the internationally renowned therapist and author Ron Kurtz and members of his training staff. Contact the institute for trainings, workshops, and nationwide referrals.

Hellerwork International
406 Berry Street
Mount Shasta, CA 96067
(916) 926-2500
(800) 392-3900
(916) 926-6839 FAX
E-Mail: Hellerwork@aol.com
Web Site: http://www.hellerwork.com

Provides information on trainings in Hellerwork and referrals to certified practitioners.

International Institute of Reflexology
P.O. Box 12642
St. Petersburg, FL 33733
(813) 343-4811
E-Mail: ftreflex@concentrix.net

Offers a worldwide referral service for qualified reflexology practitioners and trainings in the Ingham method of reflexology.

North American Society of Teachers of the Alexander Technique
3010 Hennepin Avenue South, Suite 10
Minneapolis, MN 55408
(800) 473-0620
(612) 822-7224 FAX
E-Mail: nastat@ix.netcom.com
Web Site: http://www.prarienet.org/alexandertech/nastat1.html

For information on the Alexander Technique or a list of practitioners in your area.

The Rolf Institute
205 Canyon Boulevard
Boulder, CO 80302
(303) 449-5903
(303) 449-5978 FAX
(800) 530-8875
E-Mail: rolfinst@rolf.org
Web Site: http://www.rolf.org

Provides information on Rolfing (Structural Integration) and referrals to certified practitioners.

Upledger Institute (Craniosacral Therapy)
1211 Prosperity Farms Road
Palm Beach Gardens, FL 33410
(407) 622-4334
(800) 233-5880
E-Mail: upledger@upledger.com
Web Site: http://www.upledger.com

Offers referrals to qualified practitioners of Craniosacral Therapy in your area. Contact the Upledger Foundation, (407) 624-3888, about their community outreach programs (Share Care) to teach basic Craniosacral techniques to the lay public.

ENVIRONMENTAL MEDICINE

American Academy of Environmental Medicine
American Financial Center
7701 East Kellogg, Suite 625
Wichita, KS 67207-1705
(316) 684-5500
(316) 684-5709
E-Mail: aaem@swbell.net
Web Site: http://www.healthy.net/aaem

Write for physician referral in your geographic area and reading list of relevant literature or visit on-line referral database of AAEM members at Web site.

Human Ecology Action League
P.O. Box 49126
Atlanta, GA 30359-1126
(404) 248-1898
E-Mail: HEALN@tnl@aol.com
Web Site: http://www.members.aol.com/HEALNatnl/index.html

Support organization for sufferers of environmental illness, including food and chemical sensitivity. Provides information on self-management as well as referrals to practitioners.

Internet Resources
http://www.healthy.net/environmentalmedicine

GUIDED IMAGERY

Academy for Guided Imagery
P.O. Box 2070
Mill Valley, CA 94942
(800) 726-2070
E-Mail: agi1996@aol.com
Web Site: http://www.healthy.net/agi

Cofounded by Martin Rossman, M.D., and David Bresler, Ph.D., L.Ac., the academy offers seminars in Interactive Guided Imagery for the lay public and advanced training programs for licensed health practitioners. Referrals are available on their Web site for professionals certified in the practice of Interactive Guided Imagery. Books and audio- and videotapes are also available through mail order and the Web site.

HERBAL MEDICINE

American Botanical Council
P.O. Box 201660
Austin, TX 78720-1660
(512) 331-8868
(512) 331-1924 FAX
E-Mail: abc@herbalgram.org
Web Site: http://www.herbalgram.org

The ABC publishes the quarterly journal HerbalGram, the English translation of the German Commission E Reports on botanical medicine. Also available are books on herbs, ethnobotany, and botanical medicine.

American Herbalist Guild
P.O. Box 70
Roosevelt, UT 84066
(435) 722-8434
(435) 722-8452 FAX
E-Mail: ahgoffice@earthlink.net
Web Site: http://www.healthy.net/herbalist

*The Guild was founded in 1989 as a nonprofit, educational organiza-
tion to represent the goals and voices of herbalists. It is the only peer-
review organization for professional herbalists specializing in the
medicinal use of plants. Membership consists of professionals, general
members (including students), and benefactors.*

Herb Research Foundation
1007 Pearl Street, Suite 200
Boulder, CO 80302
(303) 449-2265
E-Mail: info@herbs.org
Web Site: http://www.herbs.org

*Provides research material on herbs to consumers, pharmacists, physi-
cians, scientists, and industry.*

Internet Resources
http://www.herbalism.com

HOLISTIC MEDICINE

American Holistic Health Association
P.O. Box 17400
Anaheim, CA 92817
(714) 779-6152
E-Mail: ahha@healthy.net
Web Site: http://www.ahha.org

*Publishes and distributes literature on holistic medicine and provides
interviews and public service announcements on TV and radio on the
holistic approach to health.*

American Holistic Medical Association
6728 Old McLean Village Drive
McLean, VA 22101-3906
(703) 556-9728
(703) 556-8729 FAX
E-Mail: HolistMed@aol.com
Web Site: http://www.ahmaholistic.com

Provides referral list of member physicians organized by state and booklets including How to Choose a Holistic Physician, What to Do When Facing an Illness, *and* Ten Most Asked Questions about Holistic Medicine and Holism.

American Holistic Nurses Association
P.O. Box 2130
Flagstaff, AZ 86003-2130
(520) 526-2196
(800) 278-AHNA
(520) 526-2752 FAX
E-Mail: ahna-flag@flaglink.com
Web Site: http://www.ahna.org

AHNA, founded in 1980 by a group of nurses, is dedicated to bringing the concepts of holism to every arena of nursing practice. AHNA is a 501(c)3 nonprofit educational organization whose international membership is open to nurses and others interested in holistically oriented health care practices. Among its objectives, AHNA supports the education of nurses, allied health practitioners, and the general public on health-related issues.

American Preventive Medical Association
459 Walker Road
Great Falls, VA 22066
(703) 759-0662
(703) 759-6711 FAX
E-Mail: apma@healthy.net
Web Site: http://www.apma.net

A nonprofit health care advocacy organization whose mission is to insure the existence of a health care system in which practitioners can practice in good conscience with the well-being of the patient foremost in their minds without fear of recrimination. Encourages public and professional education in alternative medicine and lobbies for the development of a health care system that gives patients a wide range of therapies.

HOMEOPATHY

American Institute of Homeopathy
801 N. Fairfax Street, Suite 306
Alexandria, VA 22314
(703) 246-9501
Web Site: http://www.healthy.net/aih

The AIH is a trade association whose membership comprises medical and osteopathic physicians and dentists. The AIH is dedicated to the promotion and improvement of homeopathic medicine and the dissemination of pertinent medical knowledge. Established in 1844, one year after the death of homeopathy's German-born founder, Samuel Hahnemann, the AIH is the oldest national medical professional organization in the United States.

British Institute of Homeopathy (USA)
PMB 423
520 Washington Boulevard
Marina del Rey, CA 90292
(310) 306-5408
(310) 827-5766 FAX
E-Mail: bihus@thegrid.net

Provides information and home study courses on homeopathy.

Homeopathic Academy of Naturopathic Physicians
12132 S.E. Foster Place
Portland, OR 97266
(503) 761-3298
(503) 762-1929 FAX
E-Mail: hanp@igc.apc.org
Web Site: http://www.healthy.net/hanp

A professional association of naturopathic physicians who are certified in homeopathy.

Homeopathic Educational Services
2124 Kittredge Street
Berkeley, CA 94704
(510) 649-0294
E-Mail: mail@homeopathic.com
Web Site: http://www.homeopathic.com

Provides a catalogue of homeopathic books, tapes, videos, and software.

National Center for Homeopathy
801 N. Fairfax Street, Suite 306
Alexandria, VA 22314
(703) 548-7790
(703) 548-7792 FAX
E-Mail: nchinfo@igc.apc.org
Web Site: http://www.homeopathic.org

The center offers referrals to physicians and other licensed health practitioners who practice homeopathy and publishes a Directory of Homeopathic Practitioners *that lists practitioners, study groups, and pharmacies throughout the United States and Canada. Provides courses for laypeople and professionals, and sponsors study groups throughout the United States.*

Internet Resources
http://www.homeopathic.net

MENTAL HEALTH AND PSYCHOLOGY

Association of Humanistic Psychology
45 Franklin Street, Suite 315
San Francisco, CA 94102
(415) 864-8850
E-Mail: ahpoffice@aol.com
Web Site: http://www.ahpweb.org

An international community of diverse people dedicated to the exploration and healing of the human mind, body, and soul and to building a society that advances the ability to choose, grow, and create. Membership is open to all.

Association for Transpersonal Psychology
P.O. Box 3049
Stanford, CA 94309
(650) 327-2066
E-Mail: atp@igc.apc.org
Web Site: http://www.igc.org/atp

Based on observations and practices from many cultures, the transpersonal perspective is informed by modern psychology, the humanities, and human sciences, as well as contemporary spiritual disciplines and the wisdom traditions. This organization has activities and publications for those wanting to develop personal, professional, and educational interests in transpersonal psychology.

MIND/BODY MEDICINE

The Center for the Improvement of Human Functioning
3100 North Hillside Avenue
Wichita, KS 67219-3904
(316) 682-3100
E-Mail: staff@brightspot.org
Web Site: www.brightspot.org

Offers clinical services, diagnostic testing, educational classes, confer-ences, and seminars on alternative approaches to healing.

The Center for Mind/Body Medicine
5225 Connecticut Avenue NW, Suite 414
Washington, DC 20015
(202) 966-7338
(202) 966-2589 FAX
E-Mail: cmbm@ids2.idsonline.com
Web Site: http://www.healthy.net/cmbm

A nonprofit, educational organization dedicated to reviving the spirit and transforming the practice of medicine. The center is actively involved in demonstrating the cost-effectiveness and universal appro-priateness of mind/body medicine as well as making it a shaping force in the current debate on health care reform. The center's services are available to all, regardless of ability to pay.

Chopra Center for Well-Being
7630 Fay Avenue
La Jolla, CA 92037
(619) 551-7788
(619) 551-9570 FAX
E-Mail: info@chopra.com
Web Site: http://www.chopra.com

This center is the vision of Dr. Deepak Chopra, world-renowned author on mind/body medicine and human potential. He envisioned the center as a healing center where guests experience a full range of natural therapies, learn techniques for personal development, and participate in classes in mind/body medicine and healthy living. The mission is to provide guests with a life-changing experience and then show them how to transform their daily lives by applying the knowl-edge and insights they have gained.

Life Sciences Institute of Mind/Body Health
2955 SW Wanamaker Drive
Topeka, KS 66614
(785) 271-8686
E-Mail: lifesci@cjnetworks.com
Web Site: http://www.healthy.net/univ/profess/schools/edu/lsi

Founded and directed by Patricia Norris, Ph.D., a pioneer in mind/body approaches to enhancing immune system competence, the institute focuses on providing clinical services and research in mind/body medicine.

Mind-Body Medical Institute
Beth Israel Deaconess Medical Center
110 Francis Street, Suite 1A
Boston, MA 02215
(617) 632-9530
(617) 632-7383 FAX
E-Mail: mbclinic@west.bidmc.harvard.edu
Web Site: http://www.med.harvard.edu/programs/mindbody

Uses yoga, meditation, and stress reduction as part of its treatment program. Cofounded by Herbert Benson, M.D., developer of the "relaxation response," and Joan Borysenko, Ph.D.

Stress Reduction and Relaxation Program
UMass Memorial Health Care
55 Lake Avenue North
Worcester, MA 01655
(508) 856-2656
E-Mail: stress.reduction@banyan.ummed.edu

The oldest and largest hospital-based, outpatient stress reduction clinic in the country, this pioneering center uses an intensive training in mindfulness meditation and yoga to help patients work with their own stress, pain, and illnesses more effectively. The program, directed by Jon Kabat-Zinn, Ph.D., consists of an eight-week course taken to complement existing treatment. Patients are referred for stress-related conditions such as heart disease, cancer, chronic pain, gastrointestinal problems, anxiety, fatigue, or insomnia.

Internet Resources
http://www.mind-body.com

NATUROPATHIC MEDICINE

American Association of Naturopathic Physicians
601 Valley Street, Suite 105
Seattle, WA 98109
(206) 298-0126
(206) 298-0129 FAX
(206) 298-0125 Referral Line
E-Mail: 74602.3715@compuserve.com
Web Site: http://www.naturopathic.org

Provides a directory of naturopathic physicians and offers referrals to a nationwide network of accredited or licensed practitioners. On-line directory available at http://www.healthy.net/referrals.

Internet Resources
http://www.naturopathy.com

NUTRITIONAL MEDICINE

American College for Advancement in Medicine
23121 Verdugo Drive, #204
Laguna Hills, CA 92653
(714) 583-7666
(714) 455-9679 FAX
E-Mail: acam@acam.org
Web Site: http://www.acam.org

Provides a global directory of physicians who have trained in nutritional and preventative medicine. Also has an extensive list of books and articles on nutritional medicine.

Council for Responsible Nutrition
1300 19th Street, N.W., Suite 310
Washington, DC 20036-1609
(202) 872-1488
(202) 872-9594 FAX
E-Mail: webmaster@crnusa.org
Web Site: http://www.crnusa.org

CRN is a trade association representing more than eighty companies in the nutritional supplements and ingredients industry. CRN members are dedicated to enhancing the public's health through improved nutrition, including the appropriate use of nutritional supplements.

International Society for Orthomolecular Medicine
16 Florence Avenue
Toronto, Ontario
Canada M2N 1E9
(416) 733-2117
E-Mail: centre@orthomed.org
Web Site: http://www.orthomed.org

Internet Resources
http://www.nutritionsite.com
http://www.healthy.net/SupplementBenefits
http://www.healthy.net/VitaminSafety

QIGONG

Qigong Institute
561 Berkeley Avenue
Menlo Park, CA 94026
E-Mail: qigonginstitute@healthy.net
Web Site: http://www.healthy.net/qigonginstitute

Promotes medical Qigong via education, research, and clinical studies, to improve health care by integrating Qigong and Western medicine. It also makes available information on Qigong, especially as developed in China, to medical practitioners, scientists, the public, and policymakers. The Qigong Institute is a 501(c)(3) nonprofit organization.

Internet Resources
http://www.healthy.net/qigong

SPIRITUAL PSYCHOLOGY / PSYCHO-SPIRITUAL INTEGRATION

Association of Transpersonal Psychology
P.O. Box 3049
Stanford, CA 94309
(415) 327-2066
E-Mail: atp@igc.apc.org
Web Site: http://www.igc.apc.org/atp
See listing under "Mental Health and Psychology."

Esalen Institute
Highway 1
Big Sur, CA 93920-9616
(408) 667-3000
(408) 667-2724 FAX
Web Site: http://www.esalen.org

A center for exploring work in the humanities and sciences that promotes human values and potentials. The institute sponsors, encourages, and attempts evaluation of work in these areas, both inside and outside their organizational framework through public seminars, residential work-study programs, invitational conferences, research, and semiautonomous projects.

Eupsychia Institute
P.O. Box 3090
Austin, TX 78764
(512) 327-2795
(512) 327-6043 FAX
E-Mail: Eupsychia1@aol.com
Web Site: www.jacquelynsmall.com

Eupsychia is a "new paradigm" educational institute founded by Jacquelyn Small in 1975. Along with a gifted and inspired team of therapists and teachers from all over North America, Eupsychia offers training and healing programs throughout the country for both health professionals and lay public. In an environment of loving support and heart-felt company, Eupsychia is committed to the process of self-discovery and a shift to higher, more integrated ways of living and serving.

HeartNet International
P.O. Box 159
Boynton Beach, FL 33425
(561) 733-2733
(561) 733-5757 FAX
E-Mail: heartnet@aol.com
Web Site: http://www.heart-net.com

HeartNet International, founded and directed by Carlos Warter, M.D., Ph.D., pioneering researcher in stress management, self-esteem, and personal development, presents programs to increase people's quality of life, efficiency, and productivity. The workshops create an environment that reduces stress and allows for the development of higher personal mastery, management, and power in individuals, groups, businesses, and organizations. The HeartNet staff combines diverse cultural experience with expertise in the fields of medicine, psychology, philosophy, business, finance, and computers to produce world-class educational and humanitarian programs. Dr. Warter's publications and tapes are available by mail order through HeartNet.

Omega Institute for Holistic Studies
Lake Drive RD 2, Box 377
Rhinebeck, NY 12572
(914) 266-4301
Web Site: http://omega-inst.org

Through workshops and retreats, Omega has been a pioneer in exploring, teaching, and embracing new ideas in a peaceful and nurturing environment.

Psychosynthesis International
P.O. Box 279
Ojai, CA 93024
(805) 646-7041
(805) 646-9338 FAX
E-Mail: psi@west.net
Web Site: http://www.healthy.net/psi

Available to students, teachers, ministers, nuns, psychiatrists, psychologists, doctors, homemakers, businesspeople, and other individuals interested in healing and spirituality, their mission is to facilitate awareness, personal healing, and educate on the mental, emotional, physical, and spiritual levels.

Spiritual Emergence Network
E-Mail: sen@cruzio.com
Web Site: http://elfi.com/sen

SEN offers information and referral service for an international population and connects those in transformational crisis with educated and compassionate helpers.

Internet Resources
http://www.bodymindspirit.com

WOMEN'S HEALTH

Christiane Northrup, M.D., *Health Wisdom for Women*
Phillips Publishing
7811 Montrose Road
Potomac, MD 20854
(800) 211-8561

A provocative monthly newsletter focusing on natural healing alternatives and the role the emotions play in health.

Mind/Body Health Sciences, Inc.
393 Dixon Road
Boulder, CO 80302
(303) 440-8460
(303) 440-7580 FAX

Offers a free annual publication featuring Joan Borysenko's lecture and workshop itinerary, and information on "A Gathering of Women" weekend spiritual retreats. Includes books, audiotapes, and videos, plus a select offering of healing music, art, and meditation tapes for adults and children.

The Natural Woman Institute
(888) 489-6626

Founded by Christine Conrad, co-author of Natural Woman Natural Menopause. *Through a program of outreach and education for women and physicians, this organization supports a greater understanding of plant-derived hormones for women at mid-life, and the importance of hormonal balance in keeping healthy, active, and vital. A database of updated doctor referrals is maintained as well as compounding pharmacies providing natural hormones.*

Yoga

International Association of Yoga Therapists
109 Hillside Avenue
Mill Valley, CA 94941
(415) 383-4587

The International Association of Yoga Therapists is a nonprofit organization focusing on education and research in yoga and yoga therapy.

Appendix C

Recommended Reading

ACUPUNCTURE AND CHINESE MEDICINE

Beinfield, Harriet, L.Ac., and Korngold, Efrem, L.Ac., O.M.D. *Between Heaven and Earth: A Guide to Chinese Medicine*. New York: Ballantine Books, 1991.

Dharmananda, Subhuti, Ph.D. *Chinese Herbal Therapies for Immune Disorders*. Portland, OR: Institute for Traditional Medicine, 1993.

Kaptchuk, Ted. *The Web That Has No Weaver: Understanding Chinese Medicine*. New York: Congdon and Weed, 1992.

Mitchell, Ellinor R. *Plain Talk About Acupuncture*. New York: Whalehall, Inc., 1987.

Worsley, J. R. *Acupuncture: Is It for You?* New York: Harper & Row, 1973.

AGING AND MENTAL/EMOTIONAL HEALTH

Butler, Robert, and Lewis, Myrna. *Aging and Mental Health*. St. Louis: C.V. Mosby Company, 1983.

Chopra, Deepak, M.D. *Ageless Body, Timeless Mind*. New York: Random House, 1993.

Luce, Gay Gaer, Ph.D. *Longer Life, More Joy: Techniques for Enhancing Health, Happiness and Inner Vision*. North Hollywood: Newcastle Publishing, 1992.

Silverston, B., and Hyman, H. K. *You and Your Aging Parent—The Modern Family's Guide to Emotional, Physical, and Financial Problems*. New York: Pantheon Books, 1976.

Alternative/Complementary (Integrative) Health

Airola, Paavo. *How to Get Well: A Handbook of Natural Healing*. Sherwood, OR: Health Plus Publications, 1974.

Bricklin, Mark and the Editors of *Prevention* magazine. *The Practical Encyclopedia of Natural Healing*. New York: Penguin Books, 1990.

The Burton Goldberg Group. James Strohecker, exec. ed. *Alternative Medicine: The Definitive Guide*. Puyallup, WA: Future Medicine Publishing, 1993.

Galland, Leo, M.D. *Power Healing: Use the New Integrative Medicine to Cure Yourself*. New York: Random House, 1997.

Gordon, James, M.D. *Manifesto for a New Medicine*. New York: Addison-Wesley, 1997.

Janiger, Oscar, and Goldberg, Philip. *A Different Kind of Healing*. Jeremy P. Tarcher/G.P. Putnam's Sons, 1993.

Morton, Mary, and Morton, Michael. *Five Steps to Selecting the Best Alternative Medicine*. San Rafael, CA: New World Library, 1997.

Murray, Michael, N.D. *Natural Alternatives to Over-the-Counter and Prescription Drugs*. New York: William Morrow, 1994.

Robbins, John. *Reclaiming Our Health: Exploding the Medical Myth and Embracing the Source of True Healing*. Tiburon, CA: HJ Kramer, 1996.

Weil, Andrew, M.D. *8 Weeks to Optimum Health: A Proven Program for Taking Full Advantage of Your Body's Natural Healing Power*. New York: Alfred A. Knopf, 1996.

Weil, Andrew, M.D. *Natural Health, Natural Medicine: A Comprehensive Manual for Wellness and Self-Care*. New York: Houghton Mifflin, 1990.

Werbach, Melvyn R., M.D. *Third Line Medicine: Modern Treatment for Persistent Symptoms*. New York: Arkana, 1986. (Available from Third Line Press, 800-916-0076; in California and Canada, 818-996-0076; or http://www.third-line.com)

Zand, Janet, N.D., L.Ac., Spreen, Allan, M.D., Lavalle, James B., M.D. *Smart Medicine for Healthier Living: Practical A–Z Reference to Natural and Conventional Treatments for Adults*. Garden City Park, NY: Avery Publishing, 1999.

Ayurveda

Chopra, Deepak, M.D. *Perfect Health*. New York: Harmony Books, 1991.

Chopra, Deepak, M.D. *Quantum Healing*. New York: Bantam Books, 1990.

Frawley, David, O.M.D. *Ayurvedic Healing: A Comprehensive Guide*. Salt Lake City: Passage Press, 1989.

Lad, Vasant. *Ayurveda: The Science of Self-Healing.* Santa Fe, NM: Lotus Press, 1984.

Lad, Vasant. *Ayurveda: The Science of Life.* (six audiocassette course) Boulder, CO: Sounds True Audio.

Lad, Vasant, and Frawley, David, O.M.D. *The Complete Book of Ayurvedic Home Remedies.* New York: Harmony Books, 1998.

Lad, Vasant, and Frawley, David, O.M.D. *The Yoga of Herbs: An Ayurvedic Guide to Herbal Medicine.* Santa Fe, NM: Lotus Press, 1986.

CHILDREN'S HEALTH

Rapp, Doris J., M.D. *Is This Your Child's World? How You Can Fix the Schools and Homes That Are Making Your Children Sick.* New York: Bantam, 1996. (Out of print: available from HealthWorld Online bookstore: http://www.healthy.net/bookstore)

Zand, Janet, N.D., L.Ac. *Smart Medicine for a Healthier Child.* Garden City Park, NY: Avery Publishing, 1995.

CHRONIC FATIGUE SYNDROME

Chaitow, Leon, N.D., D.O. *Candida Albicans: Could Yeast Be Your Problem?* Wellingborough, North Hamptonshire, England: Thorsons, 1985.

Crook, William, M.D. *Chronic Fatigue Syndrome and the Yeast Connection.* Jackson, TN: Professional Books, 1992.

Murray, Michael, N.D. *Chronic Fatigue Syndrome: How You Can Benefit from Diet, Vitamins, Minerals, Herbs, Exercise and Other Natural Methods.* Rocklin, CA: Prima Publishing, 1994.

Rogers, Sherry, M.D. *Tired or Toxic?* Syracuse, NY: Prestige Publishers, 1990.

Susser, Murray, M.D., and Rosenbaum, Michael, M.D. *Solving the Puzzle of Chronic Fatigue Syndrome.* Tacoma, WA: Life Sciences Press, 1992.

CHRONIC PAIN

Bresler, David, Ph.D. *Free Yourself from Pain.* Originally published by Simon and Schuster, reprinted by AlphaBooks, 1998. (Available from the Academy of Guided Imagery: 800-726-2070)

Catalano, Ellen Mohr, M.A. *The Chronic Pain Control Workbook: A Step-by-Step Guide for Coping With and Overcoming Your Pain.* Oakland, CA: New Harbinger Publications, 1987.

Gelb, Harold, D.M.D. *Killing Pain Without Prescription*. New York: HarperPerennial, 1982.

Linchitz, Richard, M.D. *Life Without Pain*. Reading, MA: Addison-Wesley, 1987.

Prudden, Bonnie. *Pain Erasure*. New York: M. Evans and Co., 1980.

DEPRESSION AND MENTAL HEALTH

Khalsa, Dharma Singh. *Brain Longevity: The Breakthrough Medical Program That Improves Your Mind and Memory*. New York: Warner Books, 1997.

McWilliams, Peter, Nordfors, Mikael, and Bloomfield, Harold H. *Hypericum and Depression*. Los Angeles: Prelude Press, 1997.

Murray, Michael T. *Natural Alternatives to Prozac*. New York: William Morrow and Co. 1997.

Padus, Emrika, and the Editors of *Prevention* magazine. *The Complete Guide to Your Emotions and Your Health*. Emmaus, PA: Rodale Press, 1990.

Real, Terrence. *I Don't Want to Talk About It: Overcoming the Secret Legacy of Male Depression*. New York: Fireside, 1997.

Rogers, Sherry, M.D. *Depression: Cured at Last!* Syracuse, NY: Prestige Publishers, 1997.

Ross, Harvey, M.D. *Fighting Depression: How to Lift the Cloud That Darkens Millions of Lives*. New Canaan, CT: Keats Publishing, 1992.

Slagle, Priscilla, M.D. *The Way Up from Down*. New York: St. Martin's Press, 1994.

DIET AND NUTRITION

Balch, James, M.D., and Balch, Phyllis, R.N. *Prescription for Nutritional Healing: A Practical A–Z Reference to Drug-Free Remedies Using Vitamins, Minerals, Herbs, and Food Supplements*. Garden City Park, NY: Avery Publishing, 1990.

Braverman, Eric R., M.D.; and Pfeiffer, Carl C., M.D., Ph.D. *The Healing Nutrients Within*. New Canaan, CT: Keats Publishing, 1987.

Bricklin, Mark, and Classens, Sharon. *The Natural Healing Cookbook: Over 450 Delicious Ways to Get Better and Stay Healthy*. Emmaus, PA: Rodale Press, 1981.

Calbom, Cherie, and Keane, Maureen. *Juicing for Life: A Guide to the Health Benefits of Fresh Fruit and Vegetable Juicing*. Garden City Park, NY: Avery Publishing, 1992.

Colbin, Annemarie. *Food and Healing: How What You Eat Determines Your Health, Your Well-Being, and the Quality of Your Life*. New York: Ballantine Books, 1986.

Garrison, Robert H., Jr., M.A.R., Ph.D., and Somer, Elizabeth, M.A., R.D. *The Nutrition Desk Reference*. New Canaan, CT: Keats Publishing, Inc., 1990.

Haas, Elson M., M.D. *The Detox Diet*. Berkeley, CA: Celestial Arts Publishing, 1997.

Haas, Elson M., M.D. *Staying Healthy with Nutrition*. Berkeley, CA: Celestial Arts Publishing, 1992.

Hausman, Patricia, and Hurley, Judith Benn. *The Healing Foods: The Ultimate Authority on the Curative Power of Nutrition*. Emmaus, PA: Rodale Press, 1989.

Janson, Michael, M.D. *The Vitamin Revolution in Health Care*. Greenville, NH: Arcadia Press, 1996.

Murray, Michael, N.D. *Encyclopedia of Nutritional Supplements: The Essential Guide for Improving Your Health Naturally*. Rocklin, CA: Prima Publishing, 1996.

Murray, Michael, N.D. *5-HTP: The Natural Way to Overcome Depression, Obesity and Insomnia*. New York: Bantam Books, 1998.

Ornish, Dean, M.D. *Eat More, Weigh Less: Dr. Dean Ornish's Life Choice Program for Losing Weight Safely While Eating Abundantly*. New York: HarperCollins, 1993.

Ornish, Dean, M.D. "Opening Your Heart Recipes." In *Dr. Dean Ornish's Program for Reversing Heart Disease: The Only System Scientifically Proven to Reverse Heart Disease Without Drugs or Surgery*. New York: Ballantine Books, 1990.

Robbins, John. *Diet for a New America: How Your Food Choices Affect Your Health, Happiness, and the Future of Life on Earth*. Walpole, NH: Stillpoint Publishing, 1987.

Robbins, John. *May All Be Fed: Diet for a New World*. New York: William Morrow and Co., 1992.

Turner, Lisa. *Meals That Heal: A Nutraceutical Approach to Diet and Health*. Rochester, VT: Healing Arts Press, 1997.

Werbach. Melvyn R. *Foundations of Nutritional Medicine*. Tarzana, CA: Third Line Press, 1997. (Available from Third Line Press, 800-916-0076; in California and Canada, 818-996-0076; or http://www.third-line.com)

Werbach, Melvyn R. *Healing with Food*. New York: HarperPerennial, 1994.

Werbach, Melvyn R. *Nutritional Influences on Illness*. Tarzana, CA: Third Line Press, 1993. (Available from Third Line Press, 800-916-0076; in California and Canada, 818-996-0076; or http://www.third-line.com)

Werbach, Melvyn R. *Nutritional Influences on Mental Illness*. Tarzana, CA: Third Line Press, 1991. (Available from Third Line Press, 800-916-0076; in California and Canada, 818-996-0076; or http://www.third-line.com)

Wright, Jonathan V., M.D. *Dr. Wright's Guide to Healing with Nutrition*. New Canaan, CT: Keats Publishing, 1990.

ENVIRONMENTAL ILLNESS

Rapp, Doris J., M.D. *Is This Your Child's World? How You Can Fix the Schools and Homes That Are Making Your Children Sick*. New York: Bantam, 1996. (Out of print: available from HealthWorld Online bookstore: http://www.healthy.net/bookstore)

Steinman, David, and Epstein, Samuel S., M.D. *The Safe Shopper's Bible: A Consumer's Guide to Non-Toxic Household Products, Cosmetics and Food*. New York: McMillan, 1996.

GRIEF RECOVERY

Berkus, Rusty, illustrated by Christa Wollan. *To Heal Again: Towards Serenity and the Resolution of Grief*. Los Angeles: Red Rose Press, 1984.

Colgrove, M., Bloomfield, H., M.D., and McWilliams, P. *How to Survive the Loss of a Love*. New York: Simon and Schuster, 1976.

Craig, Jean. *Between Hello and Goodbye: A Wife's Journal of Loss and Love*. Los Angeles: Jeremy P. Tarcher, 1990.

Elmer, Lon. *Why Her, Why Now: A Man's Journey Through Love and Death and Grief*. New York: Bantam Books, 1990.

Roth, Deborah, ed. *Stepping Stones to Grief Recovery*. Santa Monica: IBS Press, 1987.

Schiff, Harriet Sarnoff. *The Bereaved Parent*. New York: Crown Books, 1987.

Storr, Anthony. *Solitude: A Return to Self*. New York: Free Press, 1988.

Tatelbaum, J. *The Courage to Grieve: Creative Living, Recovery and Growth Through Grief*. New York: Harper and Row, 1980.

HEALTH & HEALING

Carlson, Richard, and Shield, Benjamin, eds. *Healers on Healing*. Los Angeles: Jeremy P. Tarcher, 1989.

Chaitow, Leon, M.D. *The Body/Mind Purification Program: How to Be Healthy in a Polluted World*. New York: Simon and Schuster, 1990.

Chopra, Deepak, M.D. *Creating Health: Beyond Prevention, Toward Perfection*. New York: Houghton Mifflin, 1987.

Dacher, Elliott. *Whole Healing: A Step-by-Step Program to Reclaim Your Power to Heal*. New York, Dutton Books, 1996.

Dossey, Barbara, and Keegan, Lynn. *Art of Caring: Holistic Healing Using Relaxation, Imagery, Music Therapy and Touch*. (four audiocassettes) Boulder, CO: Sounds True Audio.

Jampolsky, Jerry, M.D., with Hopkins, Patricia, and Thetford, William N. *Teach Only Love: Seven Principles of Attitudinal Healing*. New York: Bantam, 1983.

Kloss, Jethro. *Back to Eden: A Human Interest Story of Health and Restoration*. Loma Linda, CA: Back to Eden Books Publications, 1939/1988.

Locke, Stephen, and Colligan, Douglas. *The Healer Within*. New York: Mentor Books, 1987.

Myss, Caroline, Ph.D. *Anatomy of the Spirit: The Seven Stages of Power and Healing*. New York: Crown Publishers, 1996.

Sanford, John A. *Healing and Wholeness*. New York: Paulist Press, 1977.

Shealy, M.D., Norman, C., and Myss, Caroline, M.A. *The Creation of Health: Merging Traditional Medicine with Intuitive Diagnosis*. Walpole, NH: Stillpoint Publishing International, 1989.

Werbach, Melvyn R., M.D. *Third Line Medicine: Modern Treatment for Persistent Symptoms*. New York: Penguin Books, 1986. (Available from Third Line Press, 800-916-0076; in California and Canada, 818-996-0076; or http://www.third-line.com)

HERBAL MEDICINE

Blumenthal, Mark, senior ed., et al. *The Complete German Commission E Monographs: Therapeutic Guide to Herbal Medicines*. English trans. (Book or CD-ROM) Austin, TX: Integrative Medicine Communications/ American Botanical Council, 1998, 1999.

Brown, Donald J., N.D. *Herbal Prescriptions for Better Health: Your Everyday Guide to Prevention, Treatment and Care*. Rocklin, CA: Prima Publishing, 1996.

Cass, Hyla, M.D., and McNally, Terrence. *Kava: Nature's Answer to Stress, Anxiety and Insomnia.* Rocklin, CA: Prima Publishing, 1998.

Cass, Hyla, M.D. *St. John's Wort: Nature's Blues Buster.* Garden City Park, NY: Avery Publishing, 1997.

Castleman, Michael. *The Healing Herbs.* Emmaus, PA: Rodale Press, 1991.

Chamberlain, Logan. *What the Labels Won't Tell You: A Consumer's Guide to Herbal Supplements.* Loveland, CO: Interweave Press, 1998.

Foster, Steven. *Herbs for Your Health: A Handy Guide for Knowing and Using 50 Common Herbs.* Loveland, CO: Interweave Press, 1996.

Hobbs, Christopher. *Handbook for Herbal Healing.* Santa Cruz, CA: Botanica Press, 1994.

Hoffmann, David. *The New Holistic Herbal.* Rockport, MA: Element Books, 1992.

Hoffmann, David. *An Elders' Herbal: Natural Techniques for Promoting Health and Vitality.* Rochester, VT: Healing Arts Press, 1993.

Lad, Vasant, and Frawley, David, O.M.D. *The Yoga of Herbs: An Ayurvedic Guide to Herbal Medicine.* Santa Fe, NM: Lotus Press, 1986.

McGuffin, Michael, Hobbs, Christopher, Upton, Roy. American Herbal Products Association's *Botanical Safety Handbook.* Boca Raton, FL: CRC Press, 1997.

Murray, Michael, N.D. *The Healing Power of Herbs.* Rocklin, CA: Prima Publishing, 1992.

Werbach, Melvyn R., and Murray, Michael, N.D. *Botanical Influences on Illness.* Tarzana, CA: Third Line Press, 1994. (Available from Third Line Press, 800-916-0076; in California and Canada, 818-996-0076; or http://www.third-line.com)

HOMEOPATHY

Cummings, Steven, M.D., and Ullman, Dana, M.P.H. *Everybody's Guide to Homeopathic Medicines.* Los Angeles, CA: Jeremy P. Tarcher, 1997.

Kruzel, Thomas, N.D. *Homeopathic Emergency Guide.* Berkeley, CA: North Atlantic Books, 1992.

Lockie, Dr. Andrew. *The Family Guide to Homeopathy.* New York: Fireside/Simon and Schuster, 1989.

Reichenberg-Ullman, Judyth, N.D., M.P.H., and Ullman, Robert, N.D. *Homeopathic Self-Care: The Quick and Easy Guide for the Whole Family.* Rocklin, CA: Prima Publishing, 1997.

Reichenberg-Ullman, Judyth, N.D., M.P.H., and Ullman, Robert, N.D.

Prozac-Free: Homeopathic Medicine for Depression, Anxiety, and Other Mental and Emotional Problems. Rocklin, CA: Prima Publishing, 1999.

Ullman, Dana, M.P.H. *The Consumer's Guide to Homeopathy: The Definitive Resource for Understanding Homeopathic Medicine and Making It Work for You*. Los Angeles: Jeremy P. Tarcher, 1996.

Ullman, Dana, M.P.H. *Homeopathic Healing: A Practical Course for Learning About Homeopathy and How to Use Powerful Natural Remedies*. (six audiocassette course) Boulder, CO: Sounds True Audio.

IMAGERY & VISUALIZATION

Achterberg, Jean. *Imagery in Healing: Shamanism and Modern Medicine*. Boston: New Science Library, 1985.

Bresler, David, Ph.D. *Free Yourself from Pain*. Originally published by Simon and Schuster, reprinted by Alpha Books, 1998. (Available from the Academy of Guided Imagery: 800-726-2070)

Gawain, Shakti. *Creative Visualization*. New York: Bantam Books, 1979.

Gendlin, Eugene. *Focusing*. New York: Bantam Books, 1982.

Johnson, Robert. *Inner Work: Using Dreams and Active Imagination for Personal Growth*. New York: Harper and Row, 1987.

Rossman, Martin L., M.D. *Healing Yourself: A Step-by-Step Program for Better Health Through Imagery*. Originally published by Pocket Books, reprinted by Alpha Books, 1998. (Available from Academy for Guided Imagery: 800-726-2070)

Rossman, Martin L., M.D. *Healing Yourself: A Step-by-Step Program to Better Health Through Imagery*. (Set of six tapes: Insight Publishing, 800-234-8562; ask for free imagery tape and catalogue)

JOURNALING AND LIFE-STORY WRITING

Baldwin, Christina. *Life's Companion: Journal Writing As a Spiritual Quest*. New York: Bantam Books, 1991.

Capacchione, Lucia, Ph.D. *The Creative Journal: The Art of Finding Yourself*. North Hollywood, CA: Newcastle Publishing Co., 1989.

Capacchione, Lucia, Ph.D. *The Picture of Health: Healing Your Life with Art*. Santa Monica, CA: Hay House, 1990.

Capacchione, Lucia, Ph.D. *The Power of Your Other Hand: A Course in Channeling the Inner Wisdom of the Right Brain*. North Hollywood, CA: Newcastle Publishing Co., 1988.

Capacchione, Lucia, Ph.D. *Recovery of Your Inner Child*. New York: Simon and Schuster, 1991.

Capacchione, Lucia, Ph.D. *The Well-Being Journal: Drawing on Your Inner Power to Heal Yourself.* North Hollywood, CA: Newcastle Publishing Co., 1989.

Chapman, Joyce, M.A. *Journaling for Joy: Writing Your Way to Personal Growth and Freedom.* North Hollywood, CA: Newcastle Publishing Co., 1991.

Progoff, Ira. *The Intensive Journal* and *At a Journal Workshop: The Basic Text and Guide for Using the Intensive Journal.* New York: Dialogue House Library, 1987.

Selling, Bernard, M.A. *In Your Own Voice: Using Life Stories to Develop Writing Skills.* Alameda, CA: Hunter House, 1994.

Selling, Bernard, M.A. *Writing from Within: A Unique Guide to Writing Your Life's Stories.* Claremont, CA: Hunter House, 1989.

LIGHT THERAPY

Liberman, Jacob, O.D., Ph.D. *Light: Medicine of the Future.* Santa Fe, NM: Bear and Co., 1990.

MASSAGE, ACUPRESSURE, REFLEXOLOGY, AND HANDS-ON HEALING

Brennan, Barbara. *Hands of Light: A Guide to Healing Through the Human Energy Field.* New York: Bantam Books, 1988.

Byers, Dwight. *Better Health with Foot Reflexology.* St. Petersburg, FL: Ingham Publishing, 1987.

Chia, Mantak. *Chi Self-Massage: The Taoist Way of Rejuvenation.* Huntington, NY: Healing Tao Books, 1986.

Downing, George. *The Massage Book.* New York: Random House, 1972.

Gach, Michael Reed. *Acupressure's Potent Points: A Guide for Self-Care for Common Ailments.* New York: Bantam Books, 1990.

Gach, Michael Reed. Acu-Yoga. (five audiocassette course) Boulder, CO: Sounds True Audio.

Krieger, Dolores, Ph.D., R.N. *The Therapeutic Touch: How to Use Your Hands to Help or to Heal.* New York: Prentice-Hall Press, 1979.

Lidell, Lucinda. *The Book of Massage: The Complete Step-by-Step Guide to Eastern and Western Techniques.* New York: Simon and Schuster, 1986.

Namikoshi, Tokuhiro. *Shiatsu: Japanese Finger Pressure Therapy.* New York: Japan Publications, 1969.

Prevention Magazine Health Books, editors of. *Hands-On Healing: Mas-*

sage Remedies for Hundreds of Health Problems. Emmaus, PA: Rodale Press, 1988.

Thomas, Sara. *Massage for Common Ailments.* New York: Fireside, 1989.

Teeguarden, Iona Marsaa. *Acupressure Way of Health: Jin Shin Do.* New York: Japan Publications, 1978.

MEDITATION

Chodron, Pema. *Awakening Compassion (Tibetan Buddhist Meditation).* (six audiocassette course) Boulder, CO: Sounds True Audio.

Cornfield, Jack. *The Inner Art of Meditation.* (six audiocassettes) Boulder, CO: Sounds True Audio.

Goldstein, Joseph. *The Experience of Insight: A Simple and Direct Guide to Buddhist Meditation.* Boston: Shambhala, 1976.

Goleman, Daniel. *The Meditative Mind.* New York: E. P. Dutton, 1977.

Kabat-Zinn, Jon. *Full Catastrophe Living: Using the Wisdom of Your Body and Mind to Face Stress, Pain, and Illness.* New York: Delta, 1990.

LeShan, Lawrence. *How to Meditate.* New York: Bantam Books, 1974.

Muktananda, Swami. *Meditate.* Albany, NY: State University of New York Press, 1980.

Ram Dass. *Journey of Awakening: A Meditator's Guidebook.* New York: Bantam Books, 1990.

Suzuki, Shunryu. *Zen Mind, Beginner's Mind: Informal Talks on Zen Meditation.* Trumbull, CT: Weatherhill, 1972.

Thich Nhat Hanh. *The Present Moment: Retreat on the Practice of Mindfulness.* (six audiocassettes) Boulder, CO: Sounds True Audio.

MIND/BODY HEALTH

Chopra, Deepak, M.D. *Quantum Healing: Exploring the Frontiers of Mind/Body Medicine.* New York: Bantam Books, 1989.

Cousins, Norman. *Head First: The Biology of Hope.* New York: Thorndike Press, 1991.

Goleman, D., and Gurin, Joel. *Mind/Body Medicine: How to Use Your Mind for Better Health.* New York: Consumer Reports Books, 1993.

Gordon, James S., M.D., Jaffe, Dennis T., Ph.D., and Bresler, David E., Ph.D. *Mind, Body, and Health: Toward an Integral Medicine.* New York: Human Sciences Press, 1984.

Institute of Noetic Sciences with Bill Poole. *The Heart of Healing*. Atlanta, GA: Turner Publishing, 1993.

Locke, Stephen, and Colligan, Douglas. *The Healer Within*. New York: Mentor, 1987.

Moyers, Bill. *Healing and the Mind*. New York: Doubleday, 1993.

Pelletier, Kenneth, Ph.D. *Mind as Healer, Mind as Slayer*. New York: Delta, 1977.

Pelletier, Kenneth. *Sound Mind, Sound Body: A New Model for Lifelong Health*. New York: Simon and Schuster, 1994.

NATUROPATHIC MEDICINE

Pizzorno, Joseph, N.D., and Murray, Michael, N.D. *Encyclopedia of Natural Medicine*. Rocklin, CA: Prima Publishing, 1991.

Pizzorno, Joseph, N.D., and Murray, Michael, N.D. *A Textbook of Natural Medicine*. 2 vols. Seattle, WA: Bastyr University Press, 1990.

Pizzorno, Joseph, N.D. *Total Wellness: Improve Your Health by Understanding and Cooperating with Your Body's Natural Healing Systems*. Rocklin, CA: Prima Publishing, 1997.

RELAXATION AND STRESS REDUCTION

Benson, Herbert, and Procter, William. *Beyond the Relaxation Response*. New York: Putnam/Berkley, 1984.

Borysenko, Joan, Ph.D., *Minding the Body, Mending the Mind*. New York: Bantam Books, 1987.

Chia, Mantak. *Taoist Ways to Transform Stress into Vitality*. Huntington, NY: Healing Tao Books, 1985.

Davis, Martha, Ph.D., Eshelman, Elizabeth Robbins, M.S.W., and McKay, Matthew, Ph.D. *The Relaxation and Stress Reduction Workbook*. Oakland, CA: New Harbinger Publications, 1988.

Kabat-Zinn, Jon. *Full Catastrophe Living: Using the Wisdom of Your Body and Mind to Face Stress, Pain, and Illness*. New York: Delta, 1990.

Murray, Michael, N.D. *Stress, Anxiety and Insomnia: How You Can Benefit from Diet, Vitamins, Minerals, Herbs, and Exercise*. Rocklin, CA: Prima Publishing, 1994.

Peper, Erik, and Holt, Catherine. *Creating Wholeness: A Self-Healing Workbook Using Dynamic Relaxation, Images, and Thoughts*. New York: Plenum, 1993.

Venu. *Rainbow Stress Reduction: Play Your Stress Away with Colorful Healing Art and Stress-Reducing Games*. North Hollywood, CA: Newcastle Publishing Co., 1991.

SPIRITUALITY AND INSPIRATION

Anonymous. *The Cloud of Unknowing*. New York: Image Books, 1973.

Dossey, Larry. *Healing Words: The Power of Prayer and the Practice of Medicine*. New York: HarperCollins, 1993.

Fox, Matthew. *A Spirituality Named Compassion*. San Francisco: Winston Press, 1979.

Frankl, Victor. *Man's Search for Meaning*. New York: Simon & Schuster, 3rd ed. 1984.

French, R.M. *The Way of a Pilgrim and the Pilgrim Continues His Way*. New York: Quality Paperback Book Club, 1998.

Houston, Jean. *The Search for the Beloved: Journeys in Mythology and Sacred Psychology*. Los Angeles: Jeremy P. Tarcher, 1987.

Khan, Hazrat Inayat. *The Purpose of Life*. San Francisco: Rainbow Bridge, 1973.

Lao-tzu. *Tao Te Ching*. Translated by Stephen Mitchell. Boston: Shambhala, 1991.

Mitchell, Stephen. *The Enlightened Heart: An Anthology of Sacred Poetry*. San Francisco: Harper and Row, 1989.

Muktananda, Swami. *Where Are You Going?: A Guide to the Spiritual Journey*. South Fallsburg, NY: S.Y.D.A. Foundation, 1981.

Myss, Caroline, Ph.D. *Anatomy of the Spirit: The Seven Stages of Power and Healing*. New York: Harmony Books, 1996.

Nikhilananda, Swami. *The Bhagavad Gita or the Song of the Lord*. New York: Ramakrishna-Vivekananda Society, 1965.

Peck, M. Scott. *The Road Less Traveled*. New York: Simon and Schuster, 1978.

Rabbin, Robert. *Invisible Leadership: Igniting the Soul at Work*. Lakewood, CO: Acropolis Books, 1998.

Rabbin, Robert. *The Sacred Hub: Living in Your Real Self*. San Diego: Inner Directions Foundation, 1996.

Rumi, Jalal Al-Din. *The Essential Rumi*. Translated by Coleman Barks and John Moyne. San Francisco: HarperSanFrancisco, 1997.

Small, Jacquelyn. *Becoming a Practical Mystic: Creating Purpose for Our Spiritual Future*. Wheaton, IL: Quest Books, 1998.

Small, Jacquelyn, and Yovino, Mary. *Rising to the Call: Healing Ourselves and Helping Others in the Coming Era: A Handbook for Evolving Souls.* Marina del Rey, CA: DeVorss and Co., 1997.

St. John of the Cross. *Dark Night of the Soul.* Garden City, New York: Image Books, 1959.

Thich Nhat, Hanh. *Peace Is at Every Step: The Path of Mindfulness in Everyday Life.* New York: Bantam Books, 1991.

Warter, Carlos, M.D., Ph.D. *Psychospiritual Integration Process.* (Available in audio or video from HeartNet International: E-mail: heartnet@aol.com; Web site: http://www.heart-net.com; Phone: 561-733-2733)

Warter, Carlos, M.D., Ph.D. *Recovery of the Sacred.* Deerfield Beach, FL: Health Communications, 1995.

Warter, Carlos, M.D., Ph.D. *Soul Remembers.* Sedona, AZ: Light Technology Publications, 1995.

Warter Carlos, M.D., Ph.D. *Vive Tu Vida.* Buenos Aires, Argentina: Lumen, 1998.

Warter, Carlos, M.D., Ph.D. *Who Do You Think You Are? The Healing Power of Your Sacred Self.* New York: Bantam, 1998.

WATER THERAPY

Keegan, Lynn, R.N., Ph.D., and Keegan, Gerald T., M.D. *Healing Waters: The Miraculous Health Benefits of the Earth's Most Essential Resource.* New York: Berkley Books, 1998.

WELLNESS

Anderson, Robert A., M.D. *Wellness Medicine: A Guide and Handbook to Comprehensive Collaborative Health Care.* New Canaan, CT: Keats Publishing, 1990.

Ryan, Regina Sara, and Travis, John W., M.D. *Wellness: Small Changes You Can Use to Make a Big Difference.* Berkeley, CA: Ten Speed Press, 1991.

Travis, John W., M.D., and Ryan, Regina Sara. *Wellness Workbook.* Berkeley, CA: Ten Speed Press, 1981.

WOMEN'S HEALTH

Borysenko, Joan, Ph.D. *A Woman's Book of Life: The Biology, Psychology and Spirituality of the Feminine Life Cycle.* New York: Riverhead Books, 1996.

Hobbs, Christopher, L.Ac., and Keville, Kathi. *Women's Herbs, Women's Health*. Loveland, CO: Interweave Press, 1998.

Laux, N.D., and Conrad, Christine. *Natural Woman Natural Menopause*. New York: HarperCollins, 1997.

Lonsdorf, Nancy, M.D., Butler, Veronica, M.D., and Brown, Melanie, Ph.D. *A Woman's Best Medicine: Health, Happiness, and Long Life Through Maharishi Ayurveda*. New York: Jeremy P. Tarcher/Putnam, 1993.

Northrup, Christiane, M.D. *Women's Bodies, Women's Wisdom: Creating Physical and Emotional Health and Healing*. New York: Bantam, 1995.

YOGA, QIGONG, TAI CHI, EXERCISE, AND MOVEMENT

Barker, Sarah. *The Alexander Technique: Learning to Use Your Body for Total Energy*. New York: Bantam Books, 1990.

Bell, L., and Seyfer, E. *Gentle Yoga*. Berkeley, CA: Celestial Arts, 1987. (For wheelchair bound and those with arthritis, stroke damage, or M.S.)

Capacchione, Lucia, Ph.D., with Strohecker, James, and Johnson, Elizabeth. *Lighten Up Your Body, Lighten Up Your Life: Beyond Diet and Exercise—The Inner Path to Lasting Change*. North Hollywood, CA: Newcastle Publishing Co., 1990.

Cohen, Ken. *The Way of Chi Kung*. (six audiocassette course) Boulder, CO: Sounds True Audio.

Feldenkrais, Moshe. *Awareness Through Movement*. New York: Harper and Row, 1977.

Huang, Al Chung-liang. *Embrace Tiger, Return to Mountain: The Essence of Tai Chi*. Moab, UT: Real People Press, 1973.

Jahnke, Roger, O.M.D. *The Healer Within: The Four Essential Self-Care Methods for Creating Optimal Health*. San Francisco: HarperSanFrancisco, 1997.

Kurtz, Ron, and Prestera, Hector, M.D. *The Body Reveals: What Your Body Says About You*. San Francisco: Harper and Row, 1976.

Lusk, Julie, M.Ed., LPC. *Desktop Yoga: The Anytime, Anywhere Relaxation Program for Office Slaves, Internet Addicts, and Stressed-Out Students*. New York: Perigee Books, 1998.

Strozzi-Heckler, Richard, Ph.D. *Anatomy of Change: Awakening the Wisdom of the Body*. Boston: Shambhala, 1984.

Internet Resources on Depression and Alternative/Complementary Medicine

DEPRESSION

D/ART—Depression/Awareness, Recognition and Treatment
http://www.nimh.nih.gov/dart

D/ART—is a federal government program to educate the public, primary care providers, and mental health specialists about depressive illnesses—their symptoms, diagnosis, and treatment. Sponsored by the National Institutes of Mental Health (NIMH) and based on more than fifty years of medical and scientific research, D/ART is a collaboration between the government and community organizations to benefit the mental health of the American public.

Depression Center
http://www.healthy.net/depression

An on-line resource for alternative therapies for treating depression, including mind/body medicine, homeopathy, herbal medicine, naturopathic medicine, and nutritional medicine.

Mental Health Net
http://www.cmhc.com

The largest, most comprehensive guide to mental health on-line, features over 6,300 individual resources. This award-winning site covers information on disorders such as depression, anxiety, panic attacks, chronic fatigue syndrome, and substance abuse as well as professional resources in psychology, psychiatry and social work, journals and self-help magazines. Focus is more on conventional rather than alternative resources. Key resources in Mental Health Net include:

- Psychological Self-Help Online
  http://www.cmhc.com/psyhelp

- Disorders and Treatments: Depression
  http://www.depression.cmhc.com

- Internet Resources, Newsgroups, and Lists
  http://www.depression.cmhc.com/guide/depress.html

National Institute of Mental Health
http://www.nimh.nih.gov

NIMH is part of the National Institutes of Health (NIH), the principal biomedical and behavioral research agency of the United States government. NIH is a component of the U.S. Department of Health and Human Services. The Web site offers public information on specific mental disorders, diagnosis and treatment, "Mental Illness in America," Consensus Conference proceedings, NIMH long-range plans and research reports, publications order forms, quicktime videos, information on the DEPRESSION/Awareness, Recognition and Treatment (D/ART) and the Panic Disorder and Anxiety Disorders Education Programs, and other resources.

Online Depression Screening Tests
http://www.med.nyu.edu/Psych/screens/depre.html

A useful On-line Depression Screening Test (ODST) provided by the NYU Department of Psychiatry.

Self-Help Sourcebook Online
http://www.cmhc.com/selfhelp

The American Self-Help Clearinghouse Self-Help Sourcebook Online has been developed to act as a starting point for exploring real-life support groups and networks that are available throughout the world. The organizations listed in this directory can help one find and/or start a support group in one's community.

ALTERNATIVE/COMPLEMENTARY (INTEGRATIVE) MEDICINE

HealthWorld Online
http://www.healthy.net

The leading Internet health network focuses on wellness, self-care, and alternative and complementary medicine. Representing all major systems of health care worldwide, HealthWorld Online offers vast resources for both consumers and health professionals, including more than 40,000 pages of free content from leading health experts, over fifty searchable resource databases, free Medline search, on-line professional referral, discussion, daily health news feed, global calendar, medical cybrarian research service, as well as premium information and services. The Alternative Medicine Center (http://www.alternativemedicine.net) is the most comprehensive and in-depth on the Internet, and the Health Conditions Center (http://www.diseases.net) has articles from leading experts on over 100 health conditions. The Wellness Center (http://www.bodymindspirit.com) is a leading resource for mind/body and spiritual health. On-line commerce includes bookstore, health food store, and consumer laboratory services. Free E-mail newsletter, Healthy Update, *is available upon request by sending E-mail to update@healthy.net and typing the word "subscribe" in the body text of the E-mail.*

Diagnostic Laboratories

The following diagnostic laboratories offer innovative tests that address many of the key health factors raised in this book that have not been available as a rule from the medical laboratory industry: female and male hormone screenings, adrenal stress hormone tests, thyroid panels, platelet or urine catecholamine panels, digestive stool analysis, candida antibody tests, Chronic Fatigue Immune Dysfunction Syndrome evaluation, ELISA food allergy testing, hair analysis for toxic and essential elements, nutritional assays, amino acid assays, essential fatty acids profile, vitamin and mineral analysis.

Accu-Chem Laboratories
990 N. Bowser Rd., Suite 800
Richardson, TX 75081
(214) 234-5412
(800) 451-0116

Specialists in human toxicology, the lab has developed proprietary testing procedures and protocols for environmental and occupational chemical exposures, including pesticide and herbicides. Also specializes in substance-of-abuse screening that utilizes Gas Chromatography/Mass Spectrometry (the technology recognized by criminal justice, government, legal experts, and the private sector). Expert consultation services.

Aeron LifeCycles
1933 Davis St., Suite 310
San Leandro, CA 94577
(800) 631-7900
(510) 729-0383 FAX
E-Mail: aeron@aeron.com
Web Site: http://www.aeron.com

A licensed clinical laboratory with research interests in linking hormonal changes with many of the diseases and symptoms of aging including osteoporosis, cardiovascular disease, and cancer. Accurate salivary hormone tests are currently available for estradiol, progesterone, testosterone, DHEA, and melatonin.

AAL Reference Laboratories, Inc.
1715 E. Wilshire #715
Santa Ana, CA 92705
(714) 972-9979
(800) 522-2611
(714) 543-2034 FAX
Web Site: http://www.antibodyassay.com

Provides a wide range of services including immunology, infectious diseases, nutrition, and oxidative medicine. AAL offers tests for the following: Candida Immune Complexes Assay, Leucocyte Phagocytosis, Chronic Fatigue Immune Dysfunction Syndrome (CFIDS) Evaluation, Oxidative Protection Screen, Antioxidant Vitamin Blood Levels including CoQ_{10}, Natural Killer Cell Function, Homocysteine, Folate and Vitamin B_{12} Levels, Intestinal Permeability Evaluation, Antibodies to Chemicals, Somatomedin C (IGF-1), Male and Female Hormone Replacement Monitoring.

Biochemical Laboratories
P.O. Box 157
Edgewood, NM 87015
(505) 832-4100 phone/FAX
E-Mail: crpbio@swcp.com

Specializes in hair Trace Mineral Analysis and offers different profiles to suit the physician's needs. The TMA is the standard test with twenty-four elements. Reports include graphic presentation of results and discussion statements for each metal, with a turn-around time of twenty-four to forty-eight hours. Makes vitamin/mineral recommendations.

Doctor's Data, Inc.
P.O. Box 111
West Chicago, IL 60185
(800) 323-2784
(708) 231-3649
(708) 231-9190 FAX
E-Mail: inquiries@doctorsdata.com
Web Site: http://www.doctorsdata.com

An independent reference laboratory providing data on levels of toxic and essential elements in hair, amino acids, and metabolites in blood and urine.

Great Smokies Diagnostic Laboratory
63 Zillicoa St.
Asheville, NC 28801-1074
(704) 253-0621
(800) 522-4762
E-Mail: cs@gsdl.com
Web Site: http://www.gsdl.com

Specializes in tests of physiological function. Tests are non- or minimally invasive, using samples of stool, urine, saliva, blood, and hair. Results focus on how well the body is doing its job in six important areas: digestion (gastrointestinal), nutrition, detoxification/oxidative stress, immunology/allergy, production and regulation of hormones (endocrinology), and heart and blood vessels (cardiovascular).

Immunodiagnostic Laboratories, Inc.
P.O. Box 5755
10930 Bigge St.
San Leandro, CA 94577
(510) 635-4555
(510) 635-5667 FAX
E-Mail: webmaster@idl-labs.com
Web Site: http://www.idl-labs.com

IDL offers a broad range of specialty immunologic tests, including immunodeficiency, autoimmunity, neoplastic, and infectious diseases. Expert consultation is available from the staff to aid in test selection and interpretation.

Immuno Laboratories, Inc.
1620 W. Oakland Park Blvd.
Ft. Lauderdale, FL 33311
(305) 486-4500
(800) 231-9197
(305) 739-6563 FAX
E-Mail: info@immunolabs.com
Web Site: http://www.immunolabs.com

Offers ELISA delayed food allergy testing, a highly sensitive candida assay, as well as an ELISA gluten/gliadin assay.

Immunosciences Lab, Inc.
8730 Wilshire Blvd., Suite 305
Beverly Hills, CA 90211
(310) 657-1077
(800) 950-4686
(310) 657-1053 FAX
E-Mail: immunsci@ix.netcom.com
Web Site: http://www.immuno-sci-lab.com

A diagnostic and research facility that specializes in innovative micro-biology and immunology laboratory testing. Immunosciences Lab's continued mission is to develop esoteric tests and help clinicians in the diagnosis of very complex diseases where the immune system is directly or indirectly involved. Tests in the following categories include: allergy, autoimmune diseases, cancer and its early diagnosis, chronic fatigue syndrome, immunology and serology, immunotoxicology, and intestinal health.

King James Medical Laboratory/Omegatech
24700 Center Ridge Rd., #113
Cleveland, OH 44145
(216) 835-2150
(800) 437-1404
(216) 835-2177 FAX
E-Mail: service@kingjamesomegatech-lab.com
Web Site: http://www.kingjamesomegatech-lab.com

Provides analysis of metals in hair and water samples to both the general public and health care practitioners. Additionally, the lab offers the testing of metals and other analytes in patient specimens submitted by physicians. The laboratory also provides services to clients in many countries throughout the world by offering the service requisitions, reports of results, and other information in several languages including Spanish, Portuguese, Italian, German, and Japanese.

Meridian Valley Clinical Laboratory, Inc.
515 W. Harrison St., Suite 9
Kent, WA 98032
(253) 859-8700
(253) 859-1135 FAX
E-Mail: mvl@nwlink.com
Web Site: http://www.tahomaclinic.com/lab/home.html

*Meridian Valley Clinical Laboratory is a fully accredited clinical refer-
ence lab that provides low-cost specialized lab services to physicians in
the United States and worldwide. A pioneer in state-of-the art nutritional testing, Meridian offers the following tests: allergy (Elisa), amino
acids, bone density, complete stool and digestive analysis, essential fatty
acids profile, mineral analysis, steroid, hormone panels, thyroid panels.*

Pantox Laboratories
4622 Santa Fe St.
San Diego, CA 92109
(619) 272-3885
(800) 726-8696
E-Mail: Customer_info@pantox.com
Web Site: http://www.pantox.com

*A licensed clinical reference laboratory that analyzes and interprets the
biochemical defense system that prevents aging and degenerative diseases. The blood serum concentrations of more than twenty-five different
substances (analytes) relating to the antioxidant defense system are determined and compared with values that are obtained from others of the
same sex and age. A percentile is assigned for each analyte so that the
medical practitioner will know the relative standing of this individual in
comparison to others like him or her. These percentiles are plotted as
families of bar graphs called the Pantox Profile.*

Spectracell Laboratories, Inc.
515 Post Oak Blvd., Suite 830
Houston, TX 77027
(800) 227-5227
(713) 621-3101
(713) 621-3234 FAX
E-Mail: spec1@spectracell.com
Web Site: http://www.spectracell.com

*A CLIA-approved clinical laboratory that specializes in functional
intracellular testing. Tests offer application for assessing many clinical
conditions including cardiovascular risk, immunological disorders,
metabolism measurements, and nutritional analysis.*

Vitamin Diagnostics/European Laboratories of Nutrients
Industrial Drive and Route 35
Cliffwood Beach, N.J. 07735
(732) 583-7773
E-Mail: vitamindia@aol.com

Offers specialized nutritional testing including complete bioavailable vitamin and mineral panels (serum, whole blood, and intracellular). Amino acids (individual or panel), total homocysteine test, free homocysteine test, essential fatty acids panel (red blood cells, lymphocytes, or leucocytes) are offered as well as tests for lipoic acid, Acetyl-L-Carnitine, salivary hormones, toxic metal panel, and salivary mercury levels. Tests related to depression include: platelet or urine catecholamine panels, urinary T_3 / T_4 for subclinical hypothyroid, histamine test, amino acid panel, as well as vitamin, mineral, and essential fatty acids profile.

Compounding Pharmacies

The following pharmacies are able to provide specially compounded natural hormones according to a doctor's prescription.

Abrams Royal Pharmacy
8220 Abrams Road
Dallas, TX 75231
(214) 349-8000

Apothe'Cure, Inc.
13720 Midway Road, Suite 109
Dallas, TX 75244
(972) 960-6601
(972) 960-6921
(800) 969-6601

Bajamar Women's Healthcare Pharmacy
9609 Dielman Rock Island Street
St. Louis, MO 63132
(314) 997-3414
(314) 997-2948

California Pharmacy and Compounding Center
307 Placentia Avenue, #102
Newport Beach, CA 92663
(800) 575-7776
(714) 642-0725 FAX

College Pharmacy
833 North Tejon Street
Colorado Springs, CO 80903
(800) 888-9358
(719) 634-4861

Hazle Drugs Apothecary, Inc.
20 N. Laurel Street
Hazleton, PA 18201
(717) 454-2670
(800) 439-2026
(800) 400-8764 FAX

Hopewell Pharmacy and Compounding Center
1 West Broad Street
Hopewell, NJ 08525
(609) 466-1960
(800) 792-6670

Lakeside Pharmacy
4632 Hwy. 58 North
Chattanooga, TN 37416
(423) 894-3222
(800) 523-1486
(423) 499-8435 FAX

Madison Pharmacy Associates, Inc.
Women's Health America Group
429 Gammon Place
Madison, WI 53719
(800) 558-7046

Medical Center Pharmacy
10721 Main Street
Fairfax, VA 22030
(800) 723-7455
(703) 273-7311
(800) 238-8239 FAX
(703) 591-3604 FAX

Monument Pharmacy
115C Second Street, P.O. Box 511
Monument, CO 80132
(719) 481-2209
(800) 595-7565
(719) 481-4971 FAX

Quest Pharmaceuticals, Inc.
2951 S. Adams Road
Rochester Hills, MI 48326
(888) 455-1248
(800) 455-1248

Thayer's Colonial Pharmacy
1101 E. Colonial Drive
Orlando, FL 32803
(800) 848-4809
(407) 862-8084

Wellness Health and Pharmacy, Inc.
2800 South 18th Street
Birmingham, AL 35209
(205) 879-6551
(800) 227-2627
(205) 871-2568 FAX
(800) 369-0302 FAX

Women's International Pharmacy
5708 Monona Drive
Madison, WI 53716-3152
(608) 221-7800
(800) 279-5708

Appendix G

Contributors' Biographies

JAMES STROHECKER, EDITOR

James Strohecker, a recognized authority in the field of natural health, is cofounder and vice-president of HealthWorld Online, Inc. (www.healthy.net), a critically acclaimed Internet global health network. An advocate of a new global medicine based upon wise utilization of traditional systems of healing and spirituality, Strohecker has focused on educating the public and health professionals in natural health, wellness, and spirituality through book and Internet publishing; a public radio show; television and film projects; continuing education seminars; and consulting services.

As executive editor of the classic book *Alternative Medicine: The Definitive Guide* (Future Medicine Publishing, 1993), Strohecker directed the three-year, two-million-dollar project, including creative development, assembling the prestigious international team of 400 contributing health professionals and scientists, and coordinating a staff of over 100 writers, editors, and researchers. He served as founding vice-president for Future Medicine Publishing, Inc.

Strohecker is co-author of three books including *You Don't Have to Die: Unraveling the AIDS Myth* (Future Medicine Publishing, 1994); *In Your Own Voice: Using Life Stories to Develop Writing Skills* (Hunter House, 1994); and *Lighten Up Your Body, Lighten Up Your Life* (Newcastle, 1990). He has also collaborated or consulted on over twenty titles in the fields of natural health, psychology, creativity, human potential, yoga, meditation, and the world's spiritual traditions. He is editor of the electronic newsletter *Healthy Update*, a regular columnist in *Total Health* magazine, and a contributor to

Faulkner & Gray's 1998 *Guide to Healthcare Resources on the Internet.*

A Phi Beta Kappa graduate of the University of Tennessee with a degree in cultural anthropology, Strohecker was drawn to natural healing and spirituality while living and working among indigenous Mayan Indians as a member of a *National Geographic* archaeological expedition to the jungles of Yucatan in the early 1970s. Working among the ancient, ruined temples, Strohecker underwent a series of mystical experiences, culminating in a spiritual awakening that propelled him on a journey to India. There he engaged in three years of intensive study of yoga, meditation, and spiritual philosophy in a monastery. In India he was exposed to Ayurvedic medicine as well as other systems of natural healing, while guiding the development of an international spiritual research library.

Strohecker serves on the Board of Trustees of Currentur University and the Natural Woman Institute, as well as the advisory boards for the University of Southern California Complementary Medicine Center, the Academy for Guided Imagery, Dove Health Alliance, and the President's Advisory Council for Bastyr University, the first fully accredited multidisciplinary college of natural medicine in the United States. He is listed in the *International Who's Who of Information Technology*. He and his wife, Nancy, reside in Los Angeles, California. E-mail him at jim@healthy.net.

NANCY SHAW STROHECKER, EDITOR

Nancy Shaw Strohecker is a publicist, media consultant, writer/editor who has been involved in both the creative and business aspects of the media and communications for over twenty years, with publishing, public relations, film, and television. She has worked in public relations in the fields of travel, fashion, health, beauty, and fitness and currently has her own company, Word of Mouth Literary Publicity.

Ms. Shaw Strohecker was involved in the initial launch and promotion of the classic and highly acclaimed book *Alternative Medicine: The Definitive Guide* (Future Medicine Publishing, 1993). With her husband, Jim, she coproduced a natural health conference, "Healing Depression," in Los Angeles with leaders from the field of natural medicine.

A longtime student of yoga, meditation, vegetarian cooking, and natural approaches to healthy living, she has edited and collaborated on numerous books in the fields of health, business, psychology, personal development, creativity, and women's inspiration.

Ms. Shaw Strohecker has a B.A. in English literature from the University of California, Berkeley. She was a contributing writer to *Alternative Medicine: The Definitive Guide* and *Darshan*, a monthly magazine on spirituality distributed throughout the world. She and her husband, Jim, live in Los Angeles, California.

DAVID E. BRESLER, PH.D., L.AC.

Dr. David Bresler is renowned for his pioneering work and groundbreaking contributions to the fields of guided imagery and pain control. A well-known authority in the field of Behavioral Medicine, he serves as associate clinical professor in the UCLA School of Medicine, and codirector of the Academy of Guided Imagery in Mill Valley. He is best known as the founder and former director of the Pain Control Unit of the UCLA Hospital and Clinics.

He has directed numerous research projects in the UCLA Departments of Anesthesiology and Psychology and has acted as director of research at the National Acupuncture Association. He has served as a consultant to the World Health Organization as well as to a variety of national examining boards in the United States.

Dr. Bresler has also served on the board of directors of a number of charitable and community organizations. He is listed in several editions of *Who's Who* and *The Best Doctors in America*. He has made many radio and television appearances, including shows with Regis Philbin, Phil Donahue, Gary Collins, Merv Griffin, and Tom Snyder.

His work has been featured in national periodicals such as *Time*, *Newsweek*, *People*, and *Prevention*. From 1981 to the present, he has taught more than 250 courses on pain control, acupuncture, stress management, guided imagery, as well as the healing power of laughter and play, at universities, colleges, and professional organizations throughout the United States and abroad. He has also authored or coauthored over one hundred books and articles including the best-selling *Free Yourself from Pain* (Simon and Schuster, 1979), and served as a member of the editorial board for the highly acclaimed *Alternative Medicine: The Definitive Guide*.

Dr. Bresler's understanding of health and the human psyche is respected in both conventional and alternative medical circles. He asserts that the natural expression of emotion is often suppressed by the family and society, and if not recognized and dealt with, it may lead to serious health problems, including depression. By directly accessing emotions through guided imagery, biofeedback, and other mind/body techniques, the individual can begin to understand the needs that may be represented by an illness, and then develop healthy ways to meet those needs.

The Bresler Center
30765 Pacific Coast Highway
Malibu, CA 90265
(310) 446-1717

HYLA CASS, M.D.

Dr. Cass, an assistant clinical professor of psychiatry at UCLA School of Medicine, and a former member of the attending staff at Cedars Sinai Medical Center, is the author of *St. John's Wort: Nature's Blues Buster* (Avery, 1997) and *Kava: Nature's Answer to Stress, Anxiety and Insomnia* (Prima, 1998). A holistic psychiatrist who integrates psychotherapy and nutritional medicine in her Santa Monica–based practice, she is an authority on holistic approaches to women's health care, particularly regarding the relationship of hormone imbalances and mood. Dr. Cass also acts as a consultant to psychotherapists in evaluating the need for psychotropic medication.

Dr. Cass draws upon methods from both conventional and alternative medicine, with attention to mind, body, and spirit. Her methods stem from her belief that the patient heals him- or herself, so she acts as a facilitator, helping patients to interpret their signs and symptoms, and educating them about their own internal processes, using a wide variety of techniques such as guided imagery, EMDR, and Voice Dialogue.

Her evaluations may include a regular medical and psychiatric history and laboratory studies, as well as consulting with other medical practitioners. She often recommends dietary or lifestyle changes, supplements, a meditation program, or medication.

Dr. Cass has been a media consultant for many years. She has been featured on the radio and quoted extensively in the press, such as in the *L.A. Times*, *Cosmopolitan*, and *People*. She has also appeared on a number of television talk shows such as *Sonya Live*. She is a noted public speaker and seminar leader on topics concerning holistic health, clinical nutrition, women's issues, stress reduction, and psychotherapy techniques.

www.doctorcass.com
(500)4DR-CASS
(310)459-9466 FAX
E-mail: hcassmd@worinet.att.net

ROGER C. HIRSH, O.M.D., L.AC., B.AC. (UK), DIPL. AC. (NCCA)

Dr. Hirsh holds a doctorate in Oriental Medicine and is a licensed and practicing acupuncturist and herbalist. For the last twenty years he has worked to establish the specialization of regenerative health care within the conventional Western medical model and to integrate diverse Eastern and Western medical traditions in this work. As an Honors graduate of the International College of Oriental Medicine (B.Ac.) (London, 1976), he received his doctorate in Oriental Medicine (O.M.D.) (1984) with a specialty in Constitutional Medicine. After a 3,000-hour postgraduate internship he joined the Center for Orthomolecular Medicine in Palo Alto, California (1982), where he practiced acupuncture and herbal medicine for several years as a member of a six-physician team that established leading protocols for holistic medicine. It was within this period of time that Dr. Hirsh served as an adjunct faculty member of the American College of Traditional Chinese Medicine, the California Acupuncture College, and Emperor's College of Traditional Chinese Medicine and was one of the founders and the secretary of the California Acupuncture Association.

After being involved with educating novice acupuncturists, he became one of only three expert examiners for the California state medical licensing of acupuncturists. While working on the acupuncture examinations there were many acupuncture techniques and herbal secrets shared from Chinese, Japanese, Korean, Vietnamese, and European traditions. During this twelve-year period, Dr. Hirsh helped establish an evaluation by the California State Acupuncture Committee and the National Commission for the Certification of Acupuncturists (NCCA) of nontraditional medical techniques. Concurrently, he was trained in ancient rejuvenative techniques such as medical Qigong and martial arts, as well as cosmetic acupuncture and herbal procedures involving facial rejuvenation and body sculpting. It was as early as 1974, when he was studying with the famous Russian physician, Mickael Santaro, O.M.D. (China), that he realized how dramatically one could change a person's body with herbs and acupuncture. Dr. Hirsh was cotranslator, with Hui Shen, M.D., C.A., of *Chinese Medical Treatment of Mental Disorders* by Chang Jian-Hsu (unpublished manuscript). He is in private practice in Beverly Hills, California, specializing in work with people who have simple to complex health, rejuvenation, and reproductive concerns.

The MetaMedical Group
(800) 967-3898
www.metamed.com
E-mail: rhirsh@metamed.com

Shri Kant Mishra, M.D., M.S., Doctor of Ayurveda

Dr. Mishra is coordinator of the University of Southern California Center for Complementary Medicine, associate dean of veterans affairs of the USC School of Medicine, and a leading expert in Ayurvedic medicine. He is developing a program in integrative medicine at USC, with a major emphasis on the scientific basis of complementary health care modalities.

An internationally renowned expert in the field of neurology, he is professor of neurology at the USC School of Medicine, fellow and chair of the history section of the American Academy of Neurology, and formerly served as the head of the Neurology Department at the University of Mississippi School of Medicine. He served as chief of staff of the Los Angeles Veteran Affairs Outpatient Clinic, the largest of its kind in the United States, for ten years and is staff neurologist at the Southern California System of Clinics for Veterans Affairs. Dr. Mishra formerly served as associate professor of neurology and director of the Neuromuscular Disease Program at the University of Mississippi School of Medicine, and chief of neurology service, VA Medical Center, Jackson, Mississippi.

Dr. Mishra has a formal training in yoga and meditation as well as a degree of Doctor of Ayurveda from Benares Hindu University in India. He is one of the few individuals working in the United States who has a formal degree in Ayurvedic medicine. He is currently writing a book entitled "Ayurveda: The Art and Science of Healthy Living," and is contributing a chapter on Ayurveda and yoga to a professional resource guide on scientific and outcomes-based alternative and complementary medicine, to be published by Stanford University and the National Institutes of Health.

He has been extensively published in the medical literature with over two hundred papers, abstracts, and book reviews in peer-reviewed medical journals in neuroscience, management science, and integrative medicine, particularly in Ayurveda. He has also served on the editorial boards of the *Journal of Alternative Medicine in Clinical/Therapeutic Practice, Journal of Integrative Medicine, Journal of Neurological Sciences*, and as a reviewer for *Neurology* and *Annals of Neurology*.

Program for Complementary/Alternative Medicine
USC School of Medicine
(213) 342-1784
smishra@hsc.usc.edu
shrimishra@aol.com

JOSEPH PIZZORNO, N.D.

Dr. Pizzorno is a doctor of naturopathic medicine whose vision and dedication to the field unites the healing traditions of natural medicine with scientific methodology, resulting in major advances for natural medicine. As founding president of Bastyr University in Seattle, Washington, he has led this institution to become the first fully accredited multidisciplinary college of natural medicine in the United States.

Dr. Pizzorno is a noted lecturer, teacher, writer and leading communicator of natural medicine, wellness, and self-help. He is author of *Total Wellness: Improve Your Health by Understanding and Cooperating with Your Body's Natural Healing Systems* (Prima Publishing, 1997) and is co-author of the internationally acclaimed *A Textbook of Natural Medicine* and *Encyclopedia of Natural Medicine*. A frequent speaker on television and radio, Dr. Pizzorno also serves on several editorial boards and writes articles for numerous publications, including the *Journal of Naturopathic Medicine, Let's Live,* and *Vegetarian Times*. He was also on the editorial board for *Alternative Medicine: The Definitive Guide*.

In 1993 Dr. Pizzorno, as a representative from the naturopathic profession, was selected to present to First Lady Hillary Clinton's Health Care Reform Task Force. He was also appointed to the U.S.

Congress Office of Technology Advisory Panel on Health and Safety Assessment of Dietary Supplements, and had the opportunity to educate members of Congress on the importance of self-help and wellness lifestyle choices as well as the role of natural medicine in health care reform. He is currently consulting with pioneering insurance companies and HMOs that are investigating the inclusion of natural medicine.

Bastyr University
14500 Juanita Drive NE
Bothell, WA 98011
(425) 823-1300
(425) 823-6222 FAX
E-mail: www.bastyr.edu
Admissions information: admiss@bastyr.edu

CARLOS WARTER, M.D., PH.D.

Dr. Carlos Warter is an internationally recognized author, physician, lecturer, and pioneer in the mind-body-spirit approach to medicine for over twenty years. He is the author of numerous books in both English and Spanish including *Recovery of the Sacred, Soul Remembers* (Bantam), and his newly released book *Who Do You Think You Are? The Healing Power of Your Sacred Self* (Bantam), which has been praised by former U.S. Senator Alan Cranston, Deepak Chopra, M.D., John Gray, Ph.D., Rabbi Zalman Schachter, Bernie Siegel, M.D., Jack Canfield, and Carolyn Myss. His first book was prefaced by Nobel Prize winner Pablo Neruda. Upcoming books include *Chicken Soup for the Healing Soul*, co-authored with Jack Canfield and Mark Victor Hansen.

Dr. Warter is a transpersonal psychotherapist and trained medical doctor with Harvard postgraduate education. He has lectured extensively throughout Latin America, Europe, North America, and the Middle East. In his presentations, Dr. Warter blends science, psychology, issues of identity, self-development, productivity, and spirituality in a unique and powerful manner. His goal in teaching is to bring about the understanding that values and awareness are the greatest asset for our rapidly evolving and challenging world. His work has been studied and practiced by over 70,000 people worldwide.

Born in Chile, Dr. Warter has been awarded the United Nations Peace Messenger and the Pax Mundi awards for his humanitarian efforts. He is also the founder of the World Health Foundation for

Development and Peace, a nonprofit, educational organization whose mission is to disseminate ideas and programs that generate greater health, well-being, and a higher standard of living across the world. He currently resides in Ocean Ridge, Florida, with his wife and three children.

HeartNet International
P.O. Box 159
Boynton Beach, FL 33425
(561) 733 2733
www.heart-net.com
E-mail: heartnet@aol.com

MELVYN R. WERBACH, M.D.

Dr. Werbach is assistant clinical professor of the Department of Psychiatry, UCLA School of Medicine, and is a former director of Clinical Biofeedback at the Pain Control Unit of the UCLA Hospital and Clinics.

He has been a key contributor to the UCLA Medical Advisory Group's *Health Talk* audiotape series and also serves on the editorial boards of a number of national and international health journals. Of his many awards, he received the Book of the Year prize in 1992 for *Nutritional Influences on Mental Illness* presented by the *Journal of Alternative and Complementary Medicine* in London.

He's widely respected as an author on health, and in addition to *Nutritional Influences on Mental Illness* (Third Line Press, 1991) he has also authored *Healing with Food* (HarperCollins, 1994), *Healing Through Nutrition* (HarperCollins, 1993), *Nutritional Influences on Illness* (Keats, 1990), *Botanical Influences on Illness* (Third Line Press, 1994) and *Foundations of Nutritional Medicine* (Third Line Press, 1997). He writes a monthly column, "Nutritional Influences on Illness" for the *International Journal of Alternative and Complementary Medicine* in England, which is circulated in the United States, and served as a member of the editorial board for the highly acclaimed *Alternative Medicine: The Definitive Guide*.

Dr. Werbach has been listed in *Who's Who in Science and Engineering*, *The American Men and Women of Science*, and *Who's Who in the West*. He is considered to be a pioneer and an authority on biofeedback, pain control, psychiatry, and nutritional medicine both here and abroad.

He believes that the depressive syndrome is the expression of any of a wide variety of negative influences, including deterioration in body structure or function, psychological conflicts and losses, and environmental challenges, to name a few. Similarly, successful treatments can approach depression from any direction that influences it, whether physical, functional, psychological, behavioral, physiological, or spiritual. He is especially interested in reviewing nutritional approaches to healing depression, since the role of dietary factors, including food sensitivities, is often neglected by treatment approaches.

Third Line Press
www.third-line.com
E-mail: tlp@third-line.com

JACQUELYN J. WILSON, M.D.

Dr. Wilson has been in private family practice for twenty-five years and now consults for pharmaceutical companies with an interest in homeopathic medicine. Past president of the American Institute of Homeopathy, she is an internationally known authority in homeopathy and has been an instructor at University of California–San Diego School of Medicine.

A diplomate of the American Board of Family Practice, Dr. Wilson has led courses in illness and the family to medical students, lectured on homeopathy to naturopathic and acupuncture students, and taught women's health in university extension courses. She has written curriculum in self-care using homeopathic medicines and has frequently taught self-care seminars using a variety of natural therapies (such as homeopathic medicines, herbs, nutrition, and massage) to students and laypeople.

A diplomate of the American Board of Homeotherapeutics, Dr. Wilson is a member of the Homeopathic Pharmacopoeia Convention of the United States. She serves on the advisory board of *Let's Live Magazine* and of Bastyr University, the only accredited American university whose mission is based in natural therapies. One of her specialties is women's health care, and the chronic stress caused by abusive relationships. In her private practice, her approach has included preventative, holistic, homeopathic, and nutritional therapy.

Her articles have been published in magazines ranging from *United Airlines Flight Magazine* to *Holistic Life*. She has also been published in a number of leading professional publications on homeopathy, one of which, the authoritative *Homeopathic Pharmocopeia of the United States*, is now in its eighth edition. During the past fifteen years, she has frequently participated in television and radio talk shows on holistic and women's health. She was also a contributor to the highly acclaimed *Alternative Medicine: The Definitive Guide.*

Jacquelyn Wilson believes that by taking responsibility for our state of health and the process of healing, we can come to understand the attitudes, beliefs, and values that may have contributed to illness. She teaches people to create and maintain health by fostering self-responsibility and an understanding of the healing powers of the body. She also emphasizes the value of the patient/practitioner relationship.

Jacquelyn J. Wilson, M.D.
R&D Consultant in Homeopathy and Integrative Medicine
(760) 747-2144
(760) 747-1709 FAX
E-mail: drwilson@home.com
www.homeopathicdoctor.com

JANET ZAND, O.M.D., L.AC.

Janet Zand is a Doctor of Oriental Medicine and a licensed acupuncturist who has been a highly successful practitioner of natural medicine for the past sixteen years. She uses homeopathy, herbal medicine, acupuncture, nutritional medicine, exercise, and lifestyle modification to create an integrated approach to optimum health. She is best known by the public as the founder and creator of Zand Herbal Formulas, one of the most widely used over-the-counter herbal remedies lines in the country.

Zand is a former senior clinical instructor at the California Acupuncture College and a frequent lecturer on herbal medicine to physicians and other professionals such as the National Homeopathic Society, California Homeopathic Society, and California Acupuncturist Association and Pacific Symposium. Because of her expertise and her understanding of grass-roots conditions, she is often called upon to address the general public as well. She has been awarded dual honors for "Best Homeopath" and "Best Acupuncturist" by the *Los Angeles Weekly*.

Presently she acts as a monthly contributor to *Health World Mag-*

azine and has been featured in such national magazines as *Cosmopolitan, Mirabella, Longevity, Men's Fitness, Delicious,* and the *Los Angeles Times.* Dr. Zand is co-author of the best-selling book *Smart Medicine for a Healthier Child* and most recently co-author of *Smart Medicine for Healthier Living,* both from Avery Publishing.

E-mail: jzand@texas.net

Notes

CHAPTER 1

1. Terrence Real, *I Don't Want to Talk About It: Overcoming the Secret Legacy of Male Depression* (New York: Fireside, 1989).
2. K. Narayanaswami Aiyar, trans., *Laghu Yoga Vasishtha* (Madras, India: Adyar Library and Research Centre, 1971).
3. Mark Blumenthal, senior ed., et al., *The Complete German Commission E Monographs: Therapeutic Guide to Herbal Medicines*, English trans. (Austin, TX: American Botanical Council, 1998. This is available from American Botanical Council, 512-331-8868).
4. Melvyn R. Werbach, *Nutritional Influences on Illness* (Tarzana, CA: Third Line Press, 1993). An expanded version is also available on CD-ROM. Both are available from Third Line Press, 800-916-0076; in California and Canada, 818-996-0076; or http://www.third-line.com.

CHAPTER 2

1. *Diagnostic and Statistical Manual of Mental Disorders*, 4th ed. (Washington, DC: American Psychiatric Press, 1994).

CHAPTER 3

1. K. Lindstrom et al. "Occupational Solvent Exposure and Neuropsychiatric Disorders," *Scan J Work Environ Health* 10:321-23, 1984.
2. D. M. White et al. "Neurologic Syndromes in 25 Workers from an Aluminum Smelting Plant," *Arch Int Med* 152:1443-48, 1982.
3. "Hazardous Incinerators?" *Science News*. May 22, 1983:143-334.
4. Y. Hidehiko et al. "Effects of Aspartame and Glucose Administration on Brain and Plasma Levels of Large Neutral Amino Acids and Brain S-Hydroxyindoles," *AJCH* 40:1-7, 1984.

5. E. Robenstein and D. D. Federman, *Scientific American Medicine*, 13 Psychiatry II: Mood and Anxiety Disorders (New York: Scientific American Books, 1994).
6. L. Ganzini et al., "Drug-induced Depression in the Ages: What Can Be Done?" *Aging* 3:147-58, 1993.
7. M. Hashizume and M. Mori, "An Analysis of Hypermagnesemia and Hypomagnesemia," *Jap J Med* 28:368-472, 1990.
8. E. Robenstein and D. D. Federman, *Scientific American Medicine*, 13 Psychiatry II: Mood and Anxiety Disorders, (NY: Scientific American Books, 1994).
9. M. Moss et al. "The Decreased Availability of L-Tryptophan in Depressed Females: Clinical and Biological Correlates," *Prog Neuro-Psychopharmacol Biol Psychiat* 14:903-13, 1990.
10. G. R. Heninger et al. "Tryptophan-deficient Diet and Amino Acid Drink Deplete Plasma Tryptophan and Induce a Relapse of Depression in Susceptible Patients," *J Chem Neuroanat* 5:347-48, 1992.
11. Y. Hidehiko et al. "Effects of Aspartame and Glucose Administration on Brain and Plasma Levels of Large Neutral Amino Acids and Brain S-Hydroxyindoles," *AJCH* 40:1-7, 1984.
12. B. L. Kagan et al. "Oral S-adenosylmethionine in Depression: A Randomized, Double-blind, Placebo-controlled Trial," *Am J Psych* 147:5:601-6, 1990.
13. B. Weyerer, "Physical Inactivity and Depression in Community: Evidence from the Upper Bavarian Field Study," *Int J Sports Med* 13:482-86, 1982.
14. R. L. Sack et al. "Morning vs. Evening Light Treatment for Winter Depression: Evidence that the Therapeutic Effects of Light Are Mediated by Circadian Phase Shifts," *Arch Gen Psy* 47:343-61, 1990.
15. D. A. Oren et al. "Treatment of Seasonal Affective Disorder with Green Light and Red Light," *Am J Psych* 148:509-11, 1991.
16. Joseph Pizzorno and Michael Murray, *A Textbook of Natural Medicine,* 2 vols. (Seattle: Bastyr University, 1990).

CHAPTER 4

1. Michael Rosenbaum, M.D., and Murray Susser, M.D., *Solving the Puzzle of Chronic Fatigue Syndrome* (Tacoma, WA: Life Sciences Press, 1992).
2. Jay Goldstein, M.D., *Chronic Fatigue Syndrome: The Limbic Hypothesis* (Binghamton, NY: Haworth Medical Press, 1993).
3. William Crook, M.D., *The Yeast Connection* (Jackson, TN: Professional Books, 1983); John Parks Trowbridge, M.D., *The Yeast Syndrome* (New York: Bantam Books, 1986).
4. Leo Galland, M.D., *Power Healing: How the New Integrative Medicine Can Cure You* (New York: Random House, 1998).

5. Hal Huggins, D.D.S., *It's All in Your Head* (Tacoma, WA: Life Sciences Press, 1989).

6. Nan Fuchs, Ph.D., *The Nutrition Detective* (Los Angeles: Jeremy P. Tarcher, 1985).

7. Broda Barnes, M.D., *Hypothyroidism: The Unsuspected Illness* (New York: Harper and Row, 1976).

8. Michael Rosenbaum, M.D., and Murray Susser, M.D., *Solving the Puzzle of Chronic Fatigue Syndrome.* Tacoma, WA: Life Sciences Press, 1992.

9. Dr. Devi Nambudripad, *Say Good-bye to Illness* (Buena Park, CA: Delta Publishing, 1993).

10. Priscilla Slagle, M.D., *The Way Up from Down* (New York: Random House, 1987); Eric Braverman, M.D., and Carl Pfeiffer, M.D. *The Healing Nutrients Within* (New Canaan, CT: Keats, rev. 1997).

11. Hyla Cass, M.D., *St. John's Wort: Nature's Blues Buster* (Garden City Park, NJ: Avery Publishing, 1997).

12. Hal Stone, Ph.D., and Sidra Stone, Ph.D., *Embracing the Inner Critic* (San Francisco: HarperSanFrancisco, 1992); Hal Stone, Ph.D., and Sidra Stone, Ph.D., *Embracing Our Selves: The Voice Dialogue Manual* (Mill Valley, CA: Nataraj Publications, 1993).

13. Francine Shapiro and Margot Forrest, *EMDR* (New York: Basic Books, 1997).

CHAPTER 5

1. *Diagnostic and Statistical Manual of Mental Disorders*, 4th ed. (Washington, DC: American Psychiatric Press, 1994).

2. D. S. King, "Can Allergic Exposure Provoke Psychological Symptoms? A Double-blind Test," *Biol Psychiatry* 16(1)(1981):3-19.

3. K. Gilliland and W. Bullick, "Caffeine: A Potential Drug of Abuse," *Adv Alcohol Subst Abuse* 3(1)(1984):53-73.

4. K. Gredem, "Caffeine and Tobacco Dependence," in *Comprehensive Textbook of Psychiatry* (Baltimore: Williams & Wilkins, 1985), 1026-33.

5. K. Kreitsch, L. Christensen, and B. White, "Prevalence, Presenting Symptoms, and Psychological Characteristics of Individuals Experiencing a Diet-related Mood Disturbance," *Behav Ther* 19(1988):593-604.

6. F. K. Goodwin, "Alcoholism Research: Delivering on the Promise," *Public Health Rep* 103(6)(1988):569-74.

7. R. T. Sterner, W. R. Price, "Restricted Riboflavin: Within-Subject Behavioral Effects in Humans," *Am J Clin Nutr* 26(1973):150-60.

8. M. T. Abou-Saleh and A. Coppen, "The Biology of Folate in Depression: Implications for Nutritional Hypotheses of the Psychoses," *J Psychiatric Res* 20(2)(1986):91-101.

9. E. H. Reynolds, et al., "Methylation and Mood," *Lancet* 2(1984):196-98.

10. P.S.A. Godfrey et al., "Enhancement of Recovery from Psychiatric Illness by Methylfolate," *Lancet* (1990) 336:392-95.

11. M. I. Botez, T. Botez, J. Leveille et al. "Neuropsychological Correlates of Folic Acid Deficiency: Facts and Hypotheses," in M. I. Botez and E. H. Reynolds, eds., *Folic Acid in Neurology, Psychiatry, and Internal Medicine* (New York, Raven Press, 1979): 435-61.

12. M. W. Carney et al., "Thiamine, Riboflavin and Pyridoxine Deficiency in Psychiatric Inpatients," *Br J Psychiatry* 141(1982):271-72.

13. J. Brozek, "Psychologic Effects of Thiamine Restriction and Deprivation in Normal Young Men," *Am J Clin Nutr 5(1957)(2):109-20.*

14. R. D. Williams et al., "Induced Thiamine (B_1) Deficiency in Man: Relation of Depletion of Thiamine to Development of Biochemical Defect and of Polyneuropathy," *Arch Intern Med* 71(1943):38-53.

15. C. S. Russ et al., "Vitamin B_6 Status of Depressed and Obsessive-Compulsive Patients," *Br J Psychiatry* 141(1982): 271-72.

16. M. Carney et al., "Thiamine and Pyridoxine Lack in Newly-admitted Psychiatric patients, *Br J Psychiatry* 135(1979):249-54.

17. J. W. Stewart et al., "Low B_6 Levels in Depressed Outpatients," *Biol Psychiatry* 19(4)(1984):613-16.

18. P. Bermond, "Therapy of Side Effects of Oral Contraceptive Agents with Vitamin B_6," *Acta Vitaminol Enzymol* 4(1-2)(1982):45-54.

19. C. Hallert, J. Astrom, and A. Walan, "Reversal of Psychopathology in Adult Coeliac Disease with the Aid of Pyridoxine (Vitamin B_6)," *Scand J Gastroenterol* 18(2)(1983):299-304.

20. C. M. Reading, "Latent Pernicious Anaemia: A Preliminary Report," *Med J Aust* 1(1975):91-94.

21. D. K. Zucker et al., "B_{12} Deficiency and Psychiatric Disorders: Case Report and Literature Review," *Biol Psychiatry* 16(1981):197-205.

22. H. L. Newbold, "Vitamin B_{12}: Placebo or Neglected Therapeutic Tool?" *Med Hypotheses* 28(3)(1989):155-64.

23. F. R. Ellis, and S. Nasser, "A Pilot Study of Vitamin B_{12} in the Treatment of Tiredness," *Br J Nutr* 30(1973):277-83.

24. R. E. Hodges et al., "Clinical Manifestations of Ascorbic Acid Deficiency in Man," *Am J Clin Nutr* 24(1971):432-33.

25. C. J. Schorah, et al., "Plasma Vitamin C Concentration in Patients in a Psychiatric Hospital," *Hum Nutr Clin Nutr* 37C(1983):447-52.

26. M. Kitahara, "Insufficient Ascorbic Acid Uptake from the Diet and the Tendency for Suicide," *J Orthomol Med* 2(4)(1987):217-18.

27. G. Milner, "Ascorbic Acid in Chronic Psychiatric Patients: A Controlled Trial," *Br J Psychiatry* 109(1963):294-99.

28. S. D. Parker, "Depression and Nutrition: Anemia and Glucose Imbalances," *Anabolism*, Jan.-Feb., 1984.

29. J. Linder et al., "Calcium and Magnesium Concentrations in Affective Disorder: Difference between Plasma and Serum in Relation to Symptoms," *Acta Psychiatr Scand* 80(1989):527-37.

30. J. S. Carman et al., "Calcium and Electroconvulsive Therapy of Severe Depressive Illness," *Biol Psychiatry* 12(1)(1977):5-17.
31. C. L. Bowden et al., "Calcium Function in Affective Disorders and Healthy Controls," *Biol Psychiatry* 23(4)(1988):367-76.
32. C. M. Banki et al., "Cerebrospinal Fluid Biochemical Examination. Do They Reflect Clinical or Biological Differences?" *Biol Psychiatry* 18(9)(1983):1033-44.
33. D. C. Jimerson et al., "CSF Calcium: Clinical Correlates in Affective Illness and Schizophrenia," *Biol Psychiatry* 14(1)(1979):37-51.
34. K. Arasteh, "A Beneficial Effect of Calcium Intake on Mood," *J Orthomol Psychiatry* 9(4)(1994):199-204.
35. R.C.W. Hall and J. R. Joffe, "Hypomagnesemia: Physical and Psychiatric Symptoms," *JAMA* 224(13)(1973):1749-51.
36. G. K. Kirow, N. J. Birch, P. Steadman, R. G. Ramsey. "Plasma Magnesium Levels in a Population of Psychiatric Patients: Correlation with Symptoms," *Neuropsychobiology* 30(2-3)(1994):73-78.
37. C. M. Banki et al., "Aminergic Studies and Cerebrospinal Fluid Cations in Suicide," *Ann N Y Acad Sci* 487(1986):221-30.
38. R. Whang et al., "Predictors of Clinical Hypomagnesemia," *Arch Intern Med* 144(1984):1794-96.
39. W. L. Webb and M. Gehi, "Electrolyte and Fluid Imbalance: Neuropsychiatric Manifestations," *Psychosomatics* 22(3)(1981):199-203.
40. J. R. Cox et al., "Changes in Sodium, Potassium and Fluid Spaces in Depression and Dementia," *Gerontology Clin* 13(1971):232-45.
41. S. N. Young, "The Clinical Psychopharmacology of Tryptophan," in R. J. Wurtman, J. J. Wurtman, eds., *Nutrition and the Brain*, vol. 7. New York: Raven Press, 1986:49-88.
42. J. Walinder, "Combination of Tryptophan with MAO Inhibitors, Tricyclic Antidepressants and Selective 5-HT Reuptake Inhibitors," *Adv Biol Psychiatry* 10(1983):82-93.
43. H. M. van Praag, "Studies in the Mechanism of Action of Serotonin-Precursors in Depression," *Psychopharmacol Bull* 20(1984):599-602.
44. Van Praag et al., "Therapeutic Indications for Serotonin-Potentiating Compounds: A Hypothesis," *Biol Psychiatry* 22(2)(1987):205-12.
45. K. Zmilacher et al., "L-5-Hydroxytryptophan Alone and in Combination with a Peripheral Decarboxylase Inhibitor in the Treatment of Depression," *Neuropsychobiology* 20(1):28-35, 1988.
46. M. Simonson, "L-phenylalanine. Letter." *J Clin Psychiatry* 46(8)(1985):355.
47. J. C. Sabelli et al., "Clinical Studies on the Phenylethylamine Hypothesis of Affective Disorder: Urine and Blood Phenylacetic Acid and Phenylalanine Dietary Supplements." *J Clin Psychiatry* 47(2)(1986):6-70.
48. H. M. Kravitz, H. C. Sabelli, and J. Fawcett, "Dietary Supplements of Phenylalanine and Other Amino Acid Precursors of Brain Monoamines in the Treatment of Depressive Disorders," *J Am Osteopathic Assoc* 84(Suppl)(1984):119-23.
49. A. J. Gelenberg et al., "Tyrosine for the Treatment of Depression," *Am J Psychiatry* 137(1980):622-23.

50. C. J. Gibson and A. Gelenberg, "Tyrosine for the Treatment of Depression," *Biol Psychiatry* 10(1983):148-59.
51. M. Spillmann and M. Fava, "S-Adenosylmethionine (Ademetionine) in Psychiatric Disorders: Historical Perspective and Current Status," *CNS Drugs* 6(6)(1996):416-25.
52. M. E. Carney et al., "Switch Mechanism in Affective Illness and S-Adenosylmethionine." Letter. *Lancet* i(1983):820-1.
53. R. E. Cater II, "The Clinical Importance of Hypochlorhydria (a Consequence of Chronic Helicobacter Infection): Its Possible Etiological Role in Mineral and Amino Acid Malabsorption, Depression and Other Syndromes," *Med Hypotheses* 39(1992):375-83.
54. E.J.W. Keuter, *Nutr Abstr Rev* 29(1959):273.
55. J. V. Wright. *Dr. Wright's Book of Nutritional Therapy* (Emmaus, PA: Rodale Press, 1979).

CHAPTER 6

1. *The Complete German Commission E Monographs: Therapeutic Guide to Herbal Medicines*, English trans., Mark Blumenthal, exec. ed. (Austin, TX: American Botanical Council, 1998).
2. German Ministry of Health, "Valerian," in *Commission E. Monographs for Phytomedicines* (Bonn, Germany: German Ministry of Health, 1985).
3. ESCOP, European Scientific Cooperative for Phytotherapy. *Valerian Root* (Meppel, The Netherlands: European Scientific Cooperative for Phytotherapy, 1990).
4. German Ministry of Health, "Passion Flower Leaves," in *Commission E. Monographs for Phytomedicines* (Bonn, Germany: German Ministry of Health, 1985).
5. S. Foster, "Passion Flower," in *Botanical Series 314* (Austin, TX: American Botanical Council, 1993).
6. German Ministry of Health, "Hops," in *Commission E. Monographs for Phytomedicines* (Bonn, Germany: German Ministry of Health, 1984).
7. E. Bombardelli, A. Cirstoni, and A. Lietti, "The Effect of Acute and Chronic (Panax) Ginseng Saponins Treatment on Adrenal Function; Biochemical and Pharmacological," in Proceedings, 3rd International Ginseng Symposium 1 (1980):9-16; S. J. Fulder, "Ginseng and the Hypothalamic-Pituitary Control of Stress," *American Journal of Chinese Medicine* 9 (1981): 112-18.
8. H. Hikino et al., "Antihepatotoxic Actions of Ginsenosides from Panax Ginseng Roots," *Planta Medica* 52(1985):62-64.
9. T. B. Ng and H. W. Yeung, "Hypoglycemic Constituents of Panax Ginseng," *General Pharmacology* 69(1985): 549-52.
10. I. M. Lesser, I. Mena, et al., "Reduction in Cerebral Blood Flow in Older Depressed Patients," *Arch Psychiatr* 51(1994):677-86.
11. H. Schubert and P. Halama, "Depressive Episode Primarily Unresponsive to Therapy in Elderly Patients: Efficacy of Ginkgo Biloba Extract

(EGb 761) in Combination with Antidepressants," *Geriatr Forsch* 3(1993):45-53.

CHAPTER 7

1. Kerry Dooley, "Prozac Keeps Drugmaker Feeling Good After 10 Years," *Bloomberg News*, 1997.
2. J. Davidson, R. Morrison, J. Shore, R. Davidson, G. Bedayne, "Homeopathic Treatment of Depression and Anxiety," *Alt. Ther.* 3(1997):46-49.
3. Nicholas K. Zittell, "Medicating Kids: A Pacifier for Childhood Depression," *Medical Tribune News Service*, Jan. 9, 1998.
4. A. J. Allen, H. L. Learnard, S. E. Swedo, "Case-study: A New Infection-triggered, Autoimmune Subtype of Pediatric OCD and Tourette's Syndrome." *J Am Acad Child Adolesc Psychiatry*, 34(3)(1995):307-11.
5. Clark Baker, ed., *The Homeopathic Pharmacopoeia of the United States Revision Service,* (Washington, DC: 1996).
6. Shui-Yin Lo, A. Lo, L. Chong, L. Tianzhang, L., Hua, L. et al., "Physical Properties of Water with Ice Structures," *Modern Physics Letters* B, 10, 19 (1996): 921-30.
7. Clark Baker, ed., *The Homeopathic Pharmacopoeia of the United States Revision Service* (Washington, DC: Homeopathic Pharmacopoeia Convention of the United States, 1997).
8. J. Davidson, R. Morrison, J. Shore, R. Davidson, G. Bedayn, "Homeopathic Treatment of Depression and Anxiety," *Alt. Ther.* 3(1997):46-49.
9. W. Jonas and J. Jacobs, *Healing with Homeopathy* (New York: Warner Books, 1996).
10. J. C. Barefoot and M. Schroll, "Symptoms of Depression, Acute Myocardial Infarction, and Total Mortality in a Community Sample," *Circulation* 93(11)(1996):1976-80.
11. Roger Morrison, *Desktop Guide to Keynotes and Confirmatory Symptoms* (Albany, CA: Hahnemann Clinic Publishing, 1993).
12. Sandra Perko, *Homeopathy for the Modern Pregnant Woman and Her Infant* (Austin, TX: Morgan Book Publications).
13. Hans-Heinrich Reckeweg, *Materia Medica Homoeopathia Antihomotoxica.* Vol. 2. (Baden-Baden, Germany: Aurelia-Verlag, 1983).
14. Formur, *The Biochemic Handbook* (St. Louis, MO: Formur 1976).

CHAPTER 8

1. F. J. Schell, B. Allolio, O. W. Schonoecke, "Physiological and Psychological Effects of Hatha-Yoga Exercise in Healthy Women," *Int J Psychosom* 1(1994):46-52.
2. K. Nespor, "Occupational Stress in Health Personnel and Its Prevention: Possible Use of Yoga," *Cas Lek Cesk* 129(1990):961-964; K. N.

Udupa, R. H. Singh, R. M. Settiwar, "Studies in Physiologic, Endocrine, and Metabolic Response to the Practice of Yoga in Young, Normal Volunteers," *Journal of Research in Indian Medicine* 6(1971):345-55; K. N. Udupa, R. H. Singh, R. M. Shettiwar, M. B. Singh, "Studies on the Physiological Effects of Yogic Relaxation Postures," J. Savasana, *Res. Ind. Med. Yoga and Homoeo* 13/1(1978):147.

3. J. L. Harte, G. H. Eifert, R. Smith, "The Effects of Running and Mediation on Beta-endorphin, Corticotropin-releasing Hormone and Cortisol in Plasma, and on Mood," *Biol Psychol* 40(1995):251–65; B. G. Berger and D. R. Owen, "Mood Alteration with Yoga and Swimming: Aerobic Exercise May Not Be Necessary," *Percept Mot Skills* 75(1992):1331–43.

4. H. Gaertner, et al., "Influence of Sirsasana Headstand Postures of Thirty Minutes Duration on Blood Composition and Circulation," *Acta Physiol. Pol.* 16(1965):44.

5. M. Murphy and S. Donovan, "The Physical and Psychological Effects of Meditation—A Review of Contemporary Meditation Research with a Comprehensive Bibliography 1931–1988," Esalen Institute Study of Exceptional Functioning, 1988; P. B. Fenwick, S. Donalson, and L. Gillis, et al., "Metabolic and EEG Changes During TM: An Explanation," *Biol. Psychol.* 5(1977):101–118; R. W. Cranson, et al., "Transcendental Meditation and Improved Performance on Intelligence-related Measures: A Longitudinal Study," *Personality and Individual Differences* 12(1991):1105–16; S. Telles, R. Nagarathna, and H. R. Nagendra, "Autonomic Changes During 'OM' Meditation," *Indian J Physiol Pharmacol* 39(1995):418–20.

6. K. Nespor, "Twelve Years of Experience with Yoga in Psychiatry," *Int J Psychosom* 40:(1993):105–107; J. J. Miller, K. Fletcher, and J. Kabat-Zinn, "Three-year Follow-up and Clinical Implications of a Mindfulness Meditation-based Stress Reduction Intervention in the Treatment of Anxiety Disorders," *Gen Hosp Psychiatry* 17(1995):192–200; D. S. Shannahoff-Khalsa and L. R. Beckett, "Clincal Case Report: Efficacy of Yogic Techniques in the Treatment of Obsessive Compulsive Disorders," *Int J Neurosci* 85(1996):1–17.

CHAPTER 10

1. Jalil Al-Din Rumi, *In the Arms of the Beloved*, trans. Jonathan Star, New York: Tarcher/Putnam, 1997.

2. Plato, volume 7, *Great Books of the Western World*, ed. Wallace Brockway Chicago: William Benton Encyclopedia Britannica, 1952.

3. St. John of the Cross, *The Dark Night of the Soul*, Trans. B. Zimmerman (Cambridge: Clarke, 1973).

4. Theodore Burang, from John E. Nelson, M.D., "Healing the Split: A New Understanding of the Crisis and Treatment of the Mentally Ill?" New York: State University of New York Press, 1994.

5. S. O'Laoire, "An Experiential Study of the Effects of Distant Intercessory Prayer on Self-Esteem, Anxiety and Depression," *Alternative Therapy Health Med*, 3(Nov. 1997):38–53.
6. The Psychospiritual Integration Process (PIP) is a nine-day residential process in which participants go through biographical elements in the relationship of the preteen years with mother, father, siblings, culture, and environment and through the mediation of the elements of inner wisdom, develop an analytical moment, a cathartic moment, a compassionate and forgiving episode, thus moving the awareness to understand self-love and future directedness, a lifetime of which have been rooted in negative understanding and habits to a purposeful future. I have taught this process for twenty-five years with extraordinary results followed up over a long time.

Index

Italicized page references indicate illustrations; boldface page references indicate tables.